Writing to Reading
the Steiner Waldorf Way

Foundations of Creative Literacy in Classes 1 and 2

Hawthorn Press

Writing to Reading the Steiner Waldorf Way © 2018 Abi Allanson and Nicky Teensma

Abi Allanson and Nicky Teensma are hereby identified as the authors of this work in accordance with section 77 of the Copyright, Designs and Patent Act, 1988. They assert and give notice of their moral right under this Act.

Hawthorn Press

Published by Hawthorn Press, Hawthorn House,
1 Lansdown Lane, Stroud, Gloucestershire, GL5 1BJ, UK
Tel: (01453) 757040   Email: info@hawthornpress.com
Website: www.hawthornpress.com

Cover photograph © Christopher Triplett
Cover design and typesetting by Lucy Guenot
Printed by Short Run Press Ltd, Exeter

Every effort has been made to trace the ownership of all copyrighted material. If any omission has been made, please bring this to the publisher's attention so that proper acknowledgement may be given in future editions.

The views expressed in this book are not necessarily those of the publisher.

Printed on environmentally friendly chlorine-free paper sourced from renewable forest stock.

British Library Cataloguing in Publication Data applied for

ISBN 978-1-907359-88-0

Writing to Reading
the Steiner Waldorf Way
Foundations of Creative Literacy in Classes 1 and 2

Abi Allanson
Nicky Teensma

Hawthorn Press

Dedication

*To my grandmother, Gwladys Junor, and my mother, Viki Junor – both of them
brilliant, heartfelt English teachers.*   Abi

*To all the children who have inspired me to develop more poems,
songs, activities and games.*   Nicky

Acknowledgements

I would like to express my thanks to the many people who have shown support for
this project and lent their help for me to write, over its long gestation. In particular,
I acknowledge my grandmother for the first £500 she gave me for childcare. She
would have approved. I also thank my family – Phil, Isaac, Aaron and Seth – for
getting out of the way sometimes and cheering me on always.
Abi Allanson

I would like to thank my family who have, on so many occasions, patiently accepted
that my attention was with lesson preparations, my pupils and all those extra tasks
we will go the extra mile for as class teachers. I can't express enough how much
your support has meant to me.
Nicky Teensma

We both extend our thanks and appreciation to our colleagues at the Johannes school
in Tiel, NL, St Paul's Steiner School in London, Michael Hall Rudolf Steiner School and
at the Rudolf Steiner School Kings Langley. Our discussions about teaching and child
development have always been inspiring. It has been a huge privilege to work with
the children at these schools: working with you and refining our teaching ideas and
strategies through your feedback has been our best teaching. Without you there
would be no book! Our sincere admiration and thanks also go to Martin Large,
Richard House and Hawthorn Press for their patience and unstinting enthusiasm
for this publication.

Contents

Foreword

Alongside historical upheaval and calamity, the twentieth century was in many respects also the era of the reading wars. As became evident to leading personnel during military conscription in the First World War, despite the existence of universal education at least at a primary-school level in the West, many adults were functionally illiterate. The rapid technological expansion during and after the Second World War – including the space race, the cognitive revolution, and the shift in Western economies from production-based to service-based activities (including research and development) – has further heightened the need for a well-educated workforce.

However, economic reasons alone are never the sole driving force for cultural development. Just as in the fifteenth and sixteenth centuries the reformation brought about the teaching of reading to the peasant masses in Central Europe – so that each could read the Bible in his or her own language, independently of the authority of the Church – social reasons are also a factor in the modern emphasis on developing adequate literacy skills. It is no longer acceptable to leave un-aided those struggling with reading. Each and every citizen should have access to this emancipatory skill to allow the cultivation of true independence at both a practical (obtaining a driver's licence, reading medicine labels) and an intellectual-spiritual level (to inform and form one's own thoughts). Given the societal, military and economic forces and interests at heart, it is of little wonder that reading's role in education was a source of further conflict.

Two issues have dominated the debate around reading – the first of which considers when this should be taught, and the second focusing on how this should be 'instructed'. The argument around timing is actually quite an old one: in his treatise *Émile ou de l'éducation*, Rousseau argued that reading represented an adult activity that was tiresome for children, such that it was better left for late childhood. In the 1920s and 1930s two empirical investigations led to conflicting conclusions – namely, that children under the age of six were not cognitively ready to learn to read, whereas a second concluded that children could learn to read, provided that the materials were sufficiently tailored so as to be developmentally appropriate. For many even today, if either of these poles are not the default position, they might instead hold a stronger belief yet, namely that children must learn to read early (i.e. in preschool), lest their educational development suffer long-term disadvantage.

As with many questions, Rudolf Steiner – the founder of Steiner-Waldorf education – held a view that went above and beyond conventional ideas. He maintained that learning to read later need not negatively influence later achievement: in fact, if it were replaced with appropriate pedagogical activity, delaying reading could have long-term benefits, and early reading might even be harmful. To the modern mind, such a conclusion might seem absurd – and as a result, it has constituted one point on which Steiner-Waldorf education has repeatedly been attacked. It therefore bears closer consideration.

In empirical studies, we have looked at the reading development of children who by virtue of attending Steiner-Waldorf schools began learning to read around age seven in comparison to those who started on their fifth birthday or sooner. Findings indicated that the Steiner-Waldorf children were indeed initially well-delayed on early reading skills. However, at around age eight or nine their reading skills began to show a strong burst in development, such that by age nine, ten or eleven (depending on the individual children) they had caught up to their regular school peers. In other words, *they had gained in two to three years what their regular school peers did in four to five years*. In additional work, I was able to show empirically, using data from international reading studies (i.e. PISA), that countries with earlier school entry do not have better reading skills.

All in all, then, Steiner's first idea that delaying reading until around age seven will not lead to long-term disadvantages appears to be empirically supported – certainly as long as care is taken to provide the children with a rich preschool environment. In the current work, the current authors allude in many places to the kind of foundations that underpin the approach to writing and reading advocated here. They encourage teachers to draw upon the aesthetic, social, sensori-motor, language and attention skills that children have. Each of these, in turn, could and should be gently nurtured in a preparatory way in preschool settings.

Turning to arguments around content of reading interventions, scientists, educators and politicians have argued – at times vehemently – over the best approach for early reading instruction. The one position, loosely termed phonics, advocates for the systematic teaching of children to identify the phonemes present in words (i.e. that the word 'cat' comprises the sounds /c/ /a/ /t/) and to pair these with their corresponding letters. The other whole-language position argues that this is overly reductionist, and that because of the irregular nature of English orthography, knowledge of letter–sound combinations is confusing and superfluous. Instead, children need to learn to automatically recognise words, using contextual cues and information. Although it sounds strange, the debate between these two positions has indeed been so impassioned and absolute, that this has been termed 'the reading wars'.

A third, lesser-known position is that reading is best learned through writing. Such approaches advocate the acquisition of reading through a manual activity, whereby letter–sound correspondences are learned through noticing links between written symbols and sounds.

Again, the authors of the current book show just how non-dogmatic and well-rounded Steiner-Waldorf education can be, when the starting point is taken from the child itself, as opposed to an abstract theory. This book is built on many wise examples garnered out of practical experience with real children, representing what arises out of a synthesis of these three methods (i.e. phonics, whole-language and reading-through-writing) coupled with a holistic view of the human being as found in the Steiner-Waldorf approach.

Children are first gently eased out of early childhood through a language– and pictorially rich method that introduces them to the archetypal, then graphical forms of the letters. These graphical forms take on the shape and function of letters, out of which words are formed. At the same time, these letters are allowed to remain in context and hence more holistically experienced by the children, because these are actively embedded in and presented through song, rhyme and story. The authors recognise English's difficult orthography, and the need for children to be able to recognise frequently occurring words automatically, and hence advocate teaching automated sight-word reading of commonly occurring words.

Care and detail are also paid to the cognitive and motor-skill foundations of reading and writing. Expressed in terms of cognitive psychology, the mental representation of a concept is richer if it is anchored in sensory experience in multiple domains. With the approach outlined in the current work, children have the opportunity to experience the written and spoken forms of the language in aesthetically pleasing forms, through many senses – the auditory, visual, tactile, kinaesthetic, proprioceptive, and even vestibular. The individual strengths of children are thereby used to advantage while weaknesses are gently supported, resulting in a rich and multi-faceted approach to teaching reading, centred around knowledge of the child and an ability to observe clearly and in detail.

Accordingly, the current work promises to be useful not only for teachers seeking to guide children into the world of literacy, but it also provides a long-overdue and unique resource detailing the holistic Steiner-Waldorf approach that has hitherto been unjustly neglected in scholarly and lay discussions.

Sebastian Suggate, Ph.D.
University of Regensburg, Germany
Regensburg, Germany, Autumn 2016

Preface

Sharing our Teaching

One of the great privileges that I have been fortunate enough to enjoy over the last 40 years has come through visiting many schools and classrooms. I could probably say that most of what I know is based upon years of watching teaching as well as sharing my own teaching. This focus on the tricky business of teaching and learning has been a constant delight. Often it is a mystery, sometimes a frustration, especially when we try to unravel the creative act of teaching.

Reading this book is a joyful invitation into the classrooms of Abi Allanson and Nicky Teensma. This is a wonderful read, taking us deep in to the practice of two talented and thoughtful teachers. Great teaching is an art. Sometimes, we hardly know what it was that we did that brought about an effect in the classroom. We know what we think we did but do we really know what actually happened? Describing that clearly to others, so that they might use our teaching as a springboard, is even more of a challenge.

I know that in my own early teaching, I used to love marking! I have thought about this for many years because I meet lots of teachers who hate marking. I saw teaching as a creative act. I brought my imagination to the occasion, crafting lessons and sequences that might help children write creatively. As I taught, I thought on my feet. I tired to weave atmospheres that might set up the space for a little bit of magic as children wrote creatively. I tried to be the spark that lit the fire.

So what the children wrote was a result of the chemistry between teacher and learner. Their writing was an extension of my teaching. So it was that I came to the marking with curiosity to see what they had made of the sessions, ready to be surprised and delighted. Many, many times I have tried to write or talk about that breathless sense of excitement, trying to make the complex simple without losing the richness, challenge and depth of teaching. It is not easy to explain such things but we should try to share the gift of our teaching so that we can all broaden our repertoire of what might be possible in the classroom.

The authors' deep thinking and sharing is an act of such generosity, laced with so much classroom wisdom. They will have given much time to discussing teaching and describing learning to achieve such clarity so that we can learn from their years of reflection. Indeed, reading this book made me want to get back into the classroom and there can be no higher praise for a book about teaching.

This book will be a catalyst for many teachers, in all types of schools, prompting us to challenge the status quo and bring into harmony our work on early literacy enhanced through movement, song, rhyme and art. Indeed, the richness of the programme puts to shame the meager attempts by governments to prescribe the education of small children, too often reducing early literacy to a withered curriculum that lacks heart or sense.

Here we find the voice of authentic teachers speaking to us through their unpicking of what has worked well for them. The book provides us with a radical and responsible view of teaching early literacy that confronts the mainstream view about how we should teach reading. The key challenge to current orthodoxy is the idea that children should be taught to write before they read, placing primary importance on the need to actively create rather than passively receive. This sits alongside the significance of valuing the child's 'voice'. There is a strong focus on the need to start from the 'whole' of speaking and listening so that the analytic parts of phonics and letters enjoys a rich and meaningful context.

Central too to the work of these teachers is the role of story. Literacy is taught as an art that is about both technique and feeling. I had such a vision many years ago. What would happen if we could take a school and every year children became intimate with a bank of stories that took them on a journey from the naughtiness of the Gingerbread Man to the might of Beowulf and the great, rolling adventures of the Odyssey? Steiner schools are founded on a respect for the potency of story. This is complemented by giving space to the role of song and rhyme so that children tune to the rhythms and language patterns that lie at the heart of so many cultures. Choral speaking and learning to listen provide opportunities to develop not just listening, but also a love of language, the comfort of rhythm and the confidence that comes with community.

Time is given to the importance of growing the imagination. We process the world through our imagination but it is also developed through fruitful play as well as the story worlds that the teachers create by both telling and reading. Regular work on visualization helps to build the inner world and can be practised though visualization games. Teaching children to observe their experiences more closely and more carefully is a precursor to being able to see more vividly inside our heads. Looking outside helps you to look inside. In this way, moments in stories can be slowed down and children learn how to observe more closely what they see in their minds, searching for the details and building pictures.

The authors also recognize that our teaching should fit the rhythms of the day as well as thinking about how learning should be phased over time. Attention is given to the importance of movement, balance and spatial awareness all of which have an influence upon early literacy and well-being. Infant classrooms should be places where story is central; where children sing and chant action rhymes; where they dance and move with purpose.

They are not afraid to address the thorny issue of play and its role in education. Active and collaborative learning is central so that children develop *initiative, stamina and a confidence for inquiry*. Play can be the *staple diet for educating and engaging children's will*. Steiner believed that play should not just be there to entertain or become *mere playing about*. It should educate. When our teaching is right then almost all primary school learning is a form of play. It might be a form of serious play but great literacy, and writing in particular, requires total engagement where we tussle with words and ideas with intent and joy.

Having devoted a lifetime to the importance of creativity in education, I whooped aloud when I read an early passage which points to the importance of children's early authorship, that notices and celebrates a child's own voice. They move on to make the telling point that such children will be less likely to '*over-lay these jewels with the habits of self-doubt or self-censorship, two characteristics that frequently cripple creativity and original thought in more mature writers*' (page 30).

Fear is the enemy of creativity. In mainstream primary education in England children write with checklists of grammatical features to include, robbing them of the opportunity to think for themselves. Indeed, most young children write by numbers learning that their own ideas are not what the teacher requires. Education is becoming so criteria bound that those who succeed are those who can fulfil the criteria. Free-thinking, curiosity, questioning and creativity have less space than ever before. No wonder our businesses and universities despair at young people who know how to do what they are told but lack confidence in themselves and find independent learning and thinking a challenge. There is such wisdom in the simple words, '*a classroom quickly turns sterile if the teacher is the only one with answers*' (page 23).

This is a book not just for those working in Steiner schools. It offers a richer view of what it means to develop literacy with young children. It is a little gem glittering in the dark night of current educational thinking about early education.

Let's all work hard to share our teaching with a similar generosity. We do not have to always agree but we can think, learn and grow together. Ultimately, this book is about whom we are as human beings; how we cherish the human spirit in ourselves and within those we are fortunate enough to teach.

Pie Corbett, creator of *Talk for Writing* (see page 346), teacher, author and poet

Introduction

It would be a good idea if Waldorf teachers would work on creating decent textbooks that reflect our pedagogical principles.[1]

This book is intended to provide a rationale and practical pathway for teaching and working with foundation literacy skills in Steiner Waldorf schools where English is the first language. The material in this book provides a clear route through Classes 1 and 2, offering guidance and inspiration to Waldorf class teachers. Most new teachers have not previously studied linguistics, and it can be deceptively complex to understand the structure of one's own mother tongue. In addition to knowing one's subject – in this case literacy in English – an effective teacher needs to know their pupils. Most novices will need some experience before they can knit together their training on child development, the temperaments, learning strengths and difficulties with the reality of the live children they actually encounter in the classroom.

We hope that the framework set out in this book will enhance the essential principles of Waldorf education to help those teachers who are in the early stages of becoming expert and adept. With class teachers following the steps in this book, with some discipline and repetition, our goal is that, through the stages of mastery, they will paradoxically become creatively freer as they come to understand more deeply the craft of literacy teaching. We would like to share our work in order to encourage teachers to form a conversation with the book, and to develop their own exercises. After all, what works for one class does not always work for another, and the poems, stories, songs and exercises teachers develop themselves are often the ones that give most joy and success in their classes.

In addition, we sincerely hope that the suggestions herein will help teachers navigate around common pitfalls on the learning journey. It is quite easy to teach English literacy badly and to inadvertently leave students behind. Our aim is to help all teachers develop confidence and increase creativity in their work so that they can teach effectively, whilst successfully including all children in their classes, even those who have learning differences.

Rudolf Steiner gave inspiring indications about how to introduce the letters in Class 1, and many stories and poems have been written by teachers over the years to help us make this first introduction

---

1 Rudolf Steiner, p. 440 (Steiner, 1998).

to writing a wonderful experience for Class 1 children. But what do we do with those letters once they have been introduced? How do we practise the skills the children need to become confident writers and readers? And how can we do it in such a way that it is a joyful experience for the children – an experience that they will love, and that does not detract from the wholeness of imagination, reverence and well-being that we like to foster in the lower classes of our schools? In this book, we hope to set out a pathway that blends the best techniques of teaching from the Waldorf traditions with effective and efficient tools used by teachers everywhere to reach all the children in a class.

Finally, we have a fundamental aim regarding levels of achievement. Rudolf Steiner says,

> It would be good to try to get the children to learn to write themselves. In our opinion, between the eighth and ninth year they even ought to be able to write after a fashion... we should have brought them to the ordinary primary level by then.[2]

In our interpretation, this means that all children in a class ought to be measurably at a peer-equivalent level with those in the mainstream education system somewhere in Class 2 or 3. While later chapters will set this out in greater detail, we aim for the majority of children in any given class to reach an age-appropriate[3] level of independence and facility in writing, reading, listening and speaking by the end of Class 3. With the methods set out here, and in further volumes, we suggest that this outcome can be achieved or exceeded.

Structure of the Book

The first, Part 1 of this book sets out some core principles of good practice in Steiner education. These include foundation ideas about teaching that are both generally applicable and also essential for literacy teaching. These include teaching with authority, image-building, learning styles, multi-sensory methods, active learning, whole-class and group work. In Chapter 2, we describe specific principles for the teaching of literacy. This includes an analysis of Steiner's suggestion to teach writing before reading and the fundamental importance of facilitating a child's written 'voice'. A technical overview of English language structure is also given, with a summary of the role of story-telling, poetry, phonics, whole-word, visual and auditory learning. These principles will inform and underpin the practical methods which follow.

In Part 2, we begin with some background information about children in transit from the Kindergarten phase into the classroom environment. We set out what needs a teacher must expect to meet and how to prepare the way for effective literacy teaching. We describe practical ways for engaging with and addressing weakness in physical co-ordination and movement; form drawing and desk skills; speaking and listening; visual processing, memory and other social aspects of learning.

---

2 Steiner, *Faculty Meetings with Rudolf Steiner* 1922-1924, 1998, p. 439, 28/10/22.

3 Standards for what and when to test change according to current educational mores. Steiner schools will need to practise discernment and exercise their own judgements about the best way to demonstrate such information for comparison. We give some information about our experience of assessment throughout the book.

In Part 3, the reader will find substantial lesson content for working with sounds and symbols. This includes a variety of traditional and mainstream methods for letter introduction and developing phonemic and graphemic awareness. Suggested lesson content and real examples are given to show how to teach word craft, common word recognition and authorship. Throughout, box inserts include reminders, signposts for navigation and summaries.

In Part 4, there is an outline of good assessment techniques for checking progress, with the results also being helpful for the diagnosis of learning differences. We suggest ways for differentiating work so that all children are engaged and are learning at an appropriate level. We give further examples of practice work and extension tools.

In Part 5, we describe how to start the curriculum for Class 2, revising and consolidating after the summer holidays. We include physical exercises and Form Drawing to set the groundwork for learning. Part 6 then describes the teaching of cursive writing, more formal spelling instruction, extended authorship including elementary sentence structure and reading practice. Again, this includes assessment tools, differentiation suggestions and guidance for achievement at this age.

In Part 7, the reader will find a discussion of reading, and the teaching of reading. We explain how you back up your writing instruction with reading practice, supporting gradual independence for children at school and at home. Included here is guidance on how to communicate with parents about this and other issues around learning difficulties or delay.

In the book's many appendices, the reader will find resource lists of words, poems, games and additional references. We also provide example year, main lesson, subject and week plans showing how to pace your instruction. These are for your adaptation, and some of these include real-life notes showing how they were altered or annotated during one class year.

Note, finally, that in-text footnotes are numbered by part throughout.

PART 1

Theory and Best Practice

Chapter 1

Principles of Steiner Waldorf Education

In this chapter, we introduce some fundamentals of best practice in teaching, using familiar Steiner-Waldorf principles as well as widely used mainstream approaches. These include:

- Teaching with loving authority
- The use of imagery and rhythm in lesson design and implementation
- Understanding varied learning styles
- Active and independent learning

In this chapter, we briefly describe a few fundamentals of good practice that we believe will support all class teaching. All the examples of lesson material in this book draw upon these principles. Some of these principles are well-known, are more extensively explained elsewhere, and form part of the Waldorf paradigm.[1] Some are a blend of ideas taken from other settings.

The theory that Rudolf Steiner presented is practical because it helps us recognise and interpret classroom behaviours and respond in our teaching accordingly. Steiner Waldorf professionals use terms such as 'teaching with authority' or 'teaching with an image' as a kind of short-hand, useful for communicating and sharing with colleagues. However, this short-hand can become a 'jargon' that masks the nuances of Steiner's accounts, not to mention the particular time and place in which he worked. We fear that on occasion, classroom practice may be developed according to a thin interpretation of the concept and is therefore weakened. Whilst we absolutely defend the benefit of studying Steiner's works and of wrestling to understand them anew, we also present other teaching concepts here for their augmentation. This is not because a newer parlance of teaching is necessarily more robust – although we consider them qualitatively strong – but because they are

---

1 We hope it goes without saying that our description of these principles is only our own interpretation of the exceptionally detailed and subtle accounts that Steiner gave.

easily communicable. Many modern educationalists are striving to support creative, effective and enjoyable teaching and learning in a very sympathetic way. Teachers ought to understand what they are doing! We suggest that holding the old and new theories in a healthy tension is probably good for creative teaching, and we argue for pragmatically working with both.

Teaching with Authority

In Steiner schools, although there is a substantial traditional curriculum to follow, each class teacher is free to organise and colour the lesson content according to their own judgement. They will do so according to the characteristics and needs of the children and their personal specific skills or interests. Steiner described the art of 'loving authority' as being the hallmark of the teaching relationship in the class years.[2,3] Benevolent leadership is onerous, requiring excellent judgement and conferring formidable responsibility. It's attractive, however, because there is also an awesome freedom and creative potential in the work.

Teachers' confidence to do so stems from knowledge of three things. First, they will have a good understanding of their subject. This book is primarily an aid to supporting the class teacher's understanding of the subject of literacy teaching. Secondly, they will have a strong understanding of the full range of students as learners before them. The final requirement for confident teaching with authority is an openness to self-reflection and self-development. If a teacher has self-knowledge and some practice at how to change their own habits and behaviours, they will be able to meet the unknown and the unpredictable without fear. Such qualities will enable the teacher to organise the time and space well, and provide healthy boundaries of learning and behaviour. The result of such qualities will be a peaceful classroom of trust, with a positive attitude to learning.

The classroom is created primarily for the benefit of the *students*, even though the journey of the class teacher can be extremely rewarding. So why are the children there? They are there to learn about and develop their own relationship to two things: themselves and the world around them.[4] All education occurs in the dynamic of relationship between members of a learning community. The crucible is the classroom. In the next chapter, we will describe how the teacher–student relationship of 'loving authority' best functions to enable the student to know themselves and the world through the written word, to *become* literate.

Imagery and Rhythm

If the relationship between the teacher and child is vital for effective learning, so too is the form and timing with which the information is presented. How do we make it easier for teaching and learning to occur? By working with the grain of the natural development of the child.

---

2 Steiner, *The Education of the Child in the Light of Spiritual Science*, Berlin 10 January 1907 (1996) p. 24.
3 Steiner, Education in the Light of Spiritual Science, Koln, 1 December 1906 (1996), p. 58.
4 Robinson, 2013.

'I like it when you tell a story. It makes me feel like a giant!' This was a comment made by one of the students during the first term in Class 3. He was perhaps experiencing a feeling of expansion, of relaxation, of 'breathing out' that comes when a good story is told. He was one of those students who struggled with dyslexic-type difficulties. Since much of his school work requires intense labour, perhaps this is why he felt the different quality of the story and was able to express this feeling so eloquently.

What is it about a story? Again, much has been written elsewhere about the great pedagogical benefits of story-telling and dramatisation.[5] According to Steiner's views on child development, the child between the ages of 7 and 14 experiences the world primarily through their feelings.[6] That is to say that their emotional connection and personal response to the world have their most dominant influence during this phase. If they care about it, it will be noticed and 'taken in'. Steiner suggests that a direct way to pass on knowledge and encourage understanding is to teach using an image. In particular, he suggests (verbally) carefully describing images so that they are seen in the mind's eye or conjured in the imagination, prior to actually giving a physical picture for the eyes to see.[7] In other words, perhaps paradoxically, he suggests that it is optimal to use the child's auditory sense to listen to words that stimulate an inward, personal, visual sense. He claims that such teaching best reaches the child's heart, their sense of emotional connection. So when we teach, particularly in the earlier class years (up to the age of 11, for example), we must try to use a medium through which the child optimally relates to the world: vivid, personal pictures and images. Thus, stories are the ideal diet. A great deal of information can be conveyed in this way such that the child can 'own' it effortlessly.

> ...everything that one brings to a child at this age must be given in the form of fairy tales, legends, and stories in which everything is endowed with feeling.[8]
> The etheric body will unfold its forces if a well-ordered imagination is allowed to take guidance from the inner meaning it discovers for itself in pictures and allegories... with the mind's eye.[9]

Alongside these comments, Steiner made suggestions about the pacing of teaching. Human beings of all ages learn best when there are periods of concentration and effort, and some phases of relaxation. Steiner specifically gave us to understand that this is because of the way memory works. How do we teach and learn most effectively over time?

Steiner said that emotional engagement with the world, which is most important for learning during this age-range, takes two forms: a sympathetic or an antipathetic response. That is to say, a child will feel drawn to or repelled by something. Both types of response result in learning. Steiner

---

5 Daniel, 2011; Hollingsworth & Ramsden, 2013; Perrow, 2012.
6 Steiner says that this phase is when the child's etheric body can be developed and worked with through external education. He gives many details in foundation lectures such as 'The Education of the Child in the Light of Spiritual Science', Berlin, 10 January 1907 (publ. 1996), pp. 23–26.
7 See Lecture 4 (Steiner, *The Kingdom of Childhood*, Torquay 12–20 August 1924 (publ. 1995).
8 Steiner, *The Kingdom of Childhood*, Torquay, 12–20 August 1924 (publ. 1995) p. 31.
9 Steiner, 'The Education of the Child in the Light of Spiritual Science', Berlin, 10 January 1907 (publ. 1996) p. 23.

says that this emotional reality is akin to the physiological mechanism of breathing – we must breathe in and breathe out, receive and express, and so on. Our educational process, therefore, best operates according to these natural laws. Learning new academic skills demands concentration, but allowing them to sink into our long-term memory requires relaxation.[10] A series of activities that require concentration and relaxation, antipathy and sympathy, breathing in and breathing out, make for a healthy school experience. Such a learning experience appeals to children: 'Children now have a strong desire to experience the emerging life of soul and spirit on waves of rhythm and beat within the body – quite subconsciously, of course.'[11]

Steiner extended this principle as far as practically possible to underpin the design of main lesson practice and the school day. Designing learning around phases of the day, the week and blocks of several weeks pays off as an economical method for encouraging absorption of information and integrated understanding. Such an ecological approach has been noticed and documented by other educational thinkers.[12] Later in the book, we will describe ways for rhythmically bringing new ideas and concepts to a class especially to enhance the prospects of improved recall and remembering.

Learning Styles

While there is not the scope in this book to give a full account of learning preferences and difficulties that a class teacher may encounter in their classroom, here we set out a brief guide. We encourage readers to make every effort to learn more about this topic through experience, professional development and study. References are included in the bibliography to support this. Steiner addressed this issue – of the variability among children – through several key concepts, and we mention just two of these here. Perhaps simplest and most user-friendly for the class teacher is the idea of the four temperaments.[13] Children can be characterised as having dominant physical and personality temperament types, and Steiner gave examples of how the teacher may best address each of the four predominant child temperaments. Another way to consider meeting the child is to think about the three-fold faculties of the human being: thinking, feeling and willing.[14] We may plan our teaching so it can address each aspect appropriately. Other commentators have described this in far greater detail than we are currently able to do.[15]

In terms of addressing learning difficulties and classroom pitfalls, we think it is helpful to consider the three media of auditory, visual and kinaesthetic processing. All mainstream curricula now incorporate the requirement to teach in a multi-sensory way. This means that the same concept is brought using, at the least, auditory, visual and kinaesthetic means. The theory is that

10 This is described as learning being absorbed by the developing etheric forces. See Steiner, *Soul Economy: Body, Soul and Spirit in Waldorf Education*, Dornach, 23 December 1921 – 5 January 1922 (publ. 2003) for a full description.

11 Steiner, *Soul Economy: Body, Soul and Spirit in Waldorf Education*, Dornach, 23 December 1921 – 5 January 1922 (publ. 2003), p. 136.

12 Claxton, 1998.

13 Steiner, *Discussions with Teachers*, Stuttgart, 21 August – 6 September 1919 (1997), pp. 13–21.

14 Steiner, 'The Education of the Child in the Light of Spiritual Science', Berlin, 10 January 1907 (1996), pp. 33–35.

15 For example, see Rawson & Avison, 2013, Petrash, 2003 and Finser, 1994.

in this way, all the children will be able to access it. Another current way to understand learning is to try to design teaching that suits both the left and right brain for specific tasks. Later in the book, there will be more information about the art of teaching for different needs. You need to know a good deal about how children process and integrate new information and what can happen when this fails. You will find plenty of activities that help prevent failure, but in order that you may invent more, appropriate for your children, the more expert you yourself become about how their brains can work the better.

Active Learning: Playing and Independence

While children will ordinarily be comfortable and respectful receiving wise words from their teacher, a classroom quickly turns sterile if the teacher is the only one with answers. It's a teacher's job to proactively alert the children to how much they know and how much they can discover.

Although we promote the idea of teaching authority, the teacher is the facilitator as well as the guide. You are *training* them in self-reliance.[16] Children are very likely to digest and retain more information from each other than they will from you, or from most adults.[17] A classroom designed around active learning is one where children develop initiative, stamina and confidence for inquiry.[18]

Partner and group work is fundamental to enabling children to become independent learners. Most of the exercises set out in the next part of the book will include elements where the children work with each other, particularly to talk about learning and to practise a new skill. *Encouraging* talking in the classroom may still be imagined a risky or trivial undertaking but it is one we applaud, with appropriate boundaries.

> On one hand, talk has more official recognition now than at any time in our educational history; on the other hand, as a culture we value reading and writing more highly than oral competence and our assessment system is still conducted predominantly in the written mode. In the pre-GCSE era, there existed a deficit model of oracy, which suggested that it was a way of compensating for the lack of writing ability of lower ability pupils.[19]

We rate it as a high-quality teaching strategy, as do many mainstream educationalists. Perhaps paradoxically, we think behaviour in the class can *improve* when children are talking – independence leads to confidence; to relaxation and a peaceful environment. In the following pages, you will find many games for children to play together to learn. Play can be the staple diet for educating and engaging children's will. Steiner made the point that games must not just be entertainment.

---

16 Janis-Norton, 2004.
17 Topping, 1998, Wiliam, 2011.
18 For further examples, see Clarke, 2008 and Myhill, Jones and Hopper, 2005.
19 Introduction, p. 1, Myhill, Jones and Hopper, 2005.

He warns:

> It is not good to introduce mere playing about into education. On the contrary, it is our task to introduce the fullness of life into education; we should not bring in things that are no more than playing about. But please do not misunderstand me. I am not saying that play should not be introduced into education; what I mean is that games artificially constructed for the lesson have no place in school. There will still be a great deal to say about how play can be incorporated into the lessons.[20]

We hope the learning games set out here will educate your children easily and meaningfully.

---

20 Lecture Four, Steiner, *Practical Advice to Teachers*, Stuttgart, 21 August – 6 September 1919 (publ. 1976), p. 58.

Chapter 2

Literacy Pedagogy

In this chapter, we introduce some fundamental principles of best practice as specific to literacy teaching. These include:

- The value of literacy
- Age of starting literacy teaching
- The relationship principle of education
- Voice
- Why writing before reading?
- Authorship and editorship
- What teachers need to know about English

Occasionally, some may question the overarching assumption that it is necessary for children to become literate at all. Perhaps there is no fundamental requirement for the health of the human being that they learn this skill. In Rudolf Steiner's view, the capacity to read and write was not intrinsically important for a child's health, development or spiritual progress as an end in itself.[21] This is quite hard to grasp for people today. Steiner felt that other subjects such as mathematics, but most especially music, movement and fine arts, are much more organic and natural to the human being, and therefore of benefit to the health and well-being of the individual. For the young child, he also vigorously championed the cultivation of curiosity and 'pure science' observation. He urged the practice of detailed observation right from the start of school. Historically, literacy is indeed a relatively young educational 'discipline', and Steiner termed it as belonging to the physical world, further away from the spiritual. We encourage readers to research this question more deeply for yourselves.

---

21 Steiner, Practical Advice to Teachers, Stuttgart, 21 August –6 September 1919 (publ. 1976), p. 10.

However, and this is a big caveat, literacy is *the* mode of knowledge in our age. In order for children to participate in our culture at all, they *must* become adept at words, quite enough to practise it, enjoy it and then bump up against the limitations of text. Even if we question its status as a strand of education, we would be negligent if we didn't teach literacy – willingly, artistically and efficiently – in order that our students may achieve expressive confidence in this medium. To this end, we follow several important principles of practice.

Why Do We Start When We Start?

In a Steiner school, we believe that it is most effective and efficient to introduce children to literacy later than statutory school age in the UK at the present time. Such formal learning begins in Class 1 at age 6, rising 7.[22] Researchers have recognised that the early starting age of most UK schools can be problematic[23, 24], and we would suggest that a later starting age can be advantageous for all children, but perhaps especially for those who have learning difficulties. We argue that this 'delay' does not hold children back from reading success.[25]

Classes 1 and 2 curricula are so designed to enable the children to acquire a solid foundation in all school skills – literacy, mathematics, movement, music, art and social life – and 'proper' curriculum content could be said to start with the Old Testament stories in Class 3. Class 3 is a sort of cross-over year, where children are now skilled (or schooled) and ready to develop real independence in learning. We hope that the principles and methods for the class teacher set out here will provide the foundation for children to achieve that independence somewhere in the third school year, at the approximate age of 9 years.

We define independence as being a fluent reader[26] and a writer able to construct an intelligible series of simple sentences, with some fluency, in response to a text or story, legibly, with reasonable spelling and consistent basic punctuation. While we recognise that a few children with more significant specific difficulties or special circumstances may not achieve this in Class 3, we hold that this is a reasonable benchmark and expectation for achievement. For illustration, we would expect that for an average class of 20 or more children with a non-selective intake, 80 per cent of them would be able to demonstrate this level of working at this age, with perhaps half exceeding such a level.[27] We believe this ambition to be in line with Steiner's intentions for Waldorf students' learning success, as indicated in our introduction, taken from Steiner's conferences with teachers in the initial years of the life of the first school.[28]

---

22 This is the equivalent UK National Curriculum Year 2.

23 Sharp, 'Age of starting school and the early years curriculum', 1998; Sharp, 'School starting age: European policy and recent research, 2002; Riggal and Sharp, 2009; Whitebread, 2013; House, 2013; Palmer, 2016.

24 See the Save Childhood Movement's 'Too Much Too Soon' campaign, which sites 75–90 per cent public support of a later school starting age in Vox polls run by the *Guardian* and *Daily Telegraph* newspapers in November 2013.

25 Suggate, 'Research into early reading instruction and like effects in the development of reading, 2009a; Suggate, 'Response to reading instruction and age related development: do later starters catch up?', 2009b; Suggate, 2009c; Healy, 2004.

26 According to a standardised test, at least age-equivalent at c. 9 or 9.5 years of age.

27 This is based on our collective experience working in large, established schools and smaller, younger organisations.

28 Steiner, Faculty Meetings with Rudolf Steiner, 1922–1924 (publ. 1998), p. 439, 28/10/22.

What Are We Asking Children to Learn?

In a school setting, Class 1 children know that they are there to learn about the world and all the things in it. However, they may initially be less conscious that they are also there to learn about themselves: to come to know their own strengths, frailties and preferred modes of expression. Thus, education has public and private aspects: what is my relationship to the world and what is my relationship to myself?[29] Eventually knowing the answers will enable a person to find expression and agency in life.

Extending the last chapter's ideas on loving authority, we suggest that a good teacher consciously aims to help the child develop and learn in both areas through what we may term a *relational* approach. Teaching and learning are a form of cyclical communication. We suggest that a child actually *uses* their teacher to mediate their growing awareness of themselves. The child and teacher grow in relationship and through 'knowing' each other as they rest upon, push against, flow with and form a sort of self/other dialogue.[30] On the classroom stage, in this relational interplay the child slowly becomes aware – as if an original discovery – of their own unique features, desires and limits, by reference to and reflection of the other.[31] In terms of learning about the world around them, one core pedagogical principle articulated in the Waldorf world is that of teaching initially from the whole to the parts.[32] Without wanting to diverge into a long discussion of this concept, we suggest that the teaching of the written word is exactly this principle in practice. We work from the 'whole' of speaking and listening, to the analytic 'parts' of sounds and symbols – and in this way, we learn about the world.

So we are expecting children to convert the living, breathing, in-the-moment world of language (speaking and listening, with which they are very familiar and adept) into the symbolic world of literacy (writing and reading), which is comparatively abstract, and always refers to the past.[33, 34] As we all know, the young child will have relatively little conscious idea of why they do what they do – they just *do*! So as a teacher, how can you enable a child to feel confident in this work when, in reality, sitting down to read or write suits a sedentary adult much better? Happily, of course, most 6 year old children will be excited by learning skills that denote maturity. They are usually enthusiastic about learning in Class 1, and we aim to show you how to capitalise upon this energy and not lose it.

Voice

As children develop, they may become more aware of experiencing their own voice. Teaching literacy is the means to a person being able to use their written voice as an artistic tool.

---

29 See Robinson, 2009 for a discussion about education for learning about the Self and learning about the World.

30 Steiner had much to say on the virtuous model teachers ought to provide. See Steiner, 'The Education of the Child in the Light of Spiritual Science', Berlin, 10 January 1907 (publ. 1996); Steiner, *The Kingdom of Childhood*, Torquay, 12–20 August 1924 (publ. 1995).

31 It is no less true that the children in a class may be the greatest guides towards self-knowledge for the teacher – a humbling proposition.

32 Lecture 5, Steiner, *The Kingdom of Childhood*, Torquay, 12–20 August 1924 (publ. 1995).

33 Elbow, 2012. See 'What's good about writing' (p. 40) for a fascinating discussion of the differences between writing and speaking. Even when you are writing about the future, the written word necessarily encapsulates a thought that has already happened.

34 See also Townend and Walker, 2006 for in-depth history of spoken and written English in the UK.

A child at age 7 may experience their inner voice as anything from the merest whisper to something quite strident. They may inwardly hear their own thoughts, feelings and desires and vocalise them in a certain way.[35] The term we use here – voice – is a subtle and difficult one to nail down. Using it, we refer to the way in which a person, and in this case a school child, articulates their own particular nature, their individual self. We can tell it is their authentic voice because there is something resonant, consistent and connected when we listen.[36]

We would suggest that many experienced teachers have struggled to draw out vivid, varied and technically strong writing from their children.[37] However, we believe that if we construct our literacy teaching around the principle of enabling children to become artists of written self-expression, then we have the best chance of setting the tone for life-long confidence in the written word. How can we allow our students to freely and healthily develop their *written* voice? How can we appropriately encourage and channel that voice in those children who are inhibited about, or unaware of, the subtleties of their own?[38] It's no wonder that children want to learn this grown-up skill – it may be a gateway to their own becoming.[39]

Writing before Reading

...as children become authors, as they struggle to express, refine, and reach audiences through their own writing, they actively come to grips with the most important reading insights of all.

Through writing, children learn that text is not preordained or immutable truth. It is human voice....Through writing, children learn that the purpose of text is not to be read but to be understood. (Adams, 1990, p. 405)

We advocate the fundamental Waldorf pedagogical principle that children should be shown how to write before they read; they should work with the active principle before the passive, initially prioritising the *creative* over the *receptive*.[40]

This is deceptively radical. Literacy, and literacy teaching, constitute a powerfully emotive subject – the debate about the best ways to teach and learn is seemingly constant, and surprisingly

---

35 The *loudest* children may not actually be the ones who speak most authentically; they may only be vocalising reactively or anxiously, for example.

36 If a person is voicing inauthentically, we, the listeners, are less likely to pick up resonance, to be convinced and to feel that communication has truly occurred. See Peter Elbow (1998), Chapter 25, for a detailed exposition of this term and the process of recognition.

37 In conversation with a principal trainer from one of the leading DfE-recognised synthetic phonics literacy schemes used widely across the UK, this author heard her say, when asked about the elements of the programme designed to teach writing skills, that "it is hard to get children to write really well and it takes a long time."

38 Graves, among many others, advocates that teachers engage in *their own* writing of stories and poetry so that the learning is happening at all levels of the classroom community (Graves, 1983).

39 Sometimes, in mainstream or Steiner schools, good writing can be seen as difficult to teach. However, many authors have vigorously championed ways of encouraging writing creativity (not only 'creative writing' as such). We recommend inspirational teachers such as Donald H. Graves, Kenneth Koch and Sandy Brownjohn, Pie Corbett and Michael Rose. See the bibliography. There are probably many more – we are always interested to hear of them!

40 Steiner, *Practical Advice to Teachers*, 1976, p. 14.

vehement.[41] However, in all the thousands of books and essays that have emerged on this topic, only a very tiny percentage has advocated this counter-cultural approach.[42,43] Why did Rudolf Steiner suggest this? We believe that the cyclical dynamic of teaching and learning that is education ought to centre on the drawing out of what exists and develops in the child's inner life. Giving 'external' information is a means to inspire and facilitate a child in becoming themselves and finding their purpose in relation to the world around them. We contend that the cultural dominance of the pedagogy of teaching reading before writing prejudices education too far towards the notion of education as the 'filling of a bucket' and as training for compliance and uniformity.[44] Steiner did not approve of dawdling through the teaching of reading, but he left no doubt about which step should take place first:

> So you can see how the letters can be developed out of pictures and pictures again directly out of life. ... On no account should you teach reading first, but proceeding from your drawing-painting and painting-drawing, you allow the letters to arise out of these, and then you can proceed to reading.[45]

Guiding Two Aspects of the Written Voice

As a result of our classroom work and planning many lessons for children who are beginners or struggling literacy learners, we have come to find it helpful to conceptualise authorship as having two distinct cognitive aspects: sympathetic and antipathetic.[46] In order to write with enthusiasm, one needs to have an idea or impulse (a voice) and enough tools to be able to set those down in print. The impulse to express thoughts and feelings is paramount: it amounts to the *content* of the communication. This first aspect can be characterised as 'sympathetic' authorship. Next, in order to communicate effectively so that a reader can be certain of understanding the intended idea, the most appropriate words must be set down using the accurate conventions of spelling, syntax and punctuation. These perhaps determine the style or the structure of the communication. To master this, the child must use the second aspect of 'antipathetic' skills of authorship, or, one could also say, editorship.

We believe that the child needs plenty of sympathetic authorship space in Class 1 (without too much interference from other written voices, i.e. *reading*.) This means that they need to become a little accustomed to the phenomenon of expressing themselves in writing and their own written voice awakening. The child's own voice – either spoken or written – may emerge by surprise, almost – popping up out of seemingly nowhere, perhaps in bite-sized little bits. The key pedagogical quality

---

41 Adams, 1990.
42 Interestingly, this was a pedagogical point of convergence between Montessori and Steiner (Montessori, 1966).
43 See Adams, 1990, Ch. 14, and Elbow, 2004 for full discussion of trends for teaching this way in the USA, such as the 'Writer's Workshop' approach inspired by the work of Donald H. Graves (Graves, 1983).
44 See commentators such as Ken Robinson (2011) for contemporary accounts of the misconceptions underlying much public education.
45 Steiner, *The Kingdom of Childhood*, Torquay 12–20 August 1924 (1995) p. 25.
46 Elbow, *Writing with Power: Techniques for Mastering the Writing Process*, 1998.

for its effective encouragement is to *notice* it. If the teacher prepares the child with literacy tools, provides space for those moments to arise and then *notices* when they do, this is enough. The child will feel recognised and will also notice! It is moments like these that give the children continued enthusiasm, passion and stamina for learning. (For a further examination of the subtle concept of teaching the imagination, see Chapter 6 and the discussion about recall.) We suggest that in classes where children have experienced this positive quality of noticing and recognising the self in authorship early, they are less likely to later over-lay these jewels with the habits of self-doubt or self-censorship, two characteristics that frequently cripple creativity and original thought in more mature writers.

In the next phase of learning, once this phenomenon has been established, it becomes equally important to strengthen the children's work with technique: they need muscles to be able to bring form and structure to that voice. Children are then able to stand back from their work and address issues of accuracy and clarity, spelling and punctuation, with the skills to enhance them.[47]

Further, once you feel that the children in your class have experienced something of both these aspects and have even developed some awareness and confidence – *I am a writer!* – we encourage instruction in reading. In Part 7, you will find some practical suggestions for the teaching of reading, especially suitable for Class 2. Learning to read is usually faster and easier than developing authorship and editorship. In due course, a reciprocal relationship will emerge: the virtues of good reading will help inform effective writing style, and the special quality of thought required for writing will enhance reading appreciation and comprehension.

Fairy Tales and Other Curriculum Content

If you want your children to be intelligent, read them fairy tales. If you want your children to be very intelligent, read them even more fairy tales. Albert Einstein[48]

The curriculum content – of fairy tales or nature stories, for example – is the teacher's third arm, the mediator in their relationship with the child. In order to support children's writing, we try to use meaningful and beautiful text – stories and poems – to nourish them with imagery and colour[49] and to stimulate and extend their own verbal capacities. In the following lecture, Steiner aims to show that we can simultaneously draw out individual expression whilst also giving technical instruction.

---

47 It is often pedagogically most sensible to direct a class towards authorship and editorship at separate times, not simultaneously. Otherwise, it can be like asking them to do something independently with each hand – overwhelming! (Elbow, 1998, ibid.).

48 This oft-quoted sentence is difficult to attribute accurately but it seems that it comes from Einstein's discussion with a friend who wanted his advice on how to best prepare her son for eventually becoming a scientist. Apparently, Einstein said that creative imagination is the essential element in the intellectual equipment of the true scientist, and that fairy tales are the childhood stimulus to this quality.

49 We are deliberately not describing the curriculum story content for each year: resources for fairy tales, nature stories, poems, fables, Saints stories and so on are plentiful. We include some references for such resources in our bibliography. We encourage you to always use that material to help you find images to bring this skills work. If this book describes the warp of the weaving, others much more effectively describe the weft.

We avoid using passages that do not stimulate the imagination, and make as much use as possible of passages that stimulate the imagination really strongly, namely fairy tales. As many fairy tales as possible. And having practised this telling and retelling with the children for a long time, we then start in a small way to let them give brief accounts of something they have themselves experienced ... With all this telling of stories, retelling, and telling of personal experiences we develop without being pedantic about it the transition from the local dialect to educated speech ... We can do all this and in spite of it the children will have reached the desired goal by the end of their first year at school.[50]

We consciously teach literacy as an *art*, in an artistic way. This book will show you how to develop the skills needed, deriving spelling patterns from poems and sentence structure from the stories, for example. In addition, we also demonstrate structured practice out of context, through lively, organised 'play' to maintain interest and excitement in the children. Children need to learn in the spirit of play.[51] This sounds obvious, but it makes all the difference whether children love what they are doing compared to feeling forced. Even the most difficult concept can be understood by a learner who is enthusiastic, but if they are detached or stressed, this same understanding cannot occur. We aim to show the reader ways of inspiring children with meaningful, artistic and imaginative lesson content and then to capitalise on their natural abundance of playfulness to rehearse the necessary skills.[52]

The English language is complex and irregular: the children will need to develop many skills. For example, they need to be able to hear the different sounds in words, to recognise simple and complex sound–symbol correlations and to *automatically and instantly* recognise numerous spelling patterns, grammar rules and exceptions. Showing the children or telling them is often not enough. Some children may soon forget what they have learnt, some things have to be learnt through experience and some just by heart. How do you know what to repeat, and when? How can you make sure that the more able children are still engaged while the ones who need it are receiving a healthy amount of practice? How do you measure what they have learned, partially or securely?

Essentially, the more playfully and independently active the children are, following multiple ways to repeat the learning, the more likely they are to develop a solid foundation of understanding. They may need multi-sensory activities to absorb the same piece of information, such as whole-body movement, fine-motor movement, hearing, speaking and observing in order to be able to identify, recognise, categorise, organise and make links between phenomena. We shall be giving indicators that may help teachers identify children with dyslexic tendencies, who are vulnerable to failure in literacy. We also set out many dyslexia-friendly activities that can be used by the whole class or small groups to support learning. Indeed, it is widely understood that techniques that are good for those with learning difficulties are almost always good for a whole class, too.[53] By following the guidance here, it is hoped that even the dyslexic children in the class will have minimal experience

---

50 Steiner, *Practical Advice to Teachers*, Stuttgart 21 August – 6 September 1919 (1976), pp. 179–180.
51 Brock, Jarvis, & Olusoga, 2014.
52 Steiner, *Practical Advice to Teachers*, Stuttgart 21 August – 6 September 1919 (1976), Chapter 4.
53 Reid, 2009; Palmer & Corbett, 2003; Dodge, 2005.

of failure and maximum experience of success in their learning of literacy, so that the seriously debilitating effects of poor learning self-esteem can as far as possible be prevented.

What You Need to Know about English

In the English language there are 44 phonemes.[54] This is a relatively high number compared to many languages. In addition, there are multiple ways of spelling these phonemes: there are 120+ graphemes in English.[55] Other languages may have a much closer correspondence between their alphabetic symbols and their phonemes, for example Spanish and Finnish. This means that those languages are easier to encode for spelling and decode for reading.[56] English students must learn many more variations. Despite this complexity, 80 per cent of written English is phonically regular so it is possible to teach this according to a sensible, logical pathway in such a way that children are not immediately overwhelmed or confused.[57]

In principle then, it is best to introduce children to a certain quantity of the basic materials – a group of the most frequently used consonants and short vowels – and then let them practise and work with them, applying them to writing. We suggest that the children's exposure to written words is at first somewhat controlled. At this stage, only ask them to decode new words which they can also write in order to create a feeling of security from the beginning.[58] We also encourage 'emergent spelling' where a child writes what they want to write in a phonically plausible way. We tell the children that it is important to have all the sounds in a word represented by letters, so that others can read their work, but they will learn the way that grown-ups spell in due course.

In addition, when teaching poems for recitation (and perhaps memory reading) and in all other auditory activities, we suggest deliberately using a wide variety of words, many too complicated for children to spell, possibly even to understand. This is crucial so that a real richness of language is maintained. The games described here are created so that the children can easily and confidently work with most words (e.g. a blends dictation where they only write the blend and a line for the rest of the word so that its real-life spelling is unimportant).

It is important that the children are quickly made aware of the distinction between vowels and consonants.[59] Class teachers may choose to use terminology other than 'vowel' and 'consonant' at the outset of Class 1 – for example, vowels might be termed golden letters and always written in

---

54 A phoneme is a unit of sound that forms part of a whole word. The convention for showing a phoneme is to use // around the symbols. For example, we would write /sh/ to denote the phoneme that begins the word 'ship'. See Appendix 1 for a need-to-know list of English phonemes and some corresponding graphemes. A very detailed account can be found in Townend & Walker, 2006. Chapter 16.

55 A grapheme is the symbolic representation of the phoneme. An example of the conventional way to denote a grapheme in text would be 'dge,' showing the grapheme that represents the phoneme at the end of the word 'bridge'.

56 Goswami, 2005.

57 Townend & Walker, 2006.

58 In educational debate, advocates of all types of phonics have historically emphasised this approach, while phonics detractors have been set against this, instead insisting on a whole-word method that maintains rich and varied language use. See Adams (1990) for an account of the polarised argument. Here, we seek to describe a compromise.

59 Steiner, 1976, p. 180.

golden yellow – but we emphasise that it is most important that the conceptual difference ought to be made clear. We recommend that teachers choosing to use different terminology revert to the conventional terms reasonably soon. Vowels and consonants are formed differently by the vocal cords, using different places in the mouth.[60] Vowels provide the 'spaces' in language so in the spoken word there is something amorphous and movable about them according to regional accent, for example (hence such difficulties and differences in their spelling). Responsible as they are for flow and changeability in our spoken communication, ontologically one might say the vowels have a 'feeling' quality,[61] while the consonants are more structural.

After the first phase, we suggest introducing the remaining phonemes and simple corresponding graphemes until they have all 44. At this point, they would in theory be able to write anything they could speak, even though they would not yet use conventional spelling. What an empowering moment! It is a moment to cherish and exploit. Also note here that knowledge of the alphabet itself is not necessary for writing. It is useful for spelling and for navigating dictionaries, but for a *writer* it is secondary. We do not advocate teaching letter *names* in isolation until it becomes useful to know the alphabet sequence. Letter names are potentially confusing at the early stages of literacy. Teach letter names and letter sounds as every letter is introduced and make the distinction very clear. For much of the work in Class 1, letter sounds are used over letter names.

Children will eventually need to know that every syllable always has at least one vowel (Y is considered to be a vowel when it makes a vowel sound).[62] We recommend that from the start, the teacher links both the long vowel sound (/ā/ as in rain – also the name of the vowel) and the short vowel sound (/ǎ/ as in cat) to the symbol 'A'. Any other sounds this vowel could make (such as /ah/ as in 'father' or 'star') are best avoided at the introduction stage.[63]

It is most effective to encourage children to create their own free writing straight away: a sentence from a story or poem they have heard or describing something they have experienced or done.[64] So many skills are involved that we consider it constitutes the richest learning activity of all in this early stage. Before outlining further details of our approach to free writing in Parts 4 and 6, however, we set out here a caveat and describe some legitimate uses for *copying text*, from the teacher or peers.

For the teaching and practice of handwriting, it is essential to copy text that has been modelled by the teacher.[65] Copying allows the children to focus only on their handwriting and their pencil grip (rather than the content, spelling or grammar of what they write). If the teacher writes poems

---

60 Townend & Walker, 2006.
61 Steiner, 1976. For an extended discussion, see Lecture Two, p. 26.
62 The only English exception to this vowel rule is the word 'rhythm', which could be considered a two-syllable word with the second syllable missing a vowel altogether.
63 This is apparently contradicted by the discussion in Lecture Two of Steiner (1976), but we would suggest that our approach is valid both because he was referring to the German language and also because of what we know about auditory processing problems for dyslexic children.
64 This is not the same as 'imaginative' free writing, which we consider an inappropriate task at this age.
65 Steiner teachers commonly still use blackboards for presenting such written work. Blackboards have the advantage of taking chalk colour well and so providing an excellent medium for illustration. Whiteboards or visualisers may do equally well for handwriting practice. For children with visual processing weakness or who have fine motor difficulties, you may decide to give them the same text on a board or paper at their desk. Of course, teachers will additionally use Form Drawing lessons to practise fine motor control and letter formation.

or stories that the children know by heart, copying can allow practising 'memory reading'.[66] This can be a useful activity where you read a familiar text while pointing at the individual words. Other activities could follow, such as giving the children certain words to search for or playing a 'mind reader' game, as described later in Chapter 12. Finally, a little further down the line, copying from the blackboard can be useful in order to give the students a model of good sentence composition. Children do need to know what makes a good sentence, a good poem or a good story. In one school, a new teacher took over a Class 3 and expected the children to be able to write their own text. He was very frustrated with their lack of ability. It was suggested that he would let the children copy for a little while. After this, the children were far more able to produce their own writing. They had had a chance to imitate the teacher, to find out what this teacher thought good work should look like.

If you do this, make sure that you ask the children to identify the criteria for successful sentence composition, e.g. accurate punctuation, interesting adjectives etc. Even more effectively, children can also examine, compare or even copy each other's work. Frequently, if they know another child will look at their work, their standard improves considerably.[67] So, as handwriting practice, for 'memory reading' and as a model of good writing, copying can be useful. We are very wary of using copying as pedagogically valuable classroom activity for any other purpose. It is much better for children to create their own writing for all other learning activities.

Further Phonics and Keywords

After the first phases of teaching writing,[68] we will be showing you some ways to further develop phonics teaching, for long vowels, digraphs and diphthongs in particular, necessary for reading and for increased accuracy in spelling. Most children need some teaching,[69] and some will need a great deal of practice. (For example, what may happen with spelling the word that sounds like 'seem'? Do you use /ee/ or /ea/ or /e-e/ or another way to make the sound of the long /ē/? 'Seem', 'seam', and 'seme' would all be plausible spellings, but a child will need to be able to distinguish both semantic meaning and have memorised phonic rules to be able to choose the right version at the right time in the right place.)[70] Secondly, teachers will need to rehearse spelling patterns – this includes word families or clusters of rhyming words and some early spelling rules. Finally, but certainly not least, keywords or common words will need to be taught and rehearsed visually. This is particularly the case for irregular common words. These are also known as sight words, because there is no avoiding the requirement of a photographic memory. It is often said that the 200 most common words in English (some of which are also sight words) make up 80 per cent of the text of most of what we read. Many children will need much repetition of all three aspects of 'code' teaching in order to effortlessly and automatically apply them in writing or read them.

66 Bear, Invernizzi, Templeton, & Johnstone, 2012.
67 For more such peer-teaching techniques, we highly recommend Shirley Clarke, 2008.
68 This amounts to the first two or three Main Lesson blocks – until Christmas or Easter, for example. See the plans in the Appendices.
69 There are a rare few who seem to absorb the literacy code by themselves or with only one telling.
70 In this book, we set out a pattern of phonics teaching that uses both analytic and synthetic phonics principles. There are probably dozens of published versions of the same type of teaching along a spectrum of analytic and synthetic models. Find the one that works for you!

PART 2

Starting Point

Chapter 3

Pre-School Preparation

- What capacities and learned skills can you expect from most Class 1 children on day 1?
- What has been learned in Kindergarten or at home?
- Learning habits to be developed in Class 1 – the transition year

What skills that are supportive of literacy can we expect our 6 year old to have practised or to have developed naturally by the time they reach Class 1? Kindergartens vary, but there are some common aspects of their daily life that will have nourished and fed those children who attended.[1] There could be a hugely variable range of talents and skills in your class. Some children will be precocious in one area and immature in another, and it can also be very difficult to predict how an individual might mature, or not. However, below we have set out a range of tasks that we think you can reasonably expect an average, healthy child to be able to do on the first day of Class 1. We hope that you will have an immediate indication of who is advanced or delayed, and in which areas.

Balance, Rhythm and Laterality

Children will be able to achieve moderate balance, for example hopping on one leg fluidly, without jarring or frequent stopping. They will be able to stand on one leg, relatively calmly, for approximately ten seconds. They may be able to skip rhythmically in a large rope held by others, if not individually using their own rope. Even if this is not a learned skill, they should be able to clap and stamp in

---

1 Of course, you may also have some children who have already attended mainstream state-school reception or Year 1 classes. Further, it may be that others join your class along the way, already having had other exposure to literacy in some way and even having gained some mastery of it. Provided they are in the right age-group, in our experience, most children who have already learnt some literacy are happy to go with the flow of the Class 1 experience. They sometimes appreciate the opportunity to repeat and, even if that does not matter to them, they rarely experience boredom if the curriculum is busy with the universal and common language of play. Observation of your children is of course paramount, and where you perceive a pupil who does need more than is on offer for the bulk of the class, you must find ways to respond.

a basic rhythm, identifying the beat in a poem, for example, and being able to maintain it. Most children will have a securely dominant hand but will be able to use either hand for many tasks with some independence, such as cutting using scissors, folding paper with some accuracy, and drawing or writing forms. Ideally, they will know how to hold a pencil or crayon in a tripod grip.[2] They will be able to draw a rough circle, square and triangle; they will be able to draw lines to resemble basic picture forms such as a person, house and a tree. They will also know the names of colours and be able to 'colour in' or create forms out of colour.

Their foot dominance is also likely to have settled to a particular side. This means that they will kick a ball or ride on the scooter using one foot as the preferred leader. Indeed, the way in which the brain absorbs and integrates the full range of sensory information will have become less plastic, more settled and with distinct tendencies and preferences. The majority of children will also show dominance in their eye and ear. They will choose one eye to look through a telescope, for example, and one ear to listen to a shell for the sound of the sea, or answer the phone.

Spatial Awareness

Most children will have learned a range of independent self-care skills such as shoe fastening, buttons and putting on outdoor clothes, basic cleanliness and hygiene, and feeding themselves. They will know the names of parts of their own bodies and in most cases, if their eyes are shut, they will be able to tell you if a part of them is touched and what the name of that part is.

Children will have practised sitting at the table concentrating on individual craft projects such as weaving or sanding wood objects, and they ought to be able to sustain 20–30 minutes of concentrated quiet activity in something that interests them. They will be accustomed to having taken some responsibility for tidying and cleaning in the Kindergarten; they will know where things go and have some skills in preparation for tasks and putting things away afterwards. However, they will not be used to managing their own workspace, nor will they be likely to know how to order and tidy many belongings. Aside from keeping the Kindergarten tidy, children may also have engaged in the sorting and categorising of toys and materials. They will be able to organise things according to their properties, such as size or colour, or the first sound in their name. Most children will already have an understanding of 1:1 correspondence. This term means that any objects up to ten can be counted, regardless of the nature of the object. It is an essential foundation maths skill that shows that children understand the concept of numbers to represent quantity. Many children will also be able to count verbally up to 100 and may have shown curiosity about the process of basic adding up. They will be less likely to have practised any subtraction games.

Children will usually have a reasonable sense of school geography, knowing what areas are used for different activities, and will have a rough idea of their home in relation to the school and perhaps their wider locality. They will not usually have a good understanding of distances or the country around them beyond what is very familiar and relevant to their everyday lives.

---

2 See Chapter 5 for a full description. Some children will find this difficult and will gravitate towards other pencil holds.

Further, you can expect Class 1 children to be familiar with books and know that they run (in English) from left to right. They will be able to hold them up the right way and to some extent interpret a story from pictures, also knowing that each word on the page is separated by a space. They may also know some sounds and some letter names and be able to write their own, and family names and perhaps copy written text for birthday cards, for example.

Understanding Time

Children will be used to a rhythm of daily activities. Kindergartens (and many homes, of course) have a routine of meal times, play and story times that enable children to place themselves securely at any moment. Children will therefore be used to predicting what is coming next. They may have a sense of formal time though most would not know how to tell the time on a clock. Most Class 1 children will be likely to know which day it is today and the order of the days of the week. They will be able to relate simple stories about what happened yesterday and the further past, and predict or anticipate events to come within a reasonably close range. They will have some familiarity with seasons and months, especially knowing their own and family birthdays and other significant days, such as festivals.

Listening, Speaking and Socialising

Kindergarten children will usually be accustomed to hearing a fairy tale told five times – once a day for a week – and will often have memorised this word-for-word. They will sometimes have had some practice at reciting or acting out such stories. They will also have a repertoire of songs and poems that they have memorised during circle times (or at home), with accompanying movements. Some of these songs and poems will have been rhyming or alliterative, and you can expect a Class 1 child to recognise a rhyme and be able to find other words, or make up words that rhyme by changing the initial sound – for example, *ring, sing, ching, bing, ting* with some 'real' and some nonsense. In their own imaginative play, one can expect that many of them would have been accustomed to much talking and discussion. Although it can sometimes be difficult to detect, you can expect that most Class 1 children are good at 'picturing' when listening to or telling a story in play. By this, we mean that the child's imagination creates inner, 'mind's eye' illustrations of the story in question. These will be quite individual, with different colours, shapes, contexts and details.

A Class 1 child will usually be able to make simple requests and carry out simple verbal instructions, albeit not a long sequence of them at any one time. Although they may experience complex emotions, they will be likely to verbalise a simple range of emotional states and needs, such as *happy, sad, funny, comfortable, easy, cross* or *angry*. They will also be likely to need support to manage strong feelings in a social context. A Class 1 child will be unlikely to self-manage passions, fears or distress, for example, even if they are not always extrovert.

Most children will be accustomed to playing with a friend, or a small group and managing a game between them. They will be capable of forming bonds with particular individuals and will show an affiliation with a certain type of person or activity. They will understand the nature of turn taking, will have some skills at deciding what is fair and equable, will be experienced at setting the rules or parameters of a game and will enjoy using their own and benefiting from others' creative ideas. Many children will have appropriate language skills, as well as other non-verbal communications, that also facilitate and enable them to move through times of conflict or confusion. They will be well-placed to engage in partner or team learning games.

What Do You Need to Teach?

While the summary above represents what the majority of children may be expected to be able to do at the beginning of Class 1, it will be unusual for all children to be proficient in all these areas. An average child with healthy development may be able to do all these things except for fine motor skills and drawing, for example. This will be something to watch for, but it does not represent an abnormal situation. Of course, some children will have received more assistance and practice with such skills at home or school and some have a greater facility for learning them, or they may be older or younger. Summer-birthday children are often 'slow' to demonstrate capacity in these skills. There will also be a relative minority for whom there are significant difficulties in acquiring several or all of these skills. Such children would be likely to fall into the category of having learning difficulties or Special Educational Needs, and may need extra support, either from you or from specialists.

As the class teacher, there is much you can do to help teach and train the children into new habits and to support them in their maturation. You will also be able to offer guidance to other teachers and parents about how to help this growth and development. Remember that Class 1 is *the* transition year between infancy and childhood proper, the transition year from the first seven-year phase to the next. Facilitating this is the first part of your job.

Chapters 4–7 give information about exercises and activities that help children to consolidate strengths, develop new skills and good learning habits. We aim to help you settle your group into the more formal situation of Class 1 and make sure that everyone is ready for learning.

Chapter 4

Warming up for Literacy: Physical Co-ordination

- Movement exercises develop gross and fine motor skills and help with focus and concentration
- Consider your goals when designing your own movement exercises
- Creating pathways to new skills

Most children who struggle with learning also show difficulties with gross and fine motor skills as well as spatial orientation and balance. To express this in an anthroposophical manner, one might say that a child has not fully incarnated in certain areas of the body. It goes without saying that normal child development proceeds from the 'horizontal' new-born to the 'upright' year old child,[3] with intermediary stages including sitting and crawling.[4] Usually, walking precedes the beginnings of talking,[5] which precedes early independent thinking (demonstrated by linked thoughts expressed in sentences, for example, and the establishment of an individual identity),[6] rather than simple imitation and reflection. Commentators from other medical and educational arenas have shown how neurology and physiology develop during these phases and, further, have established causal links and correlations with how this can affect cognitive processing.[7,8] They have shown that

---

3 An approximate age.
4 Upright sitting at approximately 6m and crawling at 8 or 9m.
5 Approximately 18m to 2 yrs.
6 The child will usually use their own name or the pronoun 'me' for some time – e.g. 'Me do it!' – before using the word 'I' at approximately age 36m.
7 For example, see the work of Peter Blythe and Sally Goddard at the Institute of Neuro-physiological Psychology (INPP) in Chester, UK. See Bibliography.
8 Although not the subject of concern here, other practitioners have discovered that most learning difficulties, such as dyslexia, are caused by difficulties with visual, auditory or kinaesthetic processing. This means that the left and right hemispheres of the brain are not able to process visual, auditory or kinaesthetic stimuli in the most efficient way, resulting in delay with or failure to integrate new information. It is suggested that environmental or health factors such as deprived sensory environments (for example, screen entertainment for infants, rather than active physical play, or the failure to crawl) are behind the failure of children to develop healthy neural pathways. Glue ear, at the age of optimal development of auditory processing, can also inhibit the acquiring of healthy audiological acuity.

if physical development does not proceed in the optimal way, for whatever reason, the brain may not develop optimal functioning either. In some cases, the children have retained early childhood reflexes[9] such that the left and right side of the body find it hard to work either independently or in good co-ordination.[10] There can be many symptoms of retained reflexes; an example could be moving the legs and feet or the jaw and tongue when writing.[11] It is easy to imagine how fidgeting and distractibility may be interpreted as intentional 'naughtiness' or disaffection. The more knowledge and understanding that the teacher has of the underlying causes behind a child's 'inability' to sit still, for example, the more empathy they will be able to employ in behaviour management.

Movement Exercises at the Start of the Day

Movement exercises are a regular part of the first phase of the Main Lesson, commonly known as the rhythmical time. Warming up with movement helps the children awaken, imitate their teacher and follow instructions, and it improves subsequent focus in class. The activities set out below are effective for all children but can be especially important for those who need to practise coordination of movements between left, right, upper and lower parts of the body. We suggest that a class carry out each activity described below every day for around half a term. All exercises have accompanying poems or songs with a strong beat or rhythmical quality.

Creating a pathway for movement: exercises that develop strength

It is very important to design exercises so that there is a step-by-step sequence of activities leading up to the actual skill you want the children to master. We call this 'creating a pathway'. For example, if you want children to practise crossing the midline,[12] you would start with movements using both arms simultaneously or each individually before the crossing is brought in. For children for whom crossing the midline is a challenge, this creates an achievable pathway. They can get into the exercise with simpler movements, and once they are in the flow, it will be easier for them to access the harder part.

Be aware that for children who are challenged by movement exercises, it can cause a great deal of sensory and emotional discomfort if they are asked to do something that stimulates them in this area of difficulty. If your little six-year old student throws himself on the floor or hides under the desk, or makes jokes to distract his friends, the chances are that the movement is too challenging and

---

9 Primitive reflexes are present in the neurological make-up of all human babies and they function to stimulate the new-born to move and acquire muscular skill and strength. In healthy development, they are suppressed (becoming dormant, though not 'disappearing') by acquired postural reflexes as the child gains sophistication in movement. However, many children retain active primitive reflexes which then interfere with fluent and integrated movement. This may adversely affect many aspects of life, including achieving fluid rhythm, balance and laterality. In turn, movement difficulties correlate with impaired cognitive processing and attention. See Sally Goddard, *Reflexes, Learning and Behaviour*.
10 This is known as difficulty 'crossing the midline.'
11 See the work of Sally Goddard (Blythe).
12 Crossing the midline is a late Class 1/ Class 2 developmental skill. The midline is a term that refers to an 'invisible' line in the centre of the body. If you shut your right eye, you will see a certain picture; then shut your left eye and you will see a different one. The midline covers the central zone that both eyes can see, albeit from a different angle. It is one of the main tasks of cognitive maturation to ensure that the person can cross the midline confidently in all tasks – drawing, dancing, walking, writing, throwing and catching, to name a few!

leaves him feeling physically stressed or unsafe. Working with incremental steps makes this less likely.

When designing your own exercises it is important to know what you are aiming for. The following could be targets:

- Exercises to help the child gain more awareness of their own bodies in relation to the space around them, including the notion of 'personal space'.
- Exercises to help develop more finesse in the fine motor movement of the fingers.
- Exercises to support the awareness, co-ordination and independence of movements between left and right; above and below; front and back.
- Exercises to help cross the midline; use the right hand in the space to the left of the midline and vice versa.

Here are some exercises you could do with your classes in rhythmical time.

Body awareness in space

The child's awareness is generally strongest in the trunk and weakest in the periphery. Working from the centre to the periphery draws the child's attention and focus towards the hands, fingers and feet. Further, to support a child in being 'grounded', it makes most sense to work from the head down to the feet and back up again. A downward movement brings the child's awareness down to the feet. A subsequent upward movement supports a strong centre, feet firmly planted on the earth. For example, when we are clapping and stamping the beat of a song, first clap, then stamp and then add the clapping again. We suggest that a body-geography exercise start with 'hands on your hair' working down towards the feet before working back up again. Make sure the movement is not with the head; the limbs are the movers, the head remains still. Here, we also recommend a 'spiral in space' exercise given in *Take Time* by Mary Nash Wortham and Jean Hunt.[13]

Learning to relate to the space of the whole room around you

If you are a new teacher, or haven't taught young children for some time, you may be caught out by how little awareness the 6 or 7 year olds have of the space around them and their position in it. Entering a new room, especially if it is large, without furniture 'markers' indicating the function of the space, will be an invitation to them to run, whirl or zoom to fill the space up like a gas. You will need to start training them how to exercise appropriate physical control in different school spaces. You will need to be careful with your language and give them props. You may use images such as 'round as the moon' or 'walk round a pond' etc. but the children may not able to stand in that circle or walk around and maintain it. They can imagine the roundness of the moon but they may not be able to see their own position in relation to that image.

---

13 Nash Wortham & Hunt, 2008, p. 91.

To develop such a sense, we suggest using some round 'stepping stones'; rubber spots available from PE suppliers (the same quantity as there are children) which can be carefully put in a circle on the floor.

You can play a game of coloured 'lands'; the wall is yellow land, the window side of the room blue land, the circle is red, and so on. Whilst the teacher plays a drum with a rhythm for running, skipping or walking, the children move around the room. The playing stops and the teacher calls out a colour and the children run quickly, but without crashing or sliding, to the 'land' that was called out. At the colour 'red' they must stand on the spots in the circle. Later the same game can be played without the spots to help them internalise the sensation of moving from free space to an ordered, collective space.[14]

Many traditional dancing games also develop awareness in space. For example, in a Class 1 you can play *I Sent a Letter to my Love* or *Have you ever heard of the Seven?*[15] Many of the games involve standing in or dancing around the circle, standing behind, in front of or next to someone else. Through playing these games the child develops awareness of the space around them and awareness of their own position in relation to others.[16]

Learning to relate to your personal space

There is a good series of eight beanbag exercises for personal spatial orientation in the book *Take Time*.[17] These are well known in many Steiner schools and we recommend them.

Though sometimes challenging to achieve, it is crucial that the exercises are carried out correctly by all the children. We suggest using a song or poem with a strong beat. Continuing with the same song without pause throughout the whole sequence of the exercises supports concentration and accuracy. We recommend either of these accompanying songs.[18] A demonstration of the exercise can be found on YouTube, link https://www.youtube.com/watch?v=7pdNfKumVtw &feature=youtu.be.[19]

---

14 Brooking-Payne, 1996.

15 *The Clarendon Book of Singing Games* (Wiseman & Northcote, 1969)

16 Brooking-Payne, 1996.

17 Nash, Wortham & Hunt, 2008.

18 'Faja Sitóng' is a song from Suriname. The first sentence means 'Hot stone, do not burn me so much'. The second refers to 'Master Jan murdering a human child again'. There is possibly a link to the Dutch colonials branding the slaves. With the original meaning mostly forgotten, it is now played as a children's game where a hot stone is passed around the circle on the beat of the song. The child who has the stone on the last word of the song is 'out'. 'Pandoer' is a song from Hungary by Lajos Bárdos 1899–1986. There is no copyright, and this is from the Dutch school song book *Hoy, een lied*.

19 Please note this video shows exercises for classes 1 -5 so not all exercises are suitable for 1 and 2.

Faja Sitóng   Hoy ahoy

Fa - ja si - tóng no   brong mi   so, no   brong mi so,   a -

dja - ma soe - ma   sa   ki - ri   soe - ma - pi - tjien,   a -

dja - ma soe - ma   sa   ki - ri   soe - ma - pi - tjien.

Pandoer   Phalèse

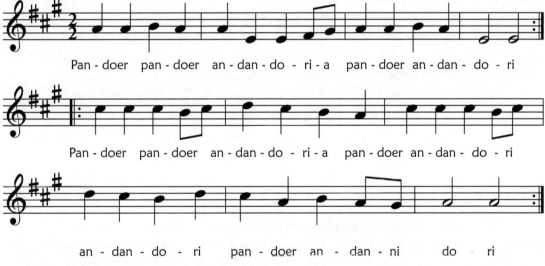

Pan - doer pan - doer an - dan - do - ri - a   pan - doer an - dan - do - ri

Pan - doer pan - doer an - dan - do - ri - a   pan - doer an - dan - do - ri

an - dan - do - ri   pan - doer an - dan - ni   do   ri

Before starting exercise 1, the children have the beanbag on their head and clap and/or stamp the beat and/or rhythm of the song. In that way, slow starters can engage and the momentum can be built up. The actual movement exercise can begin once everyone is alert. Once your class has learned the movements and become accustomed to them, the intention is to follow the sequential exercises without pause, maintaining momentum and focus. This reduces the number of transition moments, when children can be 'lost'. As a rule of thumb, children who are generally not so focused are often the ones who most benefit from doing the movement work correctly.

We have found that this sequence works better when children are standing behind their desk. You can keep a closer eye on how the children are performing the movement exercises. You will know that all the children see the same thing when following your lead and, if you turn round, will have the same left and right side as you. A circle makes this much more difficult as some children are next to you and others opposite. It also depends whether your class is able to stand and stay in a circle. Perhaps doing the beanbag exercises in a circle gives them two difficult things to do and that may be too much!

Fine motor skills

There are some who do not seem to have much awareness of what their hands are doing. In one class, a girl who was trying to improve her recorder playing did some extra practice. Every time she had to change her fingering, she wanted to look at her fingers on the instrument using her eyes since she was not able to move just by touch and feeling alone. The *Speed Up*[20] programme by Lois Addy takes a kinaesthetic approach to help children improve their handwriting and gives some interesting insights. From her Occupational Therapy background, the author explains that some children get very little kinaesthetic feedback from their hands and fingers. She suggests some physical exercises such as push-ups and circle movements with the whole arm prior to sitting down to school work in order to help children experience sensory information from their hands and fingers. This specific physical exercise gives the child a window of around 30 minutes where the hand and finger movements are more strongly experienced and therefore more easily directed. While we don't particularly recommend press-ups for a Class 1, the following exercise sequence was inspired by Addy's ideas. You might do this before any activities requiring fine motor skills such as Form Drawing, hand writing, recorder playing or lyre lessons.

> This exercise improves the kinaesthetic feedback the child gets from the fingers; following this the child is, temporarily at least, more in control. It is given in full, but you might want to start with a few elements and build it up.

A demonstration of this exercise can be found on YouTube (exercise 1–3)[21]

Start with a little story about the miller who had overslept and had to run to the mill. He turned the mill into the wind (the purpose is really that the children don't hit each other). Have arms fully stretched to each side and with the following poem start from the shoulders, each arm making small forward circles (right and left moving simultaneously) with the circles getting bigger until 'hour by hour'. Then the big circles go backwards and become smaller again until the end of the poem.

The wind turns and everyone moves the mill in the wind (this gives you the opportunity to observe the other half of the class) and does the same activity again.

---

20 Lois Addy, 2004.
21 See page 44 and Note 19.

Round and round the windmill's turning
Turning, turning hour by hour
Turning, turning ever turning
All the golden grain to flour

(When the flour is made, it must go to the baker)

There was once a baker
Who baked a big bun

(Move arms into a 'Eurythmy B')[22]

And I will show you how it was done
He took the flour and poured in the yeast

(Left arm round as if holding a bowl, pour the yeast with the right)

Then stirred it together

*(Stirring with the right whilst the left keeps holding the bowl –
this requires the children to move across the midline)*

It was such a feast
He stirred and stirred, his arm started aching
But he never got tired of all that baking
He pummeled the dough and pushed it hard

(Make kneading movements and push hard on the desk with 'pushed it hard')

He pummeled the dough and again he'd start
He pushed it down with all his weight
1,2,3,4,5,6,7,8

(Push-ups on the desk)

Now he rolled it round and round

(Roll a pretend ball between the hands)

And never a ball so round was found
He threw it up and caught it neat

(Throw the pretend ball in the air and catch it)

And then the rolling would repeat
I tell you the baker had such fun
All for the baking of one big bun

(Move arms into a 'Eurythmy B')

---

22 The archetypal Eurythmy gesture for /b/ is created by reaching with both arms backwards, deep and low, and then imaging oneself to take hold of a long cloak. One then pulls the cloak forward, in a rounded gesture, to form a round 'mantle of protection'. One experiences an inner fullness, which presses outward against the force of compression coming from the rounding arms; there is thus a tension which is ready to burst when the lips open apart with the /b/. http://www.openwaldorf.com/eurythmy.html

Then the farmer must clean his hands; use the following song.

Im - pom - pe poe-der - ne poe-der nas - ka Im - pom - pe   Im - pom

pe Im - pom - pe poe-der - ne poe-der nas - ka Im - pom - pe

- Clap hands together as though cleaning them of flour.
- Place the palm of one hand and the back of the other flat down upon the desk and then alternate these positions with the rhythm of the song.
- Right hand only – tap the thumb to the index[23] finger, then the middle, ring and little finger and back on the rhythm of the song.
- Repeat with right hand behind the back.
- Repeat with the left hand in front of the body.
- Repeat with left hand behind the back.
- Repeat with both hands in front of the body.
- Repeat with both hands behind the back.
- Bring the left and right hand together in front of the body but with only the corresponding thumbs and fingertips touching. Tap the thumbs together, then index, middle, ring and little fingers and back to the rhythm of the song.
- Repeat with the hands behind the back.

An extension would be to:
- Place one palm flat down on the desk while the other forms a clenched fist.

Alternate hand positions with the rhythm of the song.

In this way, we prepare the children for controlling their hands in a concentrated school activity.

---

23 It can be useful to give them names, such as *Peter Pointer* for the index, *Tall John, Ruby Ring, Baby Small* and *Tommy Thumb*. There are many rhymes with other variations.

Chapter 5

Warming up for Literacy:
Form Drawing and Writing

- Correct pencil grip and sitting position
- Form Drawing – supporting the development of handwriting and use of space
- Writing – forming upper-case letters first

Holding the Crayon or Pencil

Ideally, children will already have learned how to hold their crayon, pencil or pen in the correct way in Kindergarten. It is important to start out with this immediately in Class 1, teaching and encouraging children as necessary. The dynamic 'tripod' pencil grip gives the greatest control whilst placing the least strain on the wrist, hand or fingers. The thumb and index finger do most of the work. This means that the pencil is held between the tips of the thumb, index and middle fingers, the pencil is held in a relaxed way without too much pressure on the shaft of the pencil, the pencil rests on the hand between the thumb and index finger (webspace,) the webspace gap should be open (i.e. the thumb and index fingers form a circle), and the ring and little fingers are held away from the pencil bent slightly into the palm.[24]

These pictures show correct left- and right-handed tripod grip. When you are describing this grip to children, we suggest using an image of a king sitting on a throne. Make the throne with the right-hand middle, ring and little fingers (left for left-handers). Place the 'king' (pencil) on it while carefully folding the arms of the throne (thumb and index finger) around the king. The index finger will be the king's best adviser, telling him what to do and where to go at all times. You should still be able to see the king between the arms of the throne.

---

24 Children, Young People and Families Occupational Therapy Team.

Children who do not take to it by themselves will need reminding of this gently, repeatedly and consistently. Find ways of praising and rewarding good practice several times in each school day. Expect that it might take several months of repeated encouragement, and educate parents if you think this will help so that they can reward good technique at home. Learning to correct a grip, similarly to correcting something like a speech difficulty, can be a subtle but difficult challenge for a young child. When an incorrect grip persists past about age 9, we suggest using a rubber grip that supports the fingers in the correct position.[25] For left-handed children, it may be better to hold the pencil a fraction higher than right-handers so that they can more easily see what they've written.[26]

Sitting Position

The sitting position and the way the paper lies on the table are also important. Again, developing such habits requires close observation, frequent reminders and rewards for good practice. The position described here will give you the best chance of children being able to concentrate in a relaxed way whilst writing or drawing. It will also enable greater control and accuracy.

Children must be able to sit with their feet flat on the floor, with the desk or table at the correct height so that they are upright and comfortable. Thighs should be well supported and the forearm should rest comfortably on the desk. The head should be a reasonable distance from the paper, approximately 12–16 inches away.

When working on a page, the paper or book should be slightly tilted; for the right-handed child to the left, and for the left-handed child to the right (see illustration), so that the writing arm is at right angles with the bottom edge of the paper.[27] It also helps if the working page is towards the right side of the midline for the right-hander and towards the left side of the midline for the left-hander. Such considerations may help you when choosing the size of the paper or page to use.

Page position for right-handed child

Page position for left-handed child

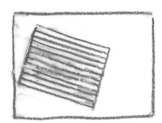

---

25 Available from a supplier such as *LDA Learning*, or many others.
26 See the HRI website for excellent information on teaching left-handers to write (Handedness Research Institute, 2003).
27 With older children, if you are able to use tilted desks, this may also help, but we haven't used these with Class 1 children. They may be too slippery to handle!

Form Drawing

In UK education, to our knowledge, Form Drawing as a distinct subject is unique to Steiner schools. It comes directly from Rudolf Steiner's suggestions for the curriculum for the lower school. The art of Form Drawing incorporates several pedagogical elements. It brings about aesthetic and geometric understanding and appreciation, and it is an ideal activity to help new school children learn how to command a page. Teaching spatial awareness and orientation is a worthwhile goal.

> ...we teach them archetypal forms in drawing by showing them how to make one angle like this or another like that; we try to reveal the circle and the spiral to them. We begin with the form as such, irrespective of whether it imitates this or that; we shall endeavour to awaken their interest in the form itself.[28]

Form Drawing aids the following:

- Handwriting – particularly running forms, but also straight line and curve exercises and mirror forms
- Fine motor co-ordination – all Form Drawing work
- Spatial awareness and orientation – mirror forms, but also organisation on the page for all Form Drawing activities
- Inner flexibility – rhythmical forms and metamorphosis exercises in particular
- Inner balance – mirror forms in particular, but also all Form Drawing activities where a balanced form is achieved
- Centring – knot forms in particular
- Social development – where Form Drawing is done with children working as pairs or in small groups

Typically, a teacher will first prepare a class by walking a form in a large space or drawing with a hand in the air. Then the children will draw freehand forms on chalk boards or paper. Usually, children use either chalk or thick, high-quality, coloured crayons such as Stockmar sticks. There are several books devoted to the teaching of Form Drawing, and we would strongly recommend the teacher explores this subject in greater depth than we are able to here.[29]

Rudolf Steiner described how you may 'teach' the straight line and the curve,[30] and this has become a classic first Main Lesson activity that many class teachers choose for the first day of Class 1. The teacher demonstrates and the children draw both forms, often on the blackboard at the front of the class, while the teacher carefully observes. Once complete, the teacher then reveals that we have now really practised all the letters already (since they are all comprised of either a straight line or a curve).

---

28 Steiner, 1976, p. 18.
29 Kutzli, 2004; Giesen, 2014; Simmonds, not dated. Christopherus homeschool resources. See www.waldorfbooks.com
30 Steiner, 1976, Chapter 4.

After this initial introduction, many drawings are made using the straight line and the curve, so that gradually the hands become steadier and the forms more regular. If the teacher has prepared upper-case name signs for the children's desks, for example, attention can also be drawn to their curves and straight lines. The teacher may have a name in mind and could ask the class, 'Who can spot a name with three straight lines and one curve?' In addition, it is particularly valuable to work on a great variety of running forms as preparation for later cursive writing.

Writing First

At the very beginning of the introduction of letters, as described in Chapter 8, the children may draw the form of the letters using Stockmar block crayons. Perhaps the first drawing of the actual letter will be done with their medium edge ('queen side'). However, we suggest that further practice must be carried out with tools that encourage a proper pencil grip as mentioned earlier in this chapter. Teachers differ in their choice of instrument, and we consider that while it may be appropriate to use the Stockmar stick crayons briefly, in our classroom we preferred to use a chunky coloured pencil such as the Lyra brand. In our view, as well as supporting the correct grip, the lead of the pencil flows more smoothly on paper. On the whole, we reserve the wax crayons for Form Drawing and the pencils for writing.

In our teaching, we have followed the tradition of introducing children to upper-case letters first. This was indicated by Rudolf Steiner because of their pictorial, distinctive forms. As such, they are less easily confused, and children distinguish and remember the upper-case letters better than print or cursive writing: 'You always use uppercase letters in the beginning so that the children can see the similarity to the picture'.[31]

Teachers must decide when the right time has come to move from upper-case to lower-case letters.[32]

When demonstrating how to write any given letter, emphasis must be given to where the letter starts and the direction of movement until it is complete. Children will need frequent demonstration and reminders to develop an automatic habit of making the letter in the right way. Appendix 2 presents a diagram of the way each capital letter ought to be formed.

Page Setting

Presentation and illustrations of written work form a significant part of literacy teaching in Class 1. We aim to invest children's writing activities with a sense of beauty, in line with content of the stories, poems and songs from which they spring. Most children who enjoy their stories and love their writing will want to express this beautifully on the page.

To this end, Class 1 children are encouraged to draw simple borders around the page to define the space they have for their writing. Writing in Class 1 is still large and children usually draw their

---

31 Steiner, 1976, Lecture 5.
32 See extended discussion in Chapter 22.

own guidelines. This develops a sense of page organisation and helps with focus. In the example below, the child has drawn a border and lines with the middle ('queen') side of a block crayon, leaving a space between the lines. It's worth persevering for some time, letting the children practise this repeatedly to develop the straightness and evenness of their lines. Only help children with this, or provide an underlay for occasional key work, when you are sure that children have reached their own capacity. Remember that every page is a work in progress rather than a gallery exhibit.

In this example, the writing space has been left blank. If this is difficult for a child, one could precede it by letting the children draw alternate bands with the 'queen' side of any colour and the pale yellow. The writing can then take place on the yellow bands. However, not all writing implements write easily over the crayon base so teachers should experiment beforehand to decide on the right approach.

In the examples here, you can see that children draw a star between each word. This is because it can be hard for children to hear when one word separates from another so the star draws their attention to this. It also forces them to make a space between words on the line.

We suggest that the teacher models the illustration of the poem or story. Children in Class 1 will frequently need to be shown how to draw, including modelling which part of the crayon to use, what movements to make and how to cover a page with colour. We would include a picture with most pieces of writing in Class 1.

Chapter 6

Warming up for Literacy:
Verbal and Social Skills

- Morning greeting and sharing news
- The class conversation and descriptive praise
- Partner work
- Choral speaking and speech difficulties
- Listening to instruction
- Listening to stories and recall

The development of speaking and listening needs your attention. This chapter will give you lots of tips and ideas for developing sophisticated communication in your class.

Although most children will speak confidently about things that interest them, there are some good classroom habits that need to be put in place; taking turns, putting your hand up if you would like to say or ask something, and so on. From the first days in Class 1, plenty of time should be devoted to the establishment of agreed rules, practising them and rewarding responsive behaviour. Some children will find it very demanding to adjust and comply. Children will often forget the rule, they may be accustomed to speaking at will, or shouting, they may experience such a sense of excitement or nervousness that they are overwhelmed... and so on. However, investing time in this really pays off in class cohesion, team work, self-reliance and confidence.

On your first day, you are likely to speak about *why* we are in Class 1. Bear in mind that all children learn when they come up with questions and answers themselves, not necessarily when information is just given. We advocate a classroom where the teacher is not just the 'self-effacing transmitter of the received wisdom'.[33] You want to start from where your class are now: they are six or seven years old, curious and enthusiastic, happy to play and be friendly, wanting to know how to do the things that older children and grown-ups can do. Steer the conversation so that classroom

---

33 Myhill, Jones & Hopper, 2006, p. 17.

rules of speaking and listening arise out of the collective wish for this end. Your aim is that the children thoroughly understand and appreciate good reasons for co-operation.

Morning Greetings and Sharing News

In Steiner schools, the class teacher customarily greets the children with a handshake at the door of the class each morning. There may also be time for a very short individual conversation – 'Is your mum better today?' 'You are really bouncy today.' 'Have you remembered your lunch box?' 'Is your finger still hurting?' – and so on. This short exchange, in addition to nurturing the relationship between the children and the teacher, consolidates conversation rules of speaking in turn, responding to questions with fully audible words, or even sentences, and using polite forms of address between adults and children.

Particularly in Class 1, we value sharing news at the beginning of the day. Aside from supporting group cohesion, the children get an opportunity to speak about something that has taken place in the past or will take place in the future, something outside the realm of here and now. They will need to develop an understanding of their audience. This is a great skill to develop!

Some children will need to learn to speak loud enough, while others need to learn to sequence their story properly so that everyone understands how the events happened. Some may need to learn to say more than one sentence and expand their story to include interesting details. Others may need to be curbed and learn to feel when their time is up and the story is told. For the teacher, it is good to take mental notes when the children are having their news time and to write them down later. It is also good to keep a record of who has shared news and who has not, and to find a way of encouraging those more reluctant speakers. Perhaps give them prior warning; 'I know you're going camping this weekend. On Monday, I will include you in the news time and you can tell us where you went and one thing that happened.'

There will be plenty of children who have a whole range of 'news' to share, from important life events to things they make up on the spot, simply because they so enjoy standing in front of the class, holding the stage. It is a good idea to set some limits. Once children have got the idea of what sharing news is, we suggest three news items per day and a requirement to tell the teacher in advance, at handshake time, if they want to share some. This brings in an element of planning which can be really helpful, and for some children quite a challenge!

Towards the end of Class 1 or in later classes, news-sharing can be reduced to special events or after holidays only. Another option may be to let the children tell their holiday news to their working partner. The partner then relates what the first child did to the whole class. This requires a new level of speaking and listening.

The Class Conversation and Encouraging Responses

It is obvious that many children love talking. Just as their propensity for game-playing and humour is a resource to capitalise upon, we encourage you to use their capacity for talking and explaining and learning from each other in the classroom. Talk for learning is a hot topic in many pedagogical settings these days.[34] Most teachers are keen to change the old-fashioned classroom culture where the teacher imparts information and only asks questions to which they already know the answer. Nonetheless, it takes confidence and high-level teaching skills to be able to manage a group who are making quite a bit of noise so that the balance between real learning and chaos or 'entertainment' is maintained. You need to be sure of the parameters of talk and of how to manage transitions. You also need to be able to discern the difference between enthusiastic and creative engagement – which can be very bubbly – and disengaged children who are setting their own agenda. How can you be in charge without constantly controlling?

The class conversation requires social sensitivity; knowing when is the right time to speak, to ask questions, and when it is right to listen and hear what others have to say. Class conversations are usually held when learning is taking place, when the teacher asks the group questions and discussion is necessary. As much as children need to know how to ask for a tissue, where the toilet is and other daily requirements, you must teach them how to ask to contribute to a conversation. Don't assume that children can intuit these things: explain and model them in a clear and down-to-earth way. There are also going to be some children who feel nervous about talking and feeding back their ideas to the class as a whole, and some who are happy to let others do the work!

Descriptive Praise

Once engaged in everyday class conversations, make sure you notice when the children do the right thing, smile and praise! The praise must be specific and descriptive rather than evaluative. 'Well done' and 'Great work' are evaluative comments. They suggest the teacher is pleased, but do not describe what the teacher is pleased about. 'I can see Freddie put his hand up when he had a question'; 'You listened well to Adam's story; you knew exactly what questions to ask him'; 'Erin was making some good choices. I could see she wanted to say something about the zoo too, but she put her hand up and listened to Tom's story first.' This is descriptive praise. The child knows what she has done well and the rest of the class knows exactly how to earn similar praise.[35]

For some children who need confirmation that they are doing the right thing more regularly than others, constant verbal praise may be overwhelming or embarrassing. Develop some non-verbal cues for these children in particular, but like the descriptive praise it would be best if the non-verbal clue could be specific too; eye contact, a finger on the lips for quiet followed by thumbs up will indicate 'I have noticed you are quiet, well done!' These non-verbal cues may need to be explained and practised for the child who struggles to manage her behaviour.

We would recommend developing descriptive praise so that it becomes second nature to the teacher and is used for all feedback, not just in Class 1.[36] Later, when the dyslexic child is more aware of her own difficulties in comparison with the others, this type of praise will be invaluable. If the

---

34 See extended discussion in Part 2; see also Wells (2009) and Myhill, Jones & Hopper, 2006.
35 Janis-Norton, 2004.
36 See Janis-Norton, 2004.

teacher simply says 'Good work' when the child knows perfectly well that others have done a much better job, she will feel that the praise is empty. The notion grows in the mind of the pupil that she is not even worthy of genuine praise any more, despite good intentions. However, if the teacher says, 'You have included three adjectives in your writing – well done!', the child has no choice but to accept the compliment.

More information about, and training in, descriptive praise can be found in the work by Noel Janis-Norton, among others.[37]

Partner Work

We suggest training children to work with partners straight away in Class 1. It's one of the easiest ways to develop independence. However, it takes some time before all children are able to work reliably without constant adult direction. Again, children will need to become aware of what makes a really good working partner, and they will need plenty of practice before it becomes a habit. Expect it to start mechanically – it's only when it happens frequently, and in lots of lessons, that it becomes second nature.

For a learning task, we suggest only very rarely using a straight-forward hands-up technique. If a question is worth considering, it's best if every child in the class engages with it, not just a few. Some children will stop putting any effort into a discussion if they think only the usual volunteers will report back. Partner work is a way of helping children talk to each other to 'discover' answers to questions or for one partner to teach something to the other. Child-teaching is a highly effective way towards mastery.

Decide how you are going to select partners. It may be that you arrange seating in a certain way so that they develop a consistent pattern with one desk partner for a phase of time. Explain that children can work well with others who are not necessarily their particular friends.

You could also choose to break this up sometimes and take names out of a hat, for example letting children work on the floor with partners for a game. Alternatively, you could sometimes nominate a child who chooses a partner for themselves, then nominate another who chooses, and so on, until the whole class is partnered. If you are sensitive about this, it can be a very powerful tool for children to show others what behaviour they like and don't like. One of the authors saw a class where a girl wasn't chosen until the end and was much chastened because the others thought she was too dominating. The message came across without words being used at all. The teacher, aware of the dynamics at play, waited until the child had 'heard' the message and then, in the activity after that, gave her something special to do, so that she still felt cared for and included. In days following, this girl tried hard to listen more to her work partners.

In general, it's good to mix genders, levels of maturity and first and second language learners. Two shy children or two dominating children together can be effective.

Also be sure that you take charge of any children who need extra help and support – you could

---

37 Janis-Norton – Calmer, Easier, Happier Parenting website.

partner the weakest children yourself, or select the right helper on a particular day. For some tasks, it's most effective to have an able and weak child partnered; for others, peer equivalence is most productive.

After trying partner work for a few tasks, let them tell you what they like about working with some children – 'They're funny, friendly, they talk in a voice I can hear' – and what can be difficult – 'They're bossy, they go too fast, they make silly noises.' This is honest feedback – children can cope with this sort of down-to-earth information if it's delivered in a way that isn't too personal and they feel included. From this, you can talk through some simple ideas on how they can support each other in learning. Do partners talk loud enough for their partner to hear, but not too loud to be interrupting? Do partners check that both really understand the question? Do partners show interest in what the other has to say? Do partners wait while the other is talking? You could also do some role-play with a child in front of the class, with you being the 'difficult' one, as a way of modelling good work.

Consider for yourself what your response might be if you notice that partners are going off task, or if there are some children who won't or can't talk. What will you do about certain children who only talk on their own terms, or another who speaks in a whisper? What if children shout, or one child is deliberately disruptive? What do you do when children are away or you have an odd number? How will you help children who don't like each other, or who rely on others to do the work for them? What will you do for those who become impatient that others can't understand things quickly, or who don't really like sharing their ideas?

Gathering Responses

These are a number of ways to get feedback from the class.[38]

Build on one
Warn one child from one partnership that he will report back. Tell the children that you will ask the rest to build on his answer.

Tell another partner
Each Partner 1 tells another Partner 1; each Partner 2 tells another Partner 2.

All together
If you have just a one-word answer, ask all the children to answer together on the count of three.

Popcorn
If there is a broad question, with many possible suggestions as answers, such as 'Can you think of any words beginning with the sound /d/?', you could give partners some time to talk and then they

---

38 Ruth Miskin Literacy, 2006.

can call out answers as you listen. However, they must sound like popcorn cooking, trying to find the spaces between others' answers, not too loudly.

This or that
If there are two alternatives, children could put their finger on their forehead if they choose the first answer, and on their knee if they choose the other.

Yes or no
Repeat one child's response and ask for thumbs up or down for agreement or disagreement.

Listening to conversations
While partners are working, listen in to a few of the conversations. Sometimes, you can report partners' ideas back to them or to the whole class. This is useful especially when you want to gather answers from less able children who have not been listened to so much, or if you want to support a quiet child's voice.

Games are ideal for starting pair work because most children will be used to following the rules of a simple game. Here are some games to develop partner work, before moving on to other learning.

Five things I know about my partner
Get the children to find out five facts about their partners and report back to the class. These can include full names, siblings, pets, sports or other interests etc. .

Animal fact file
Give each partnership a picture card of an animal (or another category) and ask the partners to prepare three fact sentences about their card. For example, 'This animal is furry; This animal is white; This animal likes human beings'. At the last minute, choose one partner to speak the sentences to the class, and they must guess what animal the partnership has.

Silent drawing
Each partnership has a piece of paper and a pencil. They must draw a fish/ animal/ house/ monster but in silence. Every ten seconds, call 'Stop!' and the children give their pencils to their partner and the partner extends the drawing. After a few swaps, ask the partners to describe the drawing to each other.

The house
The reverse of the game above, the partners talk about the house that would suit someone who wants to live underground, on the moon, in a tree, by the beach etc. Then they have turns to draw it, as above.

To and fro

Works simply to practise turn-taking – count backwards or forwards in ones, twos or fives, or say a known rhyme in alternate words/lines. See below also for choral speaking.

Once you start games that involve learning literacy material, it's a good idea to make sure that any answers are very easy for the children to find together – set the pairs up for almost constant success so that they enjoy being 'brilliant' at whatever the game is together. For example, you may play an adapted vowel game such as the ones described in Chapter 10. Let the children relish getting it right repeatedly; this way they will concentrate on following the rules appropriately and on enjoying the interaction. Your first goal is that they develop confidence that they can manage by themselves and as a team.

Save challenge and competition for later. We also suggest that you reserve discussion or problem-solving tasks for the whole class in this early stage.

Choral Speaking

Class 1 requires a rich diet of choral speaking; verses, poems and tongue-twisters learned by listening and repeating. There are several key reasons for this. It trains the auditory memory; and the momentum and energy provided by learning as a group at this age enables individuals to achieve a great deal more than they would be able to alone. There are multiple benefits provided by the content of what children learn – they absorb sounds, vocabulary, imagery and narrative. Such activity also contributes to the class's corporate identity. We suggest that at this age, most choral speaking is accompanied by physical gestures. Aim for enthusiastic participation from all. It is also a good idea to sometimes ask small groups of children or even individuals to say a verse or poem in front of the class, although this might be relatively rare in Class 1 and will increase in frequency up the school. Use working partners for individual practice of tongue-twisters too, for example.

One of the authors recently observed a French lesson in Class 1 and noticed a little girl who was not at all interested in participating with the poems and songs. She stood and watched, or 'did her own thing'. The author advised the French teacher to make it clear to the class that she was watching everyone carefully to see who would earn a chance to say the poem by herself in front of the class. Once she had realised this, the little girl in question became fully involved. Other types of children may require different coaching and coaxing!

Eventually, towards the end of the year, the class will be working towards a play (depending on readiness, you may decide to wait until Class 2). The play will have lots of choral speaking, usually in verse, and some short individual lines. The whole class learns the whole play and different children take on different parts during the daily practice.

Speech Difficulties

It is important to hear all individual children speak regularly in order to notice any speech difficulties. Some of the phoneme/grapheme games mentioned in the following chapters may flag up a difficulty; if the child makes incorrect or inconsistent choices, for example for the sound /p/, sometimes choosing /p/, sometimes /b/ or even /g/, further investigation will be needed. Do they not understand the symbol–sound correspondence; do they not hear the details clearly; or do they not speak the sound properly?

We have found these consonant sounds are commonly confused:

/b/ and /p/
/v/ and /f/
/th/ and /f/
/tr/ and /ch/
/k/ and /g/

Speech exercises to help one child can legitimately be carried out with a whole class. You may choose a riddle or poem specifically to draw that child's awareness to the sound that goes wrong. However, if you have significant concerns about speech, discuss this with parents. Although it is to be hoped that significant difficulties will have been picked up and remedied earlier, it can still be relevant for a speech therapist to assess and advise on daily exercises for improving accuracy.

Listening to Instructions

Most children in Class 1 will be able to listen and respond to simple instructions. However, there are certain teaching techniques that can make this easier and more likely. You set your class up for failure if instructions are called out over a noisy class, or children are taking things out of their desk while you deliver the information. Such conditions are difficult for everyone but very challenging for those children who have auditory difficulties, whether of perception or processing. It often leads to time being wasted when instructions have to be repeated over and over, or when children do the wrong thing.

Develop clear verbal or non-verbal signals for achieving quiet and focused listening; give instructions only under these circumstances. If there is eye-contact and a quiet environment, even children with auditory perception difficulties will be fine. However, children who don't process auditory information may well still be lost and start doing the wrong thing unintentionally. Another technique, therefore, is to give the instruction and then ask that child to repeat the instruction back to you, preferably using whole sentences, so that you can check understanding. This is also effective if the instructions are relatively complex or subtle. This facilitates mental picturing of the new activity, which is excellent for the child's memory.

Listening to Stories and Recall

In Steiner schools, teachers tell many stories for teaching, frequently from memory. In preparation, we suggest inwardly envisaging and picturing the scenes or images from the story as you learn it.

It is a memory tool but also helps you as you choose your actual words in front of the children – it improves responsiveness to the group and finding just the right expression at the right moment.

> If once or twice you have succeeded in thinking out a pictorial presentation of a lesson that you see impresses the children, then you will make a remarkable discovery about yourself. You will see that it becomes easier to invent such pictures, that by degrees you become inventive in a way you had never dreamed of. But for this you must have the courage to be very far from perfect to begin with.[39]

Story-telling is a universal language; if stories are well drawn, it is rare that children do not listen quietly.

> Let me therefore give you an example of something that can sink into the child's soul so that it grows as the child grows, something that you can come back to in later years to arouse certain feelings. Nothing is more useful and fruitful in teaching than to give the children something in picture form between the seventh and eighth years.... The child does not need to understand at once all the pictures contained in the story ...All that matters is that the child takes delight in the story because it is presented with a certain grace and charm.[40]

The day after a story, the class revisits it in order to look afresh at that which has been 'digested' overnight. We suggest the following for recall:

- Prepare questions that ask for details of the story, some of which may not have actually been directly mentioned (as described in the section on visualisation, p. 61).
- Ask children to draw part of the story.
- With working partners, one child asks the other what they most remember. After this, the first child will tell the class what the other said.
- For appropriate stories, ask the class for an alternative version. For example, what would have happened if the flounder had granted the last wish of the fisherman's wife?
- From the same story, the teacher could ask whether the children have ever wished for something that came true. This would be a speculative question drawn from the context.
- Children could re-enact a part of the story.

---

39 Steiner, 1995, Lecture 4, p. 56.
40 Steiner, 1995, Lecture 4, p. 57.

Chapter 7

Warming up for Literacy:
Auditory and Visual Attention to Detail

- Teaching detailed observation and perception
- Remembering phenomena – training the memory
- Ordering, sequencing and predicting phenomena
- Auditory detail
- Visual detail

What Do They Notice?

Becoming aware of the detailed characteristics of all sorts of phenomena is really useful! On a topic of interest, children will usually pay attention to detail without apparent effort or strain. There are two main reasons why fostering concentration and focus on detail is worthwhile. An ability to sequence information and a good memory are essential for literacy learning.

Developing a sense of order is essential for children to be able to perceive, understand and predict the underlying structure of many phenomena. Understanding structures or patterns also enables them to make links between phenomena. Further, noticing detail supports the child in remembering something: memories are stronger if the child has thoroughly noticed a whole cluster of characteristics about a given phenomena.

There will very likely be some phenomena that are necessary for literacy but that children may not automatically perceive and remember especially accurately. For example, in order to learn how to spell, the children need to start noticing details such as which individual component sounds they say when they pronounce a word. Visually, they will also need to observe the exact orientation and order of the letters in words. Some children will fail to notice these differences because of weak visual or auditory processing.

Auditory Detail

Here we set out some ideas for helping children notice auditory detail. With the introduction of every new letter, the class can play variations of the game 'I Spy'. 'I spy with my little eye something beginning with /p/' (sound rather than letter name.) Many hands will shoot up. Make sure you also notice those who don't volunteer, and those who may be enthusiastic about guessing but will just as happily respond with 'blackboard' or even 'flower.' (Alternatively, as in many other situations where children respond to questions, it may be better not to rely on 'hands up' but rather to randomly select whose turn it is to speak, for example using lollipop sticks with their names on.) Note whether the incorrect guesses are sounds that are close to the target or are way out; does the child always confuse /p/ with /b/ but never with another sound? If so, check whether the child pronounces the /p/ and /b/ correctly. This is useful information about children with poor auditory perception or processing.

As you progress, you can extend the game; 'I spy with my little eye something that ends in /p/' – or even harder, 'I spy with my little eye something that has /p/ in the middle'. Identifying sounds is easiest at the beginning, slightly harder at the end of words, and hardest in the middle.

When speaking a poem, a target letter may be emphasised with an action, such as a clap or a jump. In the following example, it may be the tip-toeing of the princesses following the introduction of the letter from Grimm's fairy tale 'The Twelve Dancing Princesses':

Pitter patter pitter patter go pretty princesses feet
Pitter patter pitter patter down the steps their prince to meet
Pipes are playing, drums are pounding,
Princes dancing, trumpets sounding.
Pitter patter pitter patter go pretty princesses feet
Pitter patter pitter patter down the steps their prince to meet

The poem can also be used for further auditory guessing games; 'Who can find a word with /p/ [sound] at the start (at the end, in the middle)?' Afterwards, once children have written the poem down, you could extend this game by asking the same questions but with the aim of training their visual perception.

Visual Detail – Classroom Games

Here we suggest a few games that you can play with your class to enhance the visual capacity to notice, to remember and to find patterns and the underlying structures of things.

One author played a game with two little classroom gnomes who are very inquisitive and wander around at night. Every morning, the children were invited to see if they could find them. The gnomes became terribly good at hiding, of course, and the children were obliged to become very observant. Later, other items such as wooden letters were hidden in the class. The children were asked to find them, make sure that they were the right way up and then make words with them.

Once the children are accustomed to everything having its particular place in the class, you could put something in the wrong place. Do the children notice the painting brush on the shelf of picture books? Make it a whole trail. Put the painting brush back and then find a piece of chalk amongst the painting brushes; put the chalk back and discover a crayon that needs tidying etc. This also encourages children to take pride in keeping an orderly room!

Word Activities

The word wall activity as described below in the section on common words[41] also fosters this ability to notice detail.

When you write a poem on the blackboard for 'memory reading' or copying, ask for visual details in this way. 'Who can spot a word with six straight lines and one curve?' 'Who can spot the word with two Ps in the middle?' – and so on. These sorts of games are similar to common 'spot the difference' puzzles.

Visualisation

Another aspect of learning that sometimes needs practice is the skill of visualisation. In our experience, some children find it genuinely difficult to see images fully in their 'mind's eye'.[42] For what ever reason, some children have a stronger imagination than others and it is possible to develop this talent where it is weak.[43] Here we describe a game that can be played and adapted to suit your lessons.

Tell the class a small vignette from a story. It should have vivid, evocative description, with detailed sensory and emotional content. While listening, the class should listen with their eyes closed and be asked to 'see' the pictures in their mind's eye. You may choose to point to their forehead to show them where they will see the images. The first time this exercise is done, after the vignette is over and the class open-eyed, the children can be asked to feed back what they saw, and encouraged to add any of their own detail. For example, you might have described a pirate and in your own words mentioned his handsome coat of dark red velvet, with gleaming, brass buttons. You may also have said he was furious, impatient and had a beard, but when you ask the children for feedback on what they saw, you can ask them what colour his hair was. If they had all been 'seeing' it, they will give different answers, but they'll be quite likely to have an answer.

---

41 See Chapter 12.

42 Steiner said that children (particularly between the ages of 7 and 14) better understand the world using the language of images rather than intellectual words. In our view, this is largely the case and remains a sterling piece of advice for economic and effective teaching. It is the brain's right hemisphere that engages with imagery and the left that houses the language centre. However, individuals differ in their hemisphere dominance and capacity and, of course, both need to be employed in learning. It is our experience that some children benefit from such image 'training' to stimulate the right brain.

43 Similarly, it is possible to prevent or inhibit its healthy development: in our view, repetition of electronic images, absorbed passively by young children, would be likely to stultify their own 'organic' generation of cognitive imagery.

As the class begins to get the idea, they will hopefully be inspired by others' imaginative inventions and also by the joy that there isn't a right answer. You can then extend this activity daily by using excerpts from poetry, or parts of your Main Lesson theme. Each time, give plenty of description of both outward visual or auditory details and more inward, abstract details of emotion or mood, leaving 'space' for a few of their own imaginings. Allow a day between the telling and the recall, for a deepening of the internalisation of the imagination, and then ask questions about what the class members have seen. With repetition, you will notice that some children are especially talented with these extensions of inner imagination, but all children ought to be able to enjoy enlivening this capacity.

To extend this, you could ask the children to imagine one or two specific things to 'see' about a story that you'll be telling in advance – information that you deliberately leave open. When re-calling it with their working partners, they will reveal the things they saw. A few pairs could be chosen to share with the class what they saw.

This will bear fruit later when they come to write from all stories or accounts they've heard; if they've had enough practice in this skill, they will use it automatically as a resource for 'thinking up' what to write.

Now we have thought about all the different ways to prepare children for learning, we can turn our attention to the content of the literacy lesson proper. Weave content and learning skills lessons together throughout the year, indeed throughout every year, so that children are prepared for success.

PART 3

Class 1 Lesson Content

Chapter 8

Introducing Sounds and Symbols

- Sequence of phonemes and graphemes
- The first consonants
- Upper-case archetype: how to use story, sound and picture

Phonemes and Graphemes: Sequence of Introduction

Now we are ready to introduce literacy properly. After the classic first lesson, as described in Chapter 5, you may then spend the first week or main lesson block of the autumn term extending and practising Form Drawing whilst you also concentrate on initial classroom management and socialisation.[1] There is a great deal to get used to in the early days, some of which may not look like as much fun as Kindergarten, and it is a good idea to include a few really grown-up elements in your early discussions so that the children know where they are heading and why you are drawing or preparing first. Let them tell you what they know already, what they would like to learn and so on. In this book, we demonstrate a term timeline often taken by one author.[2]

Once you are ready, we suggest following this method for introducing the letters. It is one of the areas where Rudolf Steiner has left fairly clear, if short, procedural indications.[3] Start with the first group of most commonly used consonants, perhaps around six or seven initially, addressing

---

1 One very well respected teacher known to the authors spends just a few days only on Form Drawing and certainly starts teaching letters within the first week. His view is that children are expecting this: they come from Kindergarten with anticipation and eager to be learning something different. We have heard children saying, 'I can't wait to learn something!' Thus, right from the start they get the message that Class 1 is a great step in maturation and agency.
2 See Appendix 9 for details.
3 Steiner, 1976, pp. 13–15.

each one individually with a story and picture, as described below. They don't need to be given in alphabetical order, but in rough order of usefulness for the children's first writing of basic words. For the very first few, you might decide to choose consonants that only have one sound associated with them.[4] We show you how to convey an understanding of the principle of how letters came into being. The purpose of this is to root the abstract literacy concepts in reality: for children of this age, story is authentic and alive, and drawing pictures which metamorphose into letters offers a genuine human experience (see description below). A suggested sequence of consonant initial sounds is listed here:

B M R T
H S N P
C K G F D
L J W
Y Z V

We suggest that after the first batch of consonants, you move straight on to vowels, as described in the next chapter, so that you can begin your first writing with the children. The whole point of acquiring this information is to be *active* with it, and no-one can write much without a vowel! We show you how to introduce them. In this author's class, the initial consonants and all the vowels were fully introduced in the first 'Letters' main lesson block.

The teacher then moved on to work with numbers, and their only language work was reciting, speaking and listening during that time. Other teachers may choose to continue with some consolidation of writing practice, perhaps extra main lessons if you have them.

After your vowels, you can return to the consonants and also the consonant digraphs,[5] but this time you may choose to bring them in a group, without the extended story, picture and writing routine described in this chapter. Once the principle of letter 'discovery' has been established, the rest of the phonemes and graphemes could legitimately be given in batches, perhaps three at a time, as simple tools to use, albeit in a playful way, using story, poem and song for facilitation.

Class Teachers vary in their approach to this. One author found so many beneficial ways to practise literacy skills during the introduction of each letter that it was still both enjoyable and economical to follow the extended, individual letter routine with more consonants. Appendix 2 gives more examples of these. Other teachers prefer to cover this introduction more quickly and then use games and other activities to rehearse all the sounds and symbols steadily in combination. Assuming you use two main lesson blocks for literacy in the first term, amounting to about seven weeks in total, plan for some core writing tasks to be completed in that time. Put yourself in the shoes of the children and ask yourself what would be satisfying for them. What

---

4 See Appendix 1 for a list of the 44 sounds and ways of spelling them.
5 You may want to introduce some of these, such as /ch/, /sh/ and /th/, before finishing the alphabet.

would they feel proud of if they finished it by Christmas, after their first term of being a Class 1 child? This may help you decide how to pace the introductions of the letters. See our suggested year plan in Appendix 7.

The First Consonants

There are three aspects to the letters that need to be conveyed and memorised by the children. These are the symbol or form of the letter, known as the grapheme; the corresponding sound or phoneme; and finally, the name of the letter, which is quite different from the sound it makes. The name of the letter is the least important aspect for initial literacy. However, it is the name of the letter that most people whom the child encounters outside the classroom will use to identify them. Make sure you're clear about which aspects you are teaching, and whenever you talk about letters, always be clear whether you're talking about the 'sound' or the 'name'.

Take note also that there are sometimes two letters that make the same sound (for example, /s/ can be made with a 's' or a 'c') or a letter that makes two sounds (for example 'g'.) In these cases, prioritise giving the most common associated sound. You would first emphasise 's' as /ss/ and 'c' as /k/, for example. But it's worth explaining to the children that letters can sometimes make mischief and change their usage. This author chose to introduce 'c' and 'k' simultaneously from the same fairy tale, for example. See Appendix 9.

We teach upper-case (capital) letters first because they represent a sort of archetype of the way the sound corresponded to form at the origin of the Aramaic alphabet.[6] Introduce upper-case letters with a strong image[7] taken from a vivid story such as a Grimm's fairy tale. Choose a word where the initial sound is clear. For example, T for 'tower' is preferable to T for 'tree' because the sound /tr/ is easily mistaken as /ch//r/. On Day 1, the teacher tells the story (from memory) and attempts to bring it alive with language designed to evoke 'mind's eye' inner pictures. On Day 2, the children re-call the story verbally and the teacher guides them through a drawing of the character or scene that she is using to introduce the letter. On Day 3, after a brief revision, class members draw a guided picture again, but this time the letter 'emerges'. This is the symbol or *grapheme*. We find that the children are very excited at their first discovery of the letters in this way and, once they're accustomed to it, many will be anticipating which letter will newly emerge.

At the same time, the class will work with the related sound, or phoneme, perhaps by reciting a poem or tongue twister, or playing a word-finding game. The class will often perform an action such as a clap or a jump during recitation in the rhythmical time – perhaps they will stamp whenever a word in the poem starts with the particular sound, or they could recite the poem sitting down, standing up for any word that begins with the newly taught sound – so that they are learning kinaesthetically as well as through auditory and visual means.

---

6 In this sense, we are aiming authentically to recapitulate the human literacy journey – drawing symbols out of an image. Steiner, *Practical Advice to Teachers*, Stuttgart, 21 August to 6 September, 1919 (1976), Chapter 5.
7 Steiner, 1995, Chapter 2.

A process for introducing a new letter

TELL A STORY

The next day
- recall the story
- draw a picture
- Introduce and practise the poem

The next day
- Practise the poem with movements on the target sound
- Play 'I spy'
- Play auditory guessing games
- Draw the letter
- 'Memory read' the poem from the blackboard

Following days
- Practise the poem with movements on the target sound
- Play 'I spy'
- Play auditory guessing games
- Play visual guessing games
- Gather and write words that begin with the target sounds
- Copy the poem or write it from memory once the children are able to do so
- Play the 'Troll Game'[8]

The following are examples of stories, poems and illustrations that could be used. The Baker poem mentioned earlier,[9] which has been used during the first Form Drawing main lesson, could be used as an image to introduce the letter 'B'.

---

8 The Troll Game is fully described in Chapter 10.
9 Part 2, Chapter 4

There was once a baker
Who baked a big bun
And I will show you how it was done
He took the flour and poured in the yeast
Then stirred it together
It was such a feast
He stirred and stirred, his arm started aching
But he never got tired of all that baking
He pummeled the dough and pushed it hard
He pummeled the dough and again he'd start
He pushed it down with all his weight
1, 2, 3, 4, 5, 6, 7, 8
Now he rolled it round and round
And never a ball so round was found
He threw it up and caught it neat
And then the rolling would repeat
I tell you the baker had such fun
All for the baking of one big bun.

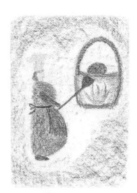

For introducing 'F', you could use the Flounder letter from the Grimms' Fairy Tale 'The Fisherman and his Wife'.[10] Steiner also gives this as an example of a suitable early letter introduction.[11] Here is a (slightly altered) poem that the fisherman cries out to call for the flounder.

Flounder, flounder in the sea
Come fulfil a wish for me.
Full of wishes I find my wife;
Never finished in all her life.
Flounder, flounder in the sea
Come fulfil a wish for me.

---

10 Grimms' Fairy Tales, 2009.
11 Steiner, 1976, p. 11.

During Michaelmas time, the 'D' could be introduced as the Dragon Letter with the story of St Michael.

Deep is the deed to be done by men.
Dangerous dragon asleep in his den.
Who dares to conquer, who dares to slay.
Who dares to banish the dragon this day?
Deep is the deed to be done by men
Dangerous dragon lies bound in his den.

The Golden Goose Letter could be introduced using Grimm's fairy tale 'The Golden Goose'.

Oh my, a golden goose I see
That golden goose must be for me
The greedy sisters grabbed the tail
Were glued together without fail
Oh goodness grace, the golden goose
Will never let the three girls loose

The 'M' could be introduced using Grimms' fairy tale 'Simeli Mountain'. It becomes the Mountain letter.

Many masked men came to the mighty mountain;
Semsi mountain, semsi mountain open, let us in.
Many masked men came out the mighty mountain;
Semsi mountain, semsi mountain shut and let us win.
Money in the measure
To collect a little treasure
But the rich man with his greed
The mighty mountain never freed.

'K' and 'C' could be introduced at the same time with Grimm's fairy tale *The Crystal Ball*.

Can the boy catch the crystal?
Can he catch the crystal ball?
Can he free the king's kind daughter
And become the king of all?

The Swan letter could be derived from Grimm's fairy tale 'The Six Swans'.

Six swans swam silently
Their souls full of sorrow
At sunset they shed their skins
But swans they'll be tomorrow.
Dear sister, dear sister please save us in our need
Sew six new shirts all silently
And your brothers will be freed.

As the 'S' is a letter that children often reverse, it will be very helpful to embroider on the story, adding for example that the swan must be looking out of the window side of the class to see whether the little sister is coming to rescue him. Adapt it to your situation but make sure they have something to help them remember its direction.

More examples and illustrations of letters are included in Appendix 2. See also Appendix 1 for a full list of all the 44 phonemes in English. You will need to teach all of these. We suggest that you teach 'Q' as 'Qu', since they are never apart in English words and pronounce them as /kw/, avoiding a schwa.

Chapter 9

Introducing Sounds and Symbols: Vowels

- Create an image to show that vowels are different from consonants
- Link both short and long vowel sounds to the symbol; leave other sounds of the same vowel for later
- Story to introduce the vowels
- Start writing!
- Time-scale of main lesson blocks

When setting out to teach the vowels, find an image to show the children how the vowels are different to consonants. If you practise making these sounds yourself, you will see that the vowels are just made by the back of the mouth and the control of air. They do not require the touching of teeth or lips or the roof of the mouth. There are several script languages which do not spell out the vowel – notably Hebrew – because the vowel is the part of speech that enables movement from one part of a word to another. Thus, they do have a less palpable quality. It is chiefly vowel pronunciation that differentiates regional accents and often many close languages, such as those in Europe.

As such airy phenomena, vowels can be very difficult to spell because the rules governing their use are so often bent and broken in English; this means that your hearing often won't help guide you to the right spelling. However, at the start it makes sense to teach the simplest and most common ways that vowels are used, namely the short vowels. These are: /ă/ as in 'hat', /ĕ/ as in 'hen', /ĭ/ as in 'hit', /ŏ/ as in 'hot', and /ŭ/ as in 'hut'.[12] We recommend also teaching the principal long vowel sound/ letter name (almost the same in English) simultaneously whilst making the difference very clear – 'Here we are teaching the short vowel, here we have the letter name or the long vowel.' You could ask the children which they would call 'long', showing them the words 'hat' and 'cake' on the board, for example. Most children will identify them easily but for those who don't, we need to agree which vowel sounds we call long and which vowel sounds we call short. To practise this, you

---

12 See Appendix 1.

could call out words in the rhythmical time and the children jump into position: a star jump for long vowels and a jump with feet together and arms crossed for short vowels.

Leave all other possible vowel sounds or diphthongs until later, e.g. /ah/ as in 'father' or 'path'. Try to avoid such words in writing at this emergent stage.

For children with auditory weakness, it will be harder to distinguish the sounds that are made in the same part of the mouth from those made slightly further apart.[13] We suggest you introduce practice games with vowels that are further apart in sound to make them easier: /ă/ and /ŏ/, /ă/ and /ĭ/, /ŏ/ and /ĕ/, /ŏ/ and /ĭ/, /ŏ/ and /ŭ/. When the children are accustomed to the whole concept of hearing vowel sounds, move on to the challenge of distinguishing the difference between /ă/ and /ĕ/ (German and Dutch children find these very difficult), /ĕ/ and /ĭ/, /ŭ/ and /ĭ/, /ŭ/ and /ĕ/.

Story for Introducing the Vowels

The children very much enjoyed the teacher's attempt to tell this vowel-less story! (It definitely requires practice.)

There once was a kingdom where the people were so hard working that there was barely any time to do anything else. Eternally, they were chopping wood, gathering the harvest, baking bread, grinding flour... Their hard work never stopped. They were so busy that they never had much time to rest; there was no time for happiness, no time for joyful birthdays, no time for any celebrations, but there was also no time for sadness, and when someone was angry, well, they would just have to get on with it; there was certainly no time to sulk.

When they spoke to each other, which they did sparingly, they used few words and you and I would have had trouble understanding them. When they wanted to say 'Hand me the spade, please', they said, 'Hnd m thspd pls'. When they wanted to say, 'We must cut that tree down', they said, 'W mstctthttr dn'. When they wanted the bread put in the oven they said, 'Pt thbrd n thvn', and when the children had to wash their hands they said, 'Wshyrhnds'.

When God looked down on this hard-working folk, he sighed. How hard they worked, but how little time they had to play, to feel happy and joyful, to feel sad and sorrowful. God decided to send down five angels to this kingdom. No-one in the kingdom noticed them, but they wandered through the kingdom nevertheless.

Whenever they came upon some hard-working soul they would gently put a hand

13 The difficulty is due to the place where the sound is formed in the palate. Some sounds are physically made near each other with very little movement between them. The other vowels are placed further apart. For details see Townend & Walker, 2006.

on that person's shoulder. As they did so, amazing things began to happen. For example, suddenly, without knowing why, the man who was cutting down the tree sighed and a big smile spread over his face as he remembered how lovingly his wife had baked him a cake for his lunch. He put down his axe and took a break from his work to enjoy the lovely food. Suddenly, the farmer who was bending over to cut the corn stretched his back and thought of his son who was today ten years old. He called out to the boy who was working hard a little further on. 'Son, it is your birthday! Go and play. You can finish your work another day.'

Suddenly, the baker who was sweating over the hot oven put down his baking tin and stretched his back while two tears rolled down his face. He remembered his old father who had died some weeks back. The baker sat down with his daughter and over a mug of hot chocolate and told her about her grandfather's life, remembering him with sadness and thankfulness.

And so the people of this kingdom were given a little time to be happy and joyful, to be sad and fearful. But the angels brought something else too. Each of them brought down a letter, and with it they touched every word the people spoke or wrote, so that every word was given a little more time. Instead of 'pls' the people said 'please', instead of 'thnks' they said 'thanks'.

The first angel brought down the A, the second the E, the third the I, the fourth the O and the fifth the U.

The A said /ā/ [as in rain] when there was lots of time, and when it had to be a bit shortened it said /ă/ [as in cat].

The E said /ē/ [as in tree] when there was lots of time, and when it had to be a bit shortened it said /ĕ/ [as in bed].

The I said /ī/ [as in pipe) when there was lots of time, and when it had to be a bit shortened it said /ĭ/ [as in sit].

The O said /ō/ [as in blow] when there was lots of time, and when it had to be a bit shortened it said /ŏ/ [as in hot].

The U said /ū/ [as in tune or rune] when there was lots of time, and when it had to be a bit shortened it said /ŭ/ [as in cut].

And to this day these letters are called the Angel Letters.

The following song for the vowels followed the story.[14]

An-gels gave us time to play, time to sing and time to pray; A – (ai)   –   –   –

–   –   –   –   –   Time for us the world to see, time to climb the high-est tree;

E – (as in tree)   –   –   –   –   –   –   –   Time to love the great blue sky,

time to fly our kites up high; I (as in high) –   –   –   –   –   –   –   –

Time to plough and seeds to sow, time to see the seed-lings grow; O (as in grow) –   –

–   –   –   –   –   Time to see the   world   a-new,   an - gels   we   are

thank-ing you;   U (as in new) –   –   –   –   –   –   –   –

14 N. Teensma.

The first, emergent whole-word writing tasks could be easy and satisfying in the following way.

- Ask the children to write the statement 'I AM ...' including their own name. Ask them to mark the space between words with a golden star, so that they understand that words are separate. It could be accompanied by a self-portrait, and join the others on the wall to show the whole class. Interesting known letters or patterns of spelling could be discussed and enjoyed, but explain that names are often very irregular.

- From a story or one of the poems above, a picture could be drawn with one word underneath. Choose short, phonically regular CVC (Consonant Vowel Consonant) words.[15] As you write them, practise sounding out and blending the letters (see below for further games and activities). Model this and ask the class to chant it back.

The next group of common vowel sounds is those influenced by 'r', especially /ar/ and /or/. We suggest that on the whole, you leave full instruction and practice on these until Class 2, after in-depth work with long vowels. You will see some examples of how to do this in that section of the book. However, since /ar/ and /or/ come up so frequently, you may find that you need to give some brief information about them. Similarly, the /er/ sound is at the end of many words with two syllables such as 'better' or 'longer', and it may be necessary to feed this in to help some writing before the end of Class 1. Indeed, some children may spot them spontaneously.

---

15 See Glossary, page 328.

Chapter 10

Introducing Sounds and Symbols: Playing to Practise Phoneme and Grapheme Awareness

- Using quick-fire games to practise phonics
- Avoid the schwa
- Teaching awareness of phonemes or sounds
- Troll game and 'Snakes and ladders' for awareness of all the phonemes in a word
- 'I Spy' and Dictation for awareness of initial and end sounds
- Cats & Dogs game for short vowels and initial blends

This chapter gives some games and exercises for practising phonological skills so that children can manipulate phonemes. 'Phonics' is the teaching of the awareness of phonemes, or individual speech sounds, automatically and at speed.[16] Effortless phonemic awareness enables accurate discernment and blending of individual speech sounds into words. Once children know at least one grapheme corresponding to each phoneme, or symbol for a sound, it means they can write what they can say. It is recognised that probably the key weakness for dyslexic children is a difficulty with phonemic awareness.[17]

---

16 The debate about the balance of whole-word and phonics (or other) methods of teaching literacy has been vigorous for decades, even centuries. For background, see Adams, 1990. In this book, we essentially take an analytic phonics approach with the underlying principle of moving from whole words (that children speak and want to write) and breaking them down into sounds and corresponding graphemes. In practice, once the process is underway, phonics instruction moves between the analysis of words and the synthesis – making words out of known sounds – and so a formal instructional definition becomes academic. For a discussion, see Bear, Invernizzi, Templeton, & Johnstone, 2012, p. 162.
17 Reid, 2009.

Supportive practice games should run simultaneously with the introduction of letters, as previously described. We suggest using the Troll Game (see p. 79) very soon after the introduction of the first few consonants. Similarly, you will need games to help distinguish between short vowel sounds. Use these as soon as you have introduced them. As soon as all your consonants have been taught, you will also find activities that play with consonant blends here.

Schedule at least three or four such supportive practice activities during every main lesson, alongside other rhythmical time work, new teaching, forming letters, listening to stories and so on. Many of the skills need to become automatic, to settle into the child's habit (this could be termed the etheric body). In order for this to happen, the activities need to be done over and over again, much more often than most teachers think. Most activities here are presented in game form. This aids the process of separating the skill from conscious control; for the child, the aim is to play and possibly win the game; for the teacher, it is to practise splitting words into sounds.

In order to stay on top of it, you will need to master your transitions, but it's best to stop an activity after 10 or 15 minutes while the children are still enjoying it and move on to the next one quickly. Leave the activity while they are still hungry for it and they will be excited to come back to it tomorrow. You could either run games as a whole-class activity or organise game-islands where the class is split and there are, say, five different activities happening at the same time. This would need helpers to manage each small group, either parents or able students. It might be especially useful to do this for assessments of how much each child has learned.

Aim for a constant buzz of interesting one-thing-after-another to do – the lesson will be finished before any of you know it, and the children will have learned without realising it – perfect.

Practising Phonics

With all these exercises, the first priority is to work with the sounds rather than the letter names.[18] We also urge you to take care in your pronunciation of the sounds. Try to enunciate them exactly as they are formed in the word, clearly but without a 'schwa' sound. This is the technical name for the guttural, non-descript vowel /uh/or /er/ sound we tend to add.[19] Demonstrate this for yourself by saying the sound /b/ for the first sound of the word 'bat'. Try to make a short, fricative sound using the lips as they come together; avoid saying 'buh'. Similarly, try not to say 'ler' for the first sound of 'lid'. The word is 'bat', not 'buh-at'; 'lid', not 'ler-id'. Practise the alphabet of sounds on your own first before going to the classroom, because it takes a little while to get the hang of it! If you can be accurate in your individual sounds, it really helps children detect them more clearly and leads to success in blending them together when they're forming their own writing.

Matching Phonemes and Graphemes

The ability to discern and distinguish the phonemes is often taken for granted but this requires

---

18 Letter names have no practical use until the children work on spelling *per se*.
19 See Appendix 1 for examples, and the Glossary for further explanation.

a cognitively analytical approach to language. All young, pre-literate children usually see the 'the whole picture', connecting images and experiences with words. When hearing the word 'splash', for example, they see the splashing water and possibly associate this with an event they've experienced. They do not automatically hear /s//p//l//a//sh/, understanding that the word is made up of five distinct speech sounds. Hearing the sounds is also different to hearing the syllables.

We work with language from the whole to the parts, helping children raise this awareness. The more times you are able to practise this skill, the better you will be in laying foundations for all the children in your class to be able to write their own words, even the ones with an auditory-processing weakness.

Consonant phonemes are much more easily aurally identified than vowels. You will also find that children are often able to identify the initial sound of a word, such as in the game 'I Spy'. The next easiest sound to identify will be the final sound of a word. Medial or middle sounds are the hardest to distinguish precisely, especially vowels. Teach and practise them in this order of difficulty.[20] See also the bibliography for further resources with ideas for practising phonic skills.

The Troll Game

The 'Troll Game' rehearses the ability to separate and distinguish the phonemes in words.

You need

- A pack of cards, each with one written word on
- Something that can serve as stepping stones. Rubber spots are useful classroom equipment for this and other games.[21]

The children sit with the teacher in a large circle on the floor. A wavy 'bridge' made of rubber spots is set out along the diameter of the circle from one side to the other. Three red spots mark the places where the 'bridge' is weak. An extra spot is put next to the bridge somewhere near the centre of the circle; this is the home of the Troll.

- Tell a little story about a troll guarding a bridge. Travellers may only pass over if they know the password.
- Choose the two children either side of the teacher in the circle; the children on your left are going to be the troll, the children on your right will try to get over the bridge. The first 'troll' goes and sits on the spot next to the bridge.
- The following chant could start the game off:

20 Bear, Invernizzi, Templeton, & Johnstone, 2012; Reid, 2009; Townend & Walker, 2006.
21 http://www.westmerciasupplies.co.uk/sequencing-spots-set.

Troll, troll, let us through. We have the mag-ic word for you.

- The teacher says the word on the first card. The whole class, including the child about to 'walk the word', chants the different sounds (phonemes) while tapping alternately with the right hand on the right knee and the left hand on the left knee. For example, 'CAT' would be right hand on right knee for the sound /k/, left hand on left knee for /ă/ and right hand on right knee for the final sound, /t/.
- The child crossing the bridge walks on the stepping stones whilst saying the individual sounds; so for 'cat', it would be three steps.
- Continue in the same way, giving new words, until the child has crossed the whole bridge.
- If the child lands on a red spot at the end of a word – weak plank in the bridge – the troll gets up and chases the child along the bridge and anti-clockwise around the circle, while the child tries to get 'home' to his place. The same also happens if the child gets to the end of the bridge.
- The troll and the child crossing the bridge may only start running when all the sounds of the word have been said. If the troll tags the child before she gets home, the two sides swap and the children on your left will be the bridge-crossers and those on your right, the trolls.
- If the troll doesn't tag the child, the sides stay as they were. The next child on your left will be the next troll, and the next child on your right will try to cross the bridge.

The next day, play the game again, reversing the sides.

In order to practise this skill, we suggest you play this game in main lesson every day for about two weeks early in Class 1, using words where the different sounds can easily be distinguished. These do not have to be only simple words: the words are read by the teacher (or by an able student) and can therefore include words the children won't be able to write or read. Avoid words where the sounds are not clear; e.g. use basketball (/b/, /ah/, /s/, /k/, /ə/, /t/, /b/, /aw/, /l/, but avoid words ending in '-er', since there can be confusion about whether we hear the /r/ sound at the end of the word. We also suggest that every now and then during Class 1, you return to it. Regularly ask the class and individual children how many steps a word would be in the Troll Game. When the children need to write a word in class, first ask them to inwardly 'do the troll game'. The children could tap the sounds of the word on their knees, so determining those they need to blend to make the word. They can then confidently write down appropriate graphemes.

Snakes and Ladders

After such a physical game, it is time to bring this activity to the desks. The children are asked to bring in snakes and ladders board games from home. Several games are played at the same time with around four or five children per game. You need counters, a snakes and ladders board game and a pack of cards with appropriate words – start with CVC (Consonant–Vowel–Consonant) words. Progress by choosing CCVC words (with initial blends), CVCC words (with end blends) and consonant digraphs (e.g. /th/, /ch/, /sh/ etc.), depending on the level you've reached with the children.[22]

- All children have a counter on the start. Cards are on the table – face down.
- Explain and model that we are counting sounds.
- The adult or more able child takes the top card and reads the first word without the players seeing.
- The first player moves his counter as many places as there are sounds, and says the sounds as he moves the counter from place to place.
- Just as with the real snakes and ladders, you climb ladders or slide down snakes as you land on the relevant squares.[23]

Initial and End Phonemes

I Spy

Play 'I spy with my little eye something beginning with /p/' when you have introduced the letter 'P'. Vary this game to include end consonants and blends.

Dictation

As soon as the class has learned a letter and its accompanying story and poem, they can start with 'dictations'. The teacher gives a word verbally and the children write it down. Simple CVC words can be given as whole words, or you could ask the children to only write the initial sound and draw a line for the remainder of the word. You could choose only words beginning with /p/ and /b/, for example, in order to help the class distinguish between these two similar phonemes. Also, if you ask children to write only the initial sound, you can use more complex words that the children wouldn't yet be able to tackle. This activity could be extended to include initial blends or other parts of the word. The children feel very proud that they are taking dictations right from the beginning!

---

22 See Glossary for terms.
23 Possible words for sound counting can be found in Appendix 4.

Distinguishing between the Short Vowel Sounds

As mentioned above, the hardest sounds for children to distinguish are the medial or middle sounds in words, especially the vowels. The simplest medial vowel sounds to work with are the short vowels. Many children have genuine difficulties hearing the difference between the short vowel sounds. This is where you could easily 'lose' the children who may be dyslexic. Such a problem may be due to auditory-processing problems, hearing difficulties (such as glue ear, past or present) or because they are bi-lingual. We need to practise this if we are to take all the children with us on the path to becoming good readers and writers.

With both these games, start with vowels that are further apart in sound: /ă/ and /ŏ/, /ă/ and /ĭ/, /ŏ/ and /ĕ/, /ŏ/ and /ĭ/, /ŏ/ and /ŭ/. Use these while the children get used to the games and the whole concept of hearing vowel sounds. Much more challenging is distinguishing the difference between /ă/ and /ĕ/, /ĕ/ and /ĭ/, /ŭ/ and /ĭ/, /ŭ/ and /ĕ/.

Run to the Vowel – Two Variations

1. This game allows you to focus specifically on the difference between two vowel sounds.
    *   Stick two large vowels (each one on a card) on opposite walls of the room. For example, choose 'A' and 'E'.
    *   While the teacher plays a drum with a rhythm for running, skipping or walking, the children move around the room. The playing stops and the teacher calls out a sound; the children run quickly, but without crashing or sliding, to the wall where the correct vowel is.
    *   If the teacher calls out a word with one of the three other vowels, the children must freeze on the spot.
    *   Extend this by calling out a CVC word so that the children have to work out what sound is in the middle.

2. Make cards with the five vowels (A5-laminated) so that you have as many of each as a half or third of the total number of children in your class. For example, in a class of 21 children, it worked well to have twelve cards of each vowel. You also need a list of short vowel words.
    *   Spread the vowels out on the floor.
    *   Teacher or able pupil calls out CVC (short vowel) words, one at a time.
    *   Children all run as fast as they can to the vowel they hear in the word. There can be a maximum of three children per card, and they must put one toe on the card.
    *   When they are all standing in the right place, ask the whole class to call out the word and the vowel it contains, e.g. 'cat' and /ă/.

Once the children know how to play this, you could start a game by calling out a word for particular individuals. The child must find the vowel on the floor by themselves. Continue on to the game as described above. This enables you to note down who just follows the others and who really knows.

Cats and Dogs

This game is also known as Crows and Cranes (when it is played in a gym lesson).[24]

Divide the class into two groups. They can be the cats and the dogs, if you want to practise distinguishing between /ă/ and /ŏ/. With a rope, make a homeland for the dogs and a land for the cats where they cannot be caught.

- Stick two vowels (A and O in this case) on opposite walls – you need a good space between them.
- The two groups walk or skip towards each other according to the teacher's drum rhythm. The teacher stops and calls out an /ŏ/ or /ă/. If it is an /ă/ the cats can chase the dogs and tag them. When a dog is caught, she becomes a cat. If the dogs manage to get back to their homeland, they're safe. The drum starts and the game continues. Extend this by calling a CVC word rather than just a sound.

Once these games have been played, it is also important to transfer the skills to written work. Show the children how to draw two 'lands' in their main lesson book, for example an /A/ and an /O/ land. Then dictate words and ask the children to write the words in the correct 'land'. Remind the class to 'tap' or 'bounce' the sounds, as in the troll game.

Create packs of CVC word cards for use later in pairs, where one child reads and dictates to the other.

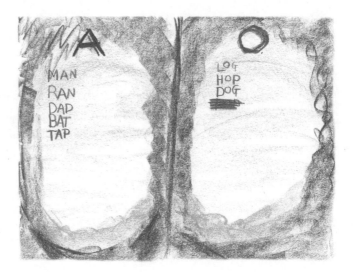

24 Brooking-Payne, 1996.

Another quick variation is for a card-caller to say the word out loud. The listener then takes the card and places it upside down in an /A/ or an /O/ pile, which they can then self-check. (This is an easy task to give parents to do at home with a child who is particularly struggling.) As with the vowel games above, start with vowels that are further apart in sound, progressing on to the more similar short vowels.

Consonant Digraphs

Digraphs can be taught alongside the early consonants because they act in the same way, albeit with a two-letter grapheme. These include /th/, /sh/, /ch/, /wh/ and /ph/. The other slightly less common digraphs are /ng/ and /nk/, especially in the form of 'ing'. Teaching children these sounds early is of great practical help in enabling their free writing – more important than knowing the alphabet, for example. In the next section, we give an example of how to work with a consonant digraph in such a way as to support accurate auditory discernment.

Confusing Phonemes

There are some consonants phonemes that can be particularly confusing for children. The following sounds can be particularly difficult to distinguish:

- /th/ and /f/
- /g/ and /k/
- /g/ and /d/
- /t/ and /d/
- /b/ and /p/ and /v/
- /f/ and /v/
- /ch/, /j/ and the blend /tr/

It is important to check whether children are actually pronouncing these sounds correctly. You can help children bring awareness and precision to their speech with poems and tongue twisters in the class. It's not uncommon for children to discover, through literacy work, that they've been saying a word 'wrong' for ever! However, be aware that those children who consistently mis-pronounce these sounds usually require individual, specialist work to iron out a specific speech problem, so it may be worth discussing this with parents.

The following is an example of a poem for distinguishing between CH and TR. When the children know the poem, draw a 'TR' on the left of the board and 'CH' on the right. The children can then jump when they say the words beginning with CH or TR; for TR jump to the left, for CH jump to the right.

A CHOO, CHOO TRAIN TRAVELLED FAST
A CHAIN OF TRAINS ARRIVED AT LAST
THE CHINESE CHILDREN CHOSE TO EMBARK
THE LAST CHAIN OF THE TRAINS WHICH WAS CHILLY AND DARK
ON BOARD THE TRAIN WAS A TREASURE CHEST
THAT THE CHILDREN FOUND AND YOU CAN THINK UP THE REST

To practise this, you could also play a game of 'Cats and Dogs' (see above), a game of run to the 'TR' or 'CH' homeland, or a simple word dictation distinguishing between those two sounds.

Pairs Game for M and N Blends

The difference between 'rig' and 'ring' is subtle. When a child is trying to write the sound /ng/, it will take some practice before they can hear the 'n'. Similarly, 'lap' and 'lamp' are different, but hearing the 'm' is a challenge. This game highlights the sounds and is suitable for children towards the end of Class 1 or early in Class 2.

Make the game together first. Give each working partnership a set of blank cards and a piece of scrap paper for practising their spelling. Explain that we are going to work with words that end in /ng/ and /mp/. Model how to do this by saying the word 'rag'. Tell the class that you can add an 'n' to make a new word and give the example, 'rang'. This shows them how the 'n' affects the consonant 'g'. Ask Partner 1 to write the first word on a card, once the pair has agreed the spelling, and then they will decide what the second word must be, and Partner 2 will then have a go at writing it on scrap paper. If this is easy, they can write it on a second card immediately to make the pair. Demonstrate again by doing this with them, using 'sag' to 'sang', for example. Then show them how to change 'lap' to 'lamp' in a similar way. See if they can discover how the 'n' partners the 'g', and the 'm' the 'p'.

Having prepared in this way, then dictate only the first word of each of the pairs set out in the table below and ask them to write the second 'n' or 'm' version themselves. So you will say out loud 'Pup', and Partner 1 will first write that word, and then Partner 2 will write on their scrap paper, 'Pump'. The first few times, check in with the class as to whether or not they have got the hang of it by asking them to say the answer out loud before everyone writes it down. As the activity progresses, to increase challenge you could reduce the number of responders, so ask half the class, then two pairs, one pair, or an individual. Check the spelling and write each one up on the board so that the correct words are now visible. Either then, or at the end of the activity, the partners will share out the remaining blank cards and complete the writing of the second-word cards.

Rag	Rang	Lap	Lamp
Cap	Camp	Rig	Ring
Dig	Ding	Rap	Ramp
Rug	Rung	Pup	Pump
Swig	Swing	Sprig	Spring
Gag	Gang	Trap	Tramp
Pin	Ping	Hag	Hang
Bet	Bent	Hug	Hung
Tag	Tang	Bag	Bang
Lip	Limp	Wig	Wing

Once all the cards are made, arrange them into playing card packs.

In another lesson, you can play pairs. Three or four children can play at a time. All the cards are shuffled and dealt. Then the children look in their hands and lay down any pairs already there (e.g. cap / camp). After this, the first child plays a card and the one who has its pair picks it up and lays the pair down. The winner has the most pairs at the end.

We are sure you can create similar activities to distinguish between the other tricky sounds!

Chapter 11

More Word Work:
Word Families and Blends

Word Families – Onset and Rime[25]

- Blends
- Making a blends game
- To play the game – blends game
- Blends dictation

In this chapter, you will be shown how to move beyond introduction and develop the children's expertise. First, we give examples of making word families to practise sounding and blending. The simplest words are the CVC words, but it's not long before you need the next level of complexity. These are often four letters in length, and can be referred to as CCVC or CVCC words. These are words where two consonants form a single-phoneme digraph such as /ch/ or /th/ or a blend with two, closely attached phonemes such as /tr/ or /st/ or /mp/. The games and activities that follow are designed to engage all the children in highly repetitive rehearsal, using multi-sensory approaches. In this way, you try to 'catch' all-comers.

Word Families: Onset and Rime

Working with onset and rime is good practice for children in Classes 1, 2 and 3. It primes the children to look for regularities and patterns in words. Good spellers tend to be those who quickly pick up etymologically similar roots, prefixes and suffixes of words and see how they fit together or adapt from one meaning to another. When teaching spelling, you are aiming to help the average or weak speller absorb the same rules of word structure.

25 See Glossary, page 329.

Hide a letter

For working with onset and rime, an initial suggestion is to develop a daily habit of 'hiding' a few letters before the children come into an English main lesson. Wooden letters are stuck with Blu-tack or put on shelves in different places in the classroom. It is a good activity for the start of the day. As soon as they have said 'good morning' to the teacher, s/he asks the children to find the letters and to make words with them. Gather the revealed letters and ask the children for suggestions for words they can make. Write them on the board, read them out loud, and then choose one to start a word family.

For example, say you have hidden M, N and A. The children will find them and suggest the words MAN, A and AN. Then write on the blackboard:

MAN
_AN
_AN

Ask them, 'Which other letters have we learnt that could go at the start of this word instead of the M? Can we make other rhyming words?'

They may come up with:

MAN
BAN
FAN
CAN
RAN
PAN
DAN

Once you have this game established, the children can make the word families in pairs. You will need to agree a rule about only choosing real words, or allowing a limited number of 'nonsense' words, but each child should make their own list.[26] Quick pairs may make little sentences, using some of their chosen words. Some are so inspired that they might create little stories.

In this way, create word families for CVC words onwards. We have used several different resources for help.[27]

---

26 The skills used here are similar to those in the game 'Boggle'. Including nonsense words still has value because the children are using their phonological understanding; it can also inject humour into the game! Make sure that it doesn't lead to confusion about which words are real – do the children know what the words really mean? – and set a behaviour parameter for coming back to order and focus.
27 Hornsy, Shear, & Pool, 2006; Bear, Invernizzi, Templeton, & Johnstone, 2012.

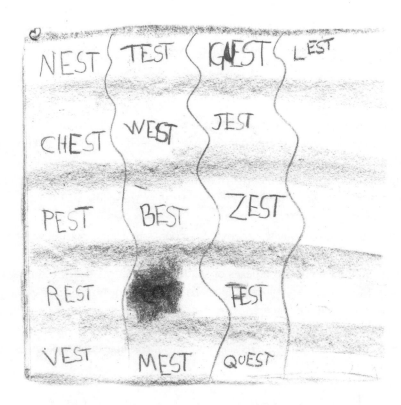

Blends

Here are some games for initial and end-blend practice. An evocative, timely poem can be used to embed this potentially rather 'dry' work in a sympathetic context. The following poem lends itself well.

IT'S **SPR**ING, IT'S **SPR**ING, LET'S DANCE AND SING
THE **SN**OW'S AWAY, THE LAMBS WILL **PL**AY
THE SKY IS **BL**UE, IT'S **BR**IGHT AND NEW
THE **GR**ASS IS **GR**EEN, A **CR**OCUS SEEN
SPROUTING **SPR**IGS, AND **TW**ISTING **TW**IGS
FLOWERS ARE HERE, AND BIRDS **FL**Y NEAR
A **BR**IGHT **GR**EEN LAWN, THE **FR**OGS WILL SPAWN
THE **FR**OGS WILL **SPL**ASH, THE KINGFISHER **FL**ASH
SWANS WILL **SW**IM, NECKS LONG AND **SL**IM
THE WORLD IS **FR**ESH, AND GOD WILL **BL**ESS
ALL **CR**EATURES BORN, ON THIS NEW MORN[28]

It contains the initial consonant blends – spr, sn, pl, sk, bl, br, gr, cr, spr, tw, fl, fr, sp, spl, fl, sw, sl.

---

28 N. Teensma.

Recite the poem and make sure the children know it well. We suggest writing it on the blackboard and asking the children to 'read' it from memory.[29] You can work with this in several ways:

- Ask a child to point at the words while they read the poem, or give them certain words to search for (visual information)
- Play a 'mind reader' game. The teacher would say, 'I have a word in my mind and it begins with "SPR", and if you walked it in the troll game you would need five steps. Who knows what word I have in mind?' The answer is, of course, 'SPRING' (uses visual and auditory information)
- Additionally, try holding up the blends from the poem on large A5 cards, shuffling them and asking the class. 'Which word from our poem starts with these letters?'

Perhaps you will ask the class to copy the poem in their books, making a lovely illustration. If you use a blackboard, be aware that there are children who find such copying very tricky due to physical difficulties with eye tracking, retained childhood reflexes or sequential visual memory.[30] Focusing on their own work, refocusing on the board at a distance and then back again many times can be visually exhausting. A good solution is to provide model copies, preferably on individual pieces of paper, handwritten in colour, just in the same way as you would like the children to write it in their main lesson books. Paper copies at the desk reduce the visual demands significantly, and enable quicker progress.

---

29 See Chapter 2 for a discussion of memory reading and the value and limitations of copying as a classroom activity. See also Bear, Invernizzi, Templeton, & Johnstone, 2012.

30 A poor visual memory may mean that a child cannot keep more than one letter at a time in mind. These children must look up and down frequently, often losing their place.

Making a Blends Game

Games are often most enjoyable for the children when they have made them themselves. There is learning involved in their making, too.

Give the children circles cut out of old paintings and ask them to write the blends from the poem on the cards. Challenge the more able students by giving them *all* other consonant blends; this way, you end up with variety among your games. The circles are laid out and stuck down on a piece of board in a clear path with a start and a finish.

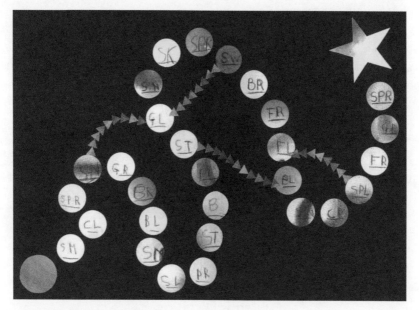

To play the game, one class of 21 children divided into groups of four or five. Each group had their own board. Even in Class 1, students can play this game without any adult help. You can repeat this and maintain enthusiasm by varying the combination of children and the board they're using.

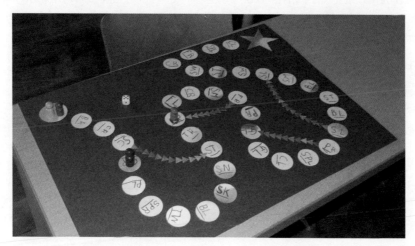

To Play Blends Game

You need a blends game board, counters and a dice.

- All students have a counter on starting.
- Each student takes it in turn to throw the dice and move her counter forward for the required number of spaces.
- The student must say the blend she has landed on and give a word that starts with that blend.
- If a student lands on a blend with an arrow, s/he must follow the arrow to the blend it points to and say both blends and give two words.
- The winner is the first to reach the finish.

The first few times you play this game it is just done verbally, but soon you can ask one student to write down all the words, or each child to write their own words. Other than the initial blend, correct spelling is not important here. It is helpful to see how the children write the blend down for you; you'll have the opportunity to assess and make a note of how well the children are managing to discern the initial blends. You can then use this information to help design your blends dictation activity.

Blends Dictation

Give the children a piece of paper that already has empty, drawn circles (see page 97 for example). With children older than Class 1, instead of a loose sheet they could draw their own in an English book or a practice book.

Using the same words the children have thought up in the blends game above, call one out and ask the children what letters they would have landed on when they were playing the blends game. The children write the appropriate blend in the circles. Extend this by asking an able child to be the word caller.

You are aiming for the whole class being able to identify the correct blend from memory. However, students who need continued support may have the original game board in front of them until they don't need it.

In a more experienced class, students write the blend and draw a line for the rest of the word. So if the teacher called out 'SPRING', the children would write 'SPR___'.

Later, any word with initial blends or end blends can be used for the same activity to cover the full range of blend types: CCVC, CCCVC, CVCC, CCVCC, CCCVCC. Remember that it is easiest for children to work with initial blends than those at the end of words, as you design tasks from easy to difficult.

Here is an example of one child's test results. The words dictated were all taken from the words the children thought of when they played the blends games:

1. SNAKE
2. FRIEND
3. STAY
4. SPRING
5. SWIM
6. BRACES
7. GLASS
8. SLITHER
9. SMART
10. SCRATCH
11. STILL
12. FRANCE
13. BRUSH
14. SPROUT
15. PRESENT

Chapter 12

More Word Work: Common Words

Activities to introduce and practise common words:

- Word Walls
- Mind Reader
- Find the Word Quiz
- Word Bingo
- Word Boxes

Common Words

Alongside practising sounds and blending, in order to help children with their writing it is necessary for students to learn to read and spell the most commonly used words in the English language. These words may also be known as keywords[31] or high-frequency words.[32] Many published versions of these common words (either the first 100 or 200) are available in books or on websites, and although there may be some disagreement on a few words, most are consistent.

Some common words are spelled in a phonically regular way, but many are not.[33] Since they occur so frequently, it is necessary for children to be able to use them automatically, without thinking twice. At first, in Class 1 you can prioritise words with regular spelling to ensure that all the children, even those with weaker visual discrimination or memory, achieve this manageable task. It's impossible to avoid certain words with unusual spelling, however, such as 'the', 'was' or 'said'. Some words will be 'irregular' to start with, such as 'she' or 'for', but become regular as the class works its way through all the phonemes.

A word bank of common words on display in the classroom for quick reference is a good idea, but you will need to work actively with such a display. See Appendix 3 for a list we have used. While

---

31 For example, Ladybird books.

32 See websites like www.highfrequencywords.org.

33 It's a good idea to use a particular term to refer to phonically regular and irregular words. For example, a green word is regular and a red word doesn't make phonic sense, like traffic lights. Odd One Out words may also be a good term.

this might initially sound rather dry, if worked with playfully it can enable children to develop a real joy in words. Patricia Cunningham and Richard Allington set out a number of excellent activities for this.[34] We start with an activity as it has been used in several Waldorf Lower School classes.

Word Wall Play in Class 1

Mind Reader
The suggestion here is for a three-week introduction to word wall work.

Word reading
- On the first Monday, stick the first six words (written in capital letters) on the word wall and ask whether anyone knows what the words say. Usually, there will be some who know but if not, read them to the class.
- Every morning, point to the words and ask the class to read them in order first, then muddled up.
- It's a good idea to point at the word and count a slow '1, 2, 3' before the whole class calls the answer. This gives more children the chance to work it out for themselves rather than call out the word they hear from the fastest children.[35]

Mind reading
- Once this is established, say to the class that you have a word in your head and that you wonder whether anyone can read your mind. Tell them it is one of the word wall words and then give them a clue. Clues are suggested in the table below.
- The children write down the word they guess.
- Tell them you have a second word in your mind, give a clue and again the children write it down. (In the first few weeks, this will be enough. Later, build this up to five a day.)
- Ask the class who knows the first word that was in your mind. When a child gives the word, ask if s/he can spell it. The child gives the letter names.
- The teacher writes the letters on the board. Ask the student who gave you the word whether they remember the clue. Don't remind them! It's a very good memory exercise. Check together whether the word matches the clue.
- Recalling the clues may involve counting the straight lines; counting the steps in the troll game – they must tap this on their knees; checking the vowel; checking whether the word rhymes, and so on.
- If correct, and there are no other suggestions, move on to the second word. If incorrect, but it was one of the word wall words, allow the children to go through the same process and let them discover where it didn't match.

---

34 Cunningham & Allington, 2002.
35 This is a good differentiation technique to use any time. Some children need 'wait time' before they can find the answer and it can be very off-putting to hear the same few voices always calling out.

- Praise the aspects that matched (if nothing else, that it was a word on the word wall!), and then ask if they or someone else has another idea.
- When all words are found, finish by asking the whole class to read each word. Point at the individual letters; the class spells the word using *letter names*.

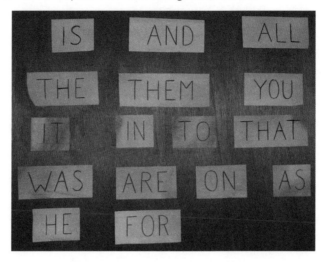

3-week Sequence of Word Wall Words and Clues

These are two sets of plans used in one class. The first clue, for example, might be: 'I'm thinking of a word from the word wall that has nine straight lines'. The second one that day would be for a word that has three straight lines, and so on.

Week 1 Words: THE, THEM, IS, ALL, AND, YOU

Monday	9 straight lines	THE
	3 straight lines	YOU
Tuesday	1 straight line	IS
	7 straight lines	ALL
Wednesday	13 straight lines	THEM
	1 curve	AND
Thursday	3 steps in the troll game & 3 letters	AND
	2 steps in the troll game & 2 letters	IS
Friday	3 steps in the troll game & 4 letters	THEM
	Rhymes with wall & ball & stall	ALL

Week 2 Words: As week 1 plus TO, IN, THAT, IT, WAS

Monday	10 straight lines	THAT
	4 straight lines	IN
Tuesday	3 straight lines, 3 letters	YOU
	3 steps in the troll game & 4 letters & it has an 'A'	THAT
Wednesday	2 steps in the troll game & an 'I'	IT, IN, IS
	Choose the word from the word wall that best fits the following sentence: 'I will give this card ___ you'	TO
Thursday	Rhymes with call	ALL
	3 steps in the troll game & 3 letters	AND, WAS
Friday	Rhymes with cat, bat, fat	THAT
	The whole word sounds just like the name of one of our vowels	YOU

Week 3 Words: As week 2 plus WE, ARE, AS, FOR, ON

Monday	3 straight lines	AS, YOU, IT, ON
	7 straight lines	HE, ALL, WAS
Tuesday	Choose the word from the word wall that best fits the following sentences: 'I have made this card _____ you'	FOR
	'How _____ you?'	ARE
Wednesday	Rhymes with me, she	HE
	Rhymes with hat'	THAT
Thursday	The whole word sounds like the name of one of our letters that is not a vowel	ARE
	The whole word sounds just like the name of one of our vowels	YOU
Friday	Dictate all words to see how many remembered	

Another example: 3-week List of Words and Clues

Week 1 Words: SAID, THE, ALL, WITH, HAVE

Monday	2 letters that are the same	ALL
	2 angel letters next to each other	SAID
Tuesday	5 straight lines	SAID
	12 straight lines	HAVE
Wednesday	A word with curves	SAID
	A word with /TH/ (unvoiced)[36]	WITH
Thursday	Rhymes with call	ALL
	Rhymes with bed	SAID
Friday	'Come _____ me'	WITH
	'_____ you washed your hands?'	HAVE

Week 2 Words: As week 1 plus: THEY, WAS, HIS

Monday	Whitsun festival[37]	
Tuesday	'Come _____ me'	WITH
	'_____ you washed your hands?'	HAVE
Wednesday	9 straight lines	THE
	4 straight lines	HIS
Thursday	/TH/ voiced[38] & four letters	THEY
	Word 'IS' hidden in it	HIS
Friday	Rhymes with call	ALL
	Rhymes with bed	SAID

36 Trying to pronounce this as gently as possible, with air but no voice!
37 This is a real-life plan, as you can see from the normal school interruptions.
38 In this word, the sound is still gentle but voiced.

Week 3 Words: As week 2 plus: THAT, AT, FOR

Monday	Has an 'A' and 2 letters	AT
	Has an 'I' and 2 letters	IS
Tuesday	Has a 'W' and ends in /S/	WAS
	Has an 'O'	FOR
Wednesday	Rhymes with more	FOR
	Rhymes with clay	THEY
Thursday	Has two vowels next to each other in the middle of the word	SAID
	Has a letter that is sometimes a vowel and sometimes a consonant	THEY
Friday	Rhymes with cat	THAT, AT
	'Here is a present ____ you.'	FOR

Find the Word Quiz

This game helps the children to notice more details within words and spellings and is a little more advanced than 'Mind Reader', mainly due to the type of clues given. Awareness of vowels, consonants, syllables, sounds, rhyming and opposite is required. Revising such terminology is essential. In addition, understanding the meaning of words in context, also known as 'listening comprehension', is necessary. Thus, the clues are multi-faceted – auditory, visual or semantic.

Even though the activity is only done with a few words, it will, if practised daily, help children to notice more details in *all* words they see.

- Five new words are introduced every week, sometimes with a mnemonic (such as 'Could Old Uncle Len Dance' to remember how to spell the word 'could'). All words are stuck on the wall and stay there, even after introduction of the new words.
- As part of the morning routine, every day the teacher gives a clue and the children write their guess down. The words can be any from the word list and not just the new words.[39] The clues

---

39 Sometimes you can set a clue to which there is more than one right answer. This self-selection gives the children an opportunity to differentiate themselves so that they work at the right level of challenge. As they become accustomed to it, you can adjust the word wall or set some rules in order that all children do, in time, move on to new words.

are visual, auditory or semantic, and require the children to search for a good match – e.g.

1. A word with five letters with the word 'quit' in it (visual clue)
2. A word with four letters and two syllables (auditory)
3. A word with four letters and two sounds (auditory)
4. A word with five letters which is the opposite of wrong (semantic)
5. A word with five letters which fits in the following sentence (semantic)

- Ask individuals to give their answers, ask whether they remember the clue, and then check whether the word indeed matched. Perhaps others had different answers because sometimes you may have allowed two possibilities.

The word wall gets bigger every week. After several weeks, perhaps four, all the words come down and you check how many are remembered. The next week, start building up the word wall again, leaving out the words everyone had spelled correctly and adding new words.

Choose words either from the list of most common or, if appropriate, from the students' own writing. Further word wall lists that can be used with older children can be found in Appendix 3.

Word Bingo

Once the children are sufficiently familiar with the common words from the word wall, you can play this word bingo game. It can help to leave time between creating the bingo sheets and playing the game since both are learning activities. For example, make the sheets at the beginning of the lesson and promise to play the game at the end, or create it at the end of one lesson and play it the next.

Making the bingo sheets
You need a blank bingo sheet of 25 squares (see Appendix 4) for each student and a pack of 25 cards with common words. Stick the cards up all around the room. Give the students ten minutes to find all the words, and write them correctly in any square on their bingo sheet.

The rules are

- You can walk to the words
- You may not take your book, pencil or paper to the words
- You may not take the words to your desk.
- The words have to be spelled correctly, otherwise it will not count when you have five in a row

Ask one child to collect the words and read them out. The children tick the words to make sure they've not missed one. When you do this checking, some of the students will find it difficult and would benefit from a desk-copy of all the words as support.

Playing bingo

- The teacher has the pack of cards
- The students have their bingo sheets and a pencil (a different colour to that used to create the sheet)
- The teacher reads out the words and the children circle the words. The first one to have five in a row wins. Check that all the words in the row of five are spelled correctly.

Prepared and played like this, the game gives the children three moments to carefully check these common spellings.

Word Boxes

This daily exercise gives children an opportunity to learn and overlearn by themselves, whilst in the classroom. We use the classic spelling technique of 'Look, Say, Cover, Write, Check'.

- Each student has a box of cards with words.
- Teach the children to Look at the word, Say the word, Cover it up, Write the word, and Check your spelling and correct if necessary.
- Some children will go through their box twice or three times, while others manage only once in the same time.
- On Friday, children pair up and check each others' words by dictating them. A correct spelling gets a tick on the card, an incorrect spelling a cross.

In a small class, the teacher can take in all the boxes and remove cards that have two ticks. In a larger class, this would be too time-consuming so the children can be trained to do this for each other. Replace them with common words that have been written incorrectly in the students' own writing or in the common word spell checks. Each child's box will then be individually suitable. The number of words practised each week can also be varied. Some children will have 10 words while others have 15, for example.

Chapter 13

Encouraging Authorship: Free Writing

- Self-expression through writing
- Modelling free writing and peer work
- Reasons to encourage invented spelling

It is pedagogically economical to encourage children to create their own free writing, re-telling a story they've heard or an event that has occurred. It helps a child start to develop the subjective art of self-expression through words, as well as the more 'objective' literacy tools and techniques.[40]

Writing in Class 1 may take many forms, including the following:

- Sound-based sentences (perhaps from known poems) – e.g. 'Charlie loves chocolate chips'
- Story-based sentences – e.g. 'Run, run, run as fast as you can!'
- Personal sentences – e.g. 'I am going to be a witch for Halloween'[41]

For the sound-based sentences, to enable the children to handle words they don't yet know how to write, you can use tongue-twister type poems they already know so that they are easy to 'read'. Alternatively, when preparing work-sheets, use the cloze (see Glossary) method to fill in some of the spaces for them, perhaps using pictures as clues for what the words mean; this will mean that children are only practising the sounding skill that you want to target. Dictation of sentences for sounds practice or for stories is also highly useful in these early stages. It is better than simply copying, because the children are not diverted by trying to retain visual information; they are just listening to the sounds of your words and applying their graphemic knowledge to that.

Here we show you an example of how to use a story to write rhyming sentences.

---

40 Please see Chapter 2 for a full discussion about the teaching of authorship.
41 Bear, Invernizzi, Templeton, & Johnstone, 2012.

Learning Free Writing

Let's say the children have heard a story about how the grass is experienced as the background for the flowers, just as the sky is the background for the stars. The children get a few minutes to talk to their working partners: you have asked them, 'How can we express something from the story in one sentence?' The ideas are gathered. One pair has come up with 'THE GRASS IS GREEN WHERE FLOWERS ARE SEEN'. The class likes it because it rhymes.[42] The teacher writes the sentence on the blackboard, asking the class for spellings that she knows they can work out. The whole class draws a picture and writes the sentence. This is the modelling stage, where the class gets used to the idea of making up writing sentences. In any class work, it is very much worth asking the children for their feedback about what makes a good main-lesson page, picture or sentence. You can give them time to look at their partner's work, or go around the class to pick out someone's work they'd like you to use as a demonstration for everyone. If done regularly, the children become expert at pointing out what is really good in the work and, in turn, this implicitly teaches them how to enhance their own.[43] It's good practice to 'ignore' the aspects that are less favourable, only emphasising the successful points.

The next day you write about a new story – perhaps the one about the crocus who was shy to come above the ground because she thought all the other flowers were prettier than she was. The story has been told the previous day and the children have had an opportunity to re-tell the story verbally today. Now it is time for the writing. The children work in pairs and decide upon a sentence to write in their practice book. They are then allowed to copy it in their main-lesson book once they've read it to the teacher or to another child. This is so that they can self-check their work, *not* so that the spelling can be corrected. Here they are practising being authors, and they may spell the words in any way they think plausible.

We suggest that correcting their spelling at this stage is demoralising for them. Spelling can be taught and practised at a different time. As the teacher, you can take note of any spelling issues that you think the child should have already known accurately. Apart from that, you will be satisfied with phonically sensible spelling; the children are thinking about the words they want to write, and listening and deciding on sound–symbol correlations. This is useful work even if they don't come up with the correct spelling. They are exercising and applying what they know; and for the words they don't know, they take an educated guess. If they ask, you can tell them that this is how children write, and that most people can read it perfectly well. If they really want to know and you think they can't work it out for themselves, you can tell them how the grown-ups would write that word.

Children's invented spelling is also really useful for a teacher. You can see which spelling issues the child has mastered, which he is unsure of and which he is not using at all. Here are some examples from a Class 1 Main Lesson. This was the first time the children were writing their own sentences.

---

42 Poetry is about the music of words (Chapter 3, Steiner, 1976) so encourage all experimentation with alliteration, rhythm and rhyme.
43 Clarke, 2008.

(The flower fairy came to see the flower of her life.)

(The crocus is here and spring is here.)

The teacher might diagnose this writing by noting that certain common words seem secure (the, is, and) and that the long vowels /ō/ and the short vowel /ĭ/ are clearly heard. The word 'HEO' for 'HERE' is interesting: the child has heard the H and a long 'e' sound, and notices that we do something with our mouth at the end. She has quite enterprisingly guessed that this may be an /o/. Both blends /cr/ and /spr/ are in place.[44]

The next day, the same child wrote...

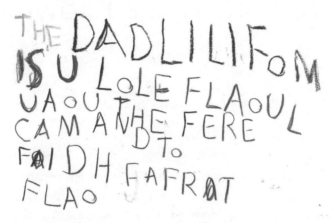

THE DADLILIFOM IS U LOLE FLAOUL UAOU THE FERE CAM AND TO FID H FAFROT FLAO
(The dandelion is a lovely flower. The fairy came to find her favourite flower.)

As the teacher you will note that four common words – 'the', 'is', 'and', 'to' – are in place. You will be likely to make sure that 'her' and 'a' come on the word wall soon. You also notice that in the longer word 'dandelion', some sounds are missing and one letter is inserted. This child needs to continue working with the troll game or other games that practise hearing all the sounds in syllables.

Another child wrote:

THE BUDDLEIA SED WAS VERY SCED HEY WAS SEPT IN THE WIND HEY MET A BRD THEN HE MAD A HOM IN A PAVMENT
(The buddleia seed was very scared. He was swept in the wind. He met a bird. Then he made a home in a pavement.)[45]

Many of the consonants are in place and this girl is clearly using what she has learned. Long vowel spellings have not yet been studied so you will not be surprised that they are guessed. Note the missing /w/ in swept. Again, the troll game or another sound splitting game will help. Common words 'the', 'was', 'very', 'in', 'a' and 'then' are in place. 'He' was initially spelled 'hey', but when she was asked to check it on the word wall, she wrote it correctly.

---

44 It is worth noting that these blends containing the /r/ are considered by speech therapists to be relatively harder to learn.
45 The word 'buddleia' was given.

Chapter 14

Encouraging Authorship:
Ways to Work with a Known Poem

- Active ways to use poems in writing

Initial writing exercises in class 1 could also involve writing a poem or song they know well. Here we set out a series of activities you could use with one song in Class 1 for teaching writing. The nursery rhyme 'Upon a hill there stood a tree' is really suitable for a first writing task as there is a lot of repetition.

Upon a hill there stood a tree
The finest tree you ever did see
And the tree was on the hill
And the hill was on the ground
And the green grass grew all around
And the green grass grew all around

And on that tree there was a trunk
The finest trunk you ever did see

And on that trunk there was a limb
The finest limb you ever did see

And on that limb there was a branch
The finest branch you ever did see

And on that branch there was a twig
The finest twig you ever did see

And on that twig there was a nest
The finest nest you ever did see

And on that nest there was an egg
The finest egg you ever did see

And on that egg there was a bird
The finest bird you ever did see

And on that bird there was a wing
The finest wing you ever did see

And on that wing there was a feather
The finest feather you ever did see

And on that feather there was some fluff
The finest fluff you ever did see

Here are two example pages:

Start with some preparatory work. Teach the children the song so that they know it, and the accompanying movements, really well.

- One day, surprise the children so that the words HILL, TREE, TRUNK, LIMB, BRANCH, TWIG, NEST, EGG, BIRD, WING, FEATHER and FLUFF appear on the blackboard all in different places. Can the class work out which is which? Whilst looking at the spelling of these words for the first time, it is a good idea to discuss the unusual spellings with the class. How unexpected, that 'B' at the end of limb! 'That is a silent letter!' shouts out one of the children. HILL, EGG and FLUFF all have double consonants. Those last letters needed a bit of help.
- Next, the teacher writes 'AND ON THAT TREE THERE WAS A TRUNK'. The children can have a go at inserting the other words, e.g. 'AND ON THAT TRUNK THERE WAS A LIMB' etc.
- The children know the song well. As it has been practised with movement, the teacher can now do the movement of one of the sentences. Can the class guess which sentence has been acted out?
- Next, when a sentence is acted out and the words needed are all still muddled up on the board, can the class work out which words are needed to write the sentence the teacher has just acted out? For example, the teacher has done the movement that goes with the sentence 'AND ON THAT TRUNK THERE WAS A LIMB'. Which words would we need for this sentence? – 'We need trunk and limb'. Now ask a child to find 'trunk' and 'limb' amongst the words on the blackboard and rub them out. Rubbing something out is a surprisingly effective task. It may sometimes imprint the word much better into the child's memory. After all, when we write something down, it gives us permission to stop thinking about it. Since in this song, most words are needed twice, there soon comes a point when the word that needs to be rubbed out is not on the board. We have a problem! We still need to rub it out – so who can write it down quickly so that James can rub it out? Another child is chosen quickly to write the word. Now James can have his turn and rub the word out that was needed for the sentence the teacher had acted out.

- Some children are now ready to write all the sentences in their books with a picture. Some would benefit from another preparation exercise such as the one below; this time a colourful work-sheet that you have prepared.

```
UPON A HILL THERE WAS A TREE
AND ON THAT TREE THERE WAS A _____
AND ON THAT _____ THERE WAS A _____
AND ON THAT _____ THERE WAS A _____
AND ON THAT _____ THERE WAS A _____
AND ON THAT _____ THERE WAS A _____
AND IN THAT _____ THERE WAS AN _____
AND IN THAT _____ THERE WAS A _____
AND ON THAT _____ THERE WAS A _____
AND ON THAT _____ THERE WAS A _____
AND ON THAT _____ THERE WAS SOME
                    _____
```

```
TRUNK    WING    TWIG    FEATHER
FLUFF    NEST    LIMB    EGG
BRANCH   BIRD
```

```
AND THE GREEN GRASS GREW ALL
AROUND AND ALL AROUND AND THE
GREEN GRASS GREW ALL AROUND.
```

- For further practice, ask the children to walk the sentence, one step per word. Then ask who can walk the sentence backwards? This is a very good exercise for sequential memory.
- Write the sentences on large strips of paper, every sentence in a different colour. Ask the children to read them and then to cut between the words. Can they put the sentence back together again? To extend this, of course, you could also cut between the letters.

Chapter 15

Extra Phonics for 1:1 Practice

- Exercises for over-learning phonological skills

Extra Practice Tools for Those Who Need It

Once you have assessed your class and identified those who need extra practice in particular areas, you need to design appropriate exercises and games to 'over-learn' these skills. As mentioned before, you may need to find time out of other lessons or break for this, or train an assistant or a parent to help. With some tasks the children may be able to help each other. Here are some suggestions that work well for 1:1 extra support, as well as further whole-class or small-group game-playing.

Sound–Symbol Confusion

This may particularly occur with words that include letters that have two sounds, or sounds that can be made by several letters or letter digraphs. Of course, vowels are also likely to be easily muddled. Check the letters in Appendix 1.

- If a child struggles to remember which letter makes which sound, do this exercise with a pack of alphabet cards. Ask the child to think up words that begin with that sound, saying both the letter sound and the letter name.
- Play 'I-spy' but with this child, point at the letter rather than give the sound: 'I spy with my little eye something beginning with this letter' (point to the card).

Identifying Sounds in Words – Phonological Awareness

- A child who has difficulties with discrimination of the sounds in words could do an 'Odd-One-Out' exercise. The adult says a short series of words to the child and the child must identify the word that does not rhyme or does not have the same initial sound etc. The following is an example of a rhyming version: The adult says 'Dad, Bad, Had, Sad, Peg', and the child answers with the odd one out. Next, the adult says, 'Can, Fan, Man, Lid, Pan' and so on. An alternative for practising short vowels could be: 'Cat, Pan, Tap, Sad, Dog' and next, 'Fed, Men, Box, Pet, Peg'. An initial letter version might start with 'Bad, Beg, Bin, Hut, Bush'. Invent your own games around this sort of practice: one class teacher embedded this work in a quiz show format complete with a showbiz 'bing' for the right answer! See Appendix 4 for game word lists in C1.

Adapting Classroom Games

Many of the games already described in Part 3 can be adapted to either give more support for those who need it or more of a challenge for the abler children.

Snakes and Ladders

For example, while playing the snakes and ladders game for sound counting (see Chapter 10), one group could be working with a teaching assistant while simultaneously, another group has the words read out by a student. The weaker children could be supported in checking that they have noticed all the sounds in the word while those in the stronger group are self-checking.

Another variant is to give the groups different sets of words.

You could also add the rule that the child may move the same word twice. First the child moves her counter for each sound of the given word (the word is spoken and she hasn't seen the spelling!). Then, for example, the child is asked to say which letter the word starts with. When she has given the first letter, she gets to see the card, and if she was correct she may move her word again, once again saying all the sounds as she moves her counter. To differentiate, one group can move each word twice if they can identify the beginning letter of the word, another if they can identify the vowel, which is a little bit harder, and the advanced group could move if they can write the whole word.

Blends & Pairs Game

- Along the same lines, in the blends game, at the point when words are written down, the weakest group might have a 'scribe' (the adult assistant) while in the other groups, all children write down their own words.
- When you follow with a blends dictation, the children who need it could have the original game board in front of them to help them identify which blend is at the beginning of a dictated word whilst the others do this from memory.
- In a pairs game, the words could be different for different groups. The group with more able children may have words that are very similar in sound, whilst in the weaker group, the words are very different.

PART 4

Class 1 Assessment

and Differentiation

Chapter 16

Learning Differences and What To Do

- Moving from whole-class to differentiated work
- Good for SEN, good for everyone!
- Three groups of needs
- Timing of support
- Multi-sensory work
- Incremental work

Teaching for different needs can be a demanding art. In this chapter, we give you some core principles for planning lessons. Active learning methods are good for those with special educational needs and the whole class. Organisation is another key to being able to reach every child in the class appropriately, achieving a balance between support and challenge. Additionally, the more you yourself understand about how children receive and process new information, the better you will be able to innovate for your particular class.

Moving from the Whole Class to Groups of Different Needs

We have described introductory work for Class 1 that ought to give you a good opportunity for engaging every child in the class from the first day, all of them progressing at a level appropriate for them. At the beginning, it is sensible to let the children all do the same activity; you don't know the detail of their different abilities and they have yet to become a 'whole class'. With literacy, they love to do the same letter learning work. It is done in such a unique way that even those who have learnt the letters already, whether at home or in a different school, usually still find great joy in doing the same work as those who have never encountered them.

As the first term progresses, you will naturally know to direct harder questions to the children who always seem to know the answers. It may start to make sense to team up more and less able children so that they can help each other practise new knowledge. This is the ideal time to start training children in the social skills necessary to exchange information helpfully and encourage each other, rather than dominate, ignore or act out. From the start, you are teaching children independence from you: they are active, not passive. You will also be watching them very closely, noticing their skills, or who doesn't want their lack of skills noticed! Develop the discipline of making post-lesson notes every day about the tiny things that the class demonstrate. It's very easy to forget detail, and writing down these observations makes a difference.

It is an often-stated truism that good teaching methods for those with special educational needs are also generally good for the whole class. An example would be the '3 counts rule'. If you ask a question and require the class to wait for '3 counts' before hands go up, it will ensure that more children are able to work things out. The classic 'put your hand up' to answer technique only ensures that one child at a time is on task, and it can be positively alienating.

In a similar way, you could use beanbags to ask individual children a question: ask the question out loud and then throw the beanbag three times up to yourself, before choosing the child you want to answer the question. Another option for call-out questions is to have a box of names on lollipop sticks and pick one at random for answering. Everybody's name could come out of the cup, so everybody is trying hard to find the answer, not just those who put their hands up. Your aim is mass engagement and mass response – in this way you get many children working at once, and those who need more processing time can participate equally.

Nonetheless, probably about half-way through Class 1 there will come a stage where it just doesn't make sense any more for them all to do *exactly* the same work. It doesn't seem right to suppress the advanced children's eagerness in order to wait for the others. It would be a particular kind of negligence. However, some will still be working hard at a more basic level.

During the first term, aim to arrange your class into roughly three groups in order that you don't become overwhelmed with trying to cater for the varied individual needs. In an average class of 20–30 children in a Steiner school, you are likely to have the following composition.[1] A handful, perhaps five, will be very able and will pick up information with one telling. Some children seem to be able to teach themselves, and if a donkey gave them the instruction, they'd still be able to learn! In time, you may have about a third of the group who can progress very well, at speed, with good independence.

There will also be a handful, probably fewer than five, who have significant learning difficulties and who will quickly demand more of your attention to make sure that they are still accessing the work appropriately. In time, you may find there are around a third of the class who need some extra, intensive input to succeed with certain aspects of basic skills. The central third of children are those who need clear explanation, modelling and repetition but who will make good progress according to your targets, provided they have this practice. This could be termed the 'on-target' group. Expert

---

1 There is a significant caveat here. Most Steiner schools in the UK are privately funded. This means that their natural constituency tends to be relatively privileged and well-educated, middle-class people. There also tend to be a large number of nationalities represented. Admissions are different at state-funded schools and in other parts of the world. In terms of learning style and literacy, there can be a great many social and environmental factors that influence children's ability, so you may find that in your school the relative proportions are different.

differentiation advice suggests that you plan tasks for this group in the middle first, secondly for those who find things more difficult, and finally adapt for those who are ahead of the game.[2]

Becoming really good at differentiation entails three main requirements: first, to know the children and what they do and don't know. This requires assessment and excellent record-keeping. Secondly, you need to really understand the subject of literacy learning and then have a repertoire of games and activities up your sleeve to address each incremental step along the path. Game playing, group working and formative assessment techniques are methods that help the children decide for themselves what is good work and how well they're doing. These are fundamental for effective differentiation.[3] Finally, you will need to develop a 'flexible thinking' muscle to enable you to be creative in the face of both the predictable and the unexpected. You can do it!

By term two, in their literacy work, your Class 1 may have the following combination:

- Some will already want to write their own stories
- Others still need to practise splitting words into sounds
- Some may confuse sound–symbol links.
- One of them may struggle to know the sounds and the letters
- Another may not be able to hear rhyme, or whether two words start with the same sound.

How will you plan for addressing those needs? The first step is good assessment. In the next chapter, we share with you some thoughts about assessing children in a useful way and ideas for helping you develop your repertoire.

---

2 Dodge, 2005; Heacox, 2012; and Cowley, 2013.
3 Bear, Invernizzi, Templeton, & Johnstone, 2012; Clarke, 2008; Myhill, Jones, & Hopper, 2005; Janis-Norton, 2004; Cunningham, 2012; and Palmer & Corbett, 2003.

Chapter 17

Record Keeping and Assessment

Continuum of assessment types, including:

- Observational notes
- Formative assessment of the teaching and learning process
- Summative assessment of progress
- Examples of tests in C1 and how to use the results

What Do They Know? – Examples of Assessment of Children in Class 1

As discussed in the previous chapter, one key to being able to plan lessons for the different needs in your class is that of good assessment. If you have taken concrete steps to measure your children's progress, you will be confident in creating the next day's lessons. You will also be demonstrating transparency so that any observers, internal or external, can see that you are aware of the way that teaching is affecting learning in your classroom. In this chapter we discuss how types of assessment run along a subjective–objective continuum, each type yielding results that are useful for different purposes. We explain two main ways in which we assess progress appropriately in Class 1. First, we discuss how to record your careful observations. Secondly, we set out some appropriate methods of testing. We aim to gain an accurate impression of each child's development and genuine knowledge, without inducing unnecessary anxiety.

Observational Notes

Rudolf Steiner was very keen on teachers observing their students, advocating a scientific method in the broadest sense of the term. While any one professional would be likely to notice different features about any one student, according to all sorts of subjective factors, he was emphatic that the teacher should cultivate their own attention to detail. He suggested that teachers note things like skin tone, warmth of the hand at the morning hand-shake, the way a child breathes or speaks... – all sorts of things that may be particular or remarkable about a child, considering them in a holistic way. He thought education could be *healing*, with a much broader remit than is usually considered the province of school. To this end, he encouraged teachers to pay attention to all possible ways in which a child might present.

One of the cornerstone practices of the College of Teachers[4] meeting is Child Study. This is a period of time dedicated to discussing details of a particular child of concern. Ideally, every member of staff who works with that child would contribute every variety of pertinent information for the group to contemplate. A rich, collective picture of that child would then emerge, and time would be given to the consideration of best practice or necessary interventions. However, this is not the same as the everyday notes that the class teacher needs.

Develop the habit of jotting down the daily thoughts you have about your class as you observe them. You may have a formal record book with lines and tables, a day journal or a notebook (or all three).[5] From the beginning of Class 1, record details of left- or right-handedness, pencil grip, vocabulary, listening and recall. For example, do any children have speech difficulties? These can have a strong effect on their ability to spell. If a child can't say /k/, can they hear it?

Further, children might demonstrate particular artistic sensibility or talents and you will perceive qualities of a child's sense of form or capacity for practical organisation. Their physical movements, sense of balance, rhythm or laterality might also interest you. You may also observe social aptitude or emotional and behavioural qualities. Notice those children who sit quietly and do not like to be conspicuous. Some children are expert at being forgotten! Writing these remarks down will help you cement impressions for more sustained contemplation; it serves as a record for remembering particular incidents or events, and this may be unpredictably useful, especially when communicating with other adults about a child, and it can feed planning and fine-tuning activities when you sit down more formally to organise upcoming work.

Assessment Using Tests

Testing sometimes has a bad name these days, with many parents and teachers wary of burdening children with stressful procedures, but we will show you ways that even in Class 1, a test can be carried out without the children being disturbed by it, perhaps not even being aware it's happening.

Testing or assessments are often classified as either formative or summative. Formative assessment is the term for multiple types of reflection in the active learning process. The key principle is that tests are not organised primarily to make judgements but to gain useful information for our teaching, and are usually administered by students *and* teacher. In formative assessment, you are taking stock of what has happened, making collaborative judgements about areas of success and

---

4 College is the word used to refer to the group of staff who take professional responsibility for pedagogy in the school. Although today, every school organises itself in a unique way with subtle differences that suit individual circumstances, in Rudolf Steiner's original vision, the College would be a sort of faculty body that would concern itself with pedagogy and student care.

5 We find it useful to have a robust, hard-backed planning book or folder with plenty of space to set out daily plans. Behind the plans section will be a record-keeping section, also with a table or chart to set out results and observations of the children. There are several such teacher's planners on the market. In addition, we find it helps to have an informal jotter or notebook to write down *any* ad hoc thoughts, questions, ideas or insights so that they are put down somewhere and won't get lost!

where there is room for improvement. You then use this information to immediately return to work, armed with new goals.[6] Summative assessment is a type of assessment where a more objective 'outcome' is established, such as a reading level. This gives a snapshot of a child's performance in comparison with appropriate benchmarks at a given point in time.

As you can see, formative assessment is useful internally in the classroom; summative can have an effective role for transparency and communication purposes with others. Formative information is usually very useful to children and teachers; summative can be useful to those overseeing the whole process – parents, teachers and their colleagues. It is the second type that usually causes most stress. It is highly problematic to try accurately to judge a person who is, by definition, growing and changing quickly! Performance isn't identical to learning or ability. There isn't space in this book to explore all the issues of how working to a test has the potential to crush creativity in both student and teacher, but we do encourage you to do so yourselves.[7]

In the early classes, we mainly use formative techniques, many of which we have described already, especially when engaging in group learning. We encourage the children to be reflective and active in their engagement with the work. See below for examples of more summative tests that would be appropriate in Class 1. You will see further information in the Appendices on suitable outcomes. These will help you consider in a judicious and mindful way when to use summative tests and what to do with the results.

Testing Word Work

After the introduction and practice of a certain teaching point, how will you know that every individual student can really tell short vowels apart, for example? Indeed, after each Main Lesson block, on whatever topic, it is very important to have one or two sessions that include a summary and some kind of assessment in order to see how much each child has absorbed.

Vowel countries
Here is an example of a mini-test after a teaching point. For working out whether the children know short vowels, ask the children to draw two 'countries', an /a/ 'country' and an /o/ 'country', and then dictate some words for them to write in the correct 'country'.

Blind words
For testing knowledge of common words, at the end of a three-week block of daily work, you can put a cloth over the word-wall words and dictate them. Tell the children that you need to know which words must stay on the word wall and which can be taken off. Explain that if they don't know how to spell the words, they can draw lines for the sounds. For example, if they know only the first letter, they can write that and draw lines for the rest of the sounds. With children late in Class 1 or

---

6 Clarke, 2008.
7 Robinson, 2015. There are many educational authors who tackle the subject of testing and assessment. Please see the book's bibliography.

into the next year, you will want to assess their spelling of common words regularly so that you can be really responsive to individual practice needs.

Blends Dictation

Having worked for a while with blends, it is also worth doing a blends dictation like the one described in Chapter 11. Use the words the children came up with in the blends game and a 'snaking' worksheet to make it more fun.

Assessment of Free Writing

A teacher can learn much from studying students' free writing. It is especially worth doing regular spelling analyses. However, be aware that children who create their own writing can sometimes confine themselves to words they can spell. They may look at words on the word wall or get their spellings from a neighbour. In their free writing, their spelling may appear better than it really is. Alternatively, children's spelling in a free writing task may present poorly as they concentrate on getting their thoughts on paper and forget their spelling. Either way, investigate what type of mistakes the children make.

- Are there missed sounds? If so, the troll game or snakes and ladders for sound counting will be useful.
- Does the child forget common words they have seen often? This would suggest possible difficulties or weakness in visual memory. Mnemonics might help as an alternative method of memorisation, or increased frequency of visual exposure.
- Does a child persist with symbol reversals? Form Drawing and gross motor spatial orientation exercises would help.

Once or twice a year, you may also decide to administer a more general spelling assessment, for example the one from the book *Words Their Way* described here.[8] The results directly feed into your planning.

In the book, learning is categorised into three areas: this test helps you understand what the child gets right most times, what they 'use but confuse' and what they are getting wrong most of the time. The authors suggest that we primarily direct our teaching to the middle area. If you present material that the child knows already, you risk frustration; there is a similar result if you present material that they are not ready for. The book provides several inventories and three levels of word dictations, each using around 25–30 words that will help you identify the areas in each child's spelling in which he is confident, that he 'uses but confuses' and that he is not yet aware of. The book is also full of teaching suggestions and games.

This is the first inventory we gave at the end of Class 1. As preparation, the children were told that many of the words they were going to be asked to write were Class 2 or even Class 3 words.

---

8 Bear, Invernizzi, Templeton, & Johnstone, 2012.

They were told that the dictation was for the teacher to know what she should teach them next year. They were also told that for many words, they would probably get some bits right even if they did not know the whole word. The teacher modelled what to do if they did not know how to spell the word giving the example of 'BRACELET'. The teacher explained that she knew that they would probably not yet know how to spell it in the grown-up way, but they might know some bits. 'You might know it starts with BR and ends in T. If you know that you could write BR_____T, or you could have a guess at the other letters and perhaps write BRASLUT.' If the teacher introduces a spelling assessment like this, the children feel good about what they are achieving.

After this test, one girl later told her mum that they had had to write lots of really difficult words; she continued proudly that she had got them all right. According to formal spelling rules, she was not in fact correct, but the result was perfect: the teacher had gained valuable insight into her spelling strategies and she maintained pride and confidence in her work. Here are some examples of spelling results with diagnostic comments.

SHARA

1 FAN	14 FRIT
2 PET	15 C⬤HOQD
3 DIG	16 CRUL
4 ROB	17 WISH
5 ~~HOB~~	18 FO⬤N
6 WAT	19 SHATIG
7 GUM	20 STOG
8 SLEDD	21 GRAL
9 STI⬤K	22 ~~FHD~~FROUL
10 SHIN	23 KANT
11 DREM	24 TRIS
12 BLAD	25 CLATIN
13 CLO⬤P	26 RIDIG

Shara is confident about initial consonants, end consonants and short vowels. She is using digraphs /SH/, /CH/, /TH/ but is not certain of them. She hears /TH/ as /F/. She is confident in her blends. She is not using any long vowel or diphthong spellings yet. Shara should do some more work with digraphs before being introduced to the first long vowel spellings. Her confusion between /TH/ and /F/ needs some further investigation. Does she speak /TH/ correctly? Some speech exercises such as tongue-twisters might help, as well as simple activities to distinguish /F/ and /TH/. This could be a cranes and crows game with /F/ and /TH/ words, a sorting activity with cards, an auditory sorting activity or a dictation with a /F/ land and a /TH/ land.

1 FAN	14 FRITE
2 PET	15 CHOOD
3 DIG	16 CROLE
4 ROB	17 WISHISE
5 HOPE	18 THORN
6 ~~WAIT~~ WAIT	19 SHADUTID
7 GUM	20 SPOIEL
8 SLED	21 GRALE
9 STICK	22 THAD
10 ~~SHINE~~ SHIN	23 CAMPDE
11 DREAM	24 TRISE
12 BLADE	25 CLAPING
13 COTCHE	26 RYDING

Erin is confident about initial consonants, end consonants and short vowels, digraphs and blends. She is using some long vowel spellings and some other vowel spellings but makes regular mistakes with those. Erin is ready to work with long vowels and other vowel spellings.

Chapter 18

Further Writing Tasks, Including Differentiation

- Developing writing with differentiation
- Using a story
- Using poetry – two poems and a song

Here are a few examples of writing exercises with possible differentiation.

Writing a Story from a Fairy Tale

The teacher has told the fairy tale of the cat and the mouse who lived together. The next day the children remember the story and, in pairs, they are invited to act it out. On the third day, in pairs again, the children work out a 'start' sentence for the story, and one of those is chosen to be written on the board. Discuss what makes a good sentence and what makes good writing; the children mention that all the letters need to be the same size and that there need to be clear spaces between the words. Some have understood that we need a full stop at the end. Those children can be encouraged to include what they know in their writing.[9] The children are reminded that they can use the 'troll game' (tapping the sounds on their knees) if they are not sure how to write a word.

The next day after some more rehearsing of sentences, most of the class is able to write the story in their pairs. You may still have a group of perhaps four children who would be struggling significantly with this. (If something is very difficult, for more children than this, it is generally not a useful classroom exercise.) What do you do? If you simply asked them to copy text you've written, this will not really help them eventually achieve the same as the others. Instead, prepare an example sentence on strips of paper or card. First, read it out to them. Then the children are asked to identify different words; who can find 'cat'? Who can find 'fat'? Then cut the story into sentences. In pairs or a small group, their next step is to try to put the story together again. Then one or two sentences

---

9 See the principles of active learning using formative assessment techniques (Clarke, 2008).

are cut up into words. Can they put a whole sentence together again? Finally, they can copy the text straight into their Main Lesson book. Simultaneously, the others will have written their first draft in their practice book, also to be copied into their Main Lesson book; this group will not end up behind and will also have worked on skills of decoding and sequencing to help them understand how a good sentence is created.

Word Work with Three Poems: 'The House that Jack Built'

The class recites 'This is the house that Jack built' every morning with movements so they know it really well. In their Main Lesson book they've drawn a picture of the poem and the teacher has written out the whole of the final verse on the blackboard.

This is the house that Jack built.

This is the malt
That lay in the house that Jack built.

This is the rat,
That ate the malt
That lay in the house that Jack built.

This is the cat,
That killed the rat,
That ate the malt
That lay in the house that Jack built.

This is the dog,
That worried the cat,
That killed the rat,
That ate the malt
That lay in the house that Jack built.

This is the cow with the crumpled horn,
That tossed the dog,
That worried the cat,
That killed the rat,
That ate the malt
That lay in the house that Jack built.

This is the maiden all forlorn,
That milked the cow with the crumpled horn,
That tossed the dog,
That worried the cat,
That killed the rat,
That ate the malt
That lay in the house that Jack built.

This is the man all tattered and torn,
That kissed the maiden all forlorn,
That milked the cow with the crumpled horn,
That tossed the dog,
That worried the cat,
That killed the rat,
That ate the malt
That lay in the house that Jack built.

This is the priest all shaven and shorn,
That married the man all tattered and torn,
That kissed the maiden all forlorn,
That milked the cow with the crumpled horn,
That tossed the dog,
That worried the cat,
That killed the rat,
That ate the malt
That lay in the house that Jack built.

This is the cock that crowed in the morn,
That waked the priest all shaven and shorn,
That married the man all tattered and torn,
That kissed the maiden all forlorn,
That milked the cow with the crumpled horn,
That tossed the dog,
That worried the cat,
That killed the rat,
That ate the malt
That lay in the house that Jack built.

This is the farmer sowing his corn,
That kept the cock that crowed in the morn,
That waked the priest all shaven and shorn,
That married the man all tattered and torn,
That kissed the maiden all forlorn,
That milked the cow with the crumpled horn,
That tossed the dog,
That worried the cat,
That killed the rat,
That ate the malt
That lay in the house that Jack built.

In the activity described below, children practise scanning from left to right and increase their awareness of words. As they read, they observe word details, recognising similarities and also unusual spelling features.

- First, the class recites the poem in sequence as the teacher points at the words.
- Next, 'trick' the class and move unexpectedly to another line. You could try making silly sentences – 'This is the cow all tattered and torn that kissed the cat all shaven and shorn'.
- Further develop this with a guessing game. The teacher models noticing details of the words. For example, say 'I have spotted a word with a double L' (or double R; or noticing that the digraph 'OR' makes a repeated appearance; or an unusual place where 'IE' says long vowel /ē/). Who can spot it too?' A final guessing game could be a free space where the children come up with things they've spotted.
- The sentences can then be cut up to look something like this:

THIS IS THE FARMER SOWING HIS CORN,
THAT KEPT THE COCK THAT CROWED IN THE MORN,
THAT WAKED THE PRIEST ALL SHAVEN AND SHORN,
THAT MARRIED THE MAN ALL TATTERED AND TORN,
THAT KISSED THE MAIDEN ALL FORLORN,
THAT MILKED THE COW WITH THE CRUMPLED HORN,
THAT TOSSED THE DOG,
THAT WORRIED THE CAT,
THAT KILLED THE RAT,
THAT ATE THE MALT
THAT LAY IN THE HOUSE THAT JACK BUILT.

- Give each pair the last verse cut up into sentences and ask them to put it back together again (cover the verse on the blackboard).

    Differentiated activity: the teaching assistant or able student reads the verse first. Then the children cut their sentences up themselves before putting them together again. They may have the whole poem handy nearby to check whether they get it right.

- The next day the verse is already cut up into words for each pair to put together.

    Differentiated activity: some pairs have part of the poem cut up into sentences, and part into words.

    Differentiated activity: the teaching assistant or able student reads the verse aloud first. Ask the children to find just the first sentence and write this in their Main Lesson books.

- Create a pairs game: in pairs, the children choose any words from the poem. Agreeing on a word, each one writes the word on a card in their neatest writing. They check each others' spelling for mistakes and there will be two clearly written word cards as a result. Children are asked to choose only words they can read easily so that this activity will differentiate itself.[10]

- Cards are laid out in a grid face down, and players take turns flipping over pairs of cards. On each turn, the player will first turn one card over, then a second. If the two cards match, the player scores one point, the two cards are removed from the game, and the player gets another turn. If they don't match, the cards are turned back over.

Eventually, the whole class copies the verse from the blackboard.

- *Differentiated activity*: some children turn their desk and try to do it from memory; some children do the same but are given a few key words, while some children copy from cut-up sentences given one at a time and laid on their desk.

'Key of the Kingdom'

A similar sequence can be followed using the poem 'Key of the Kingdom'.

> This is the key of the kingdom.
> In that kingdom there is a city.
> In that city there is a town.
> In that town there is a street.
> In that street there is a lane.
> In that lane there is a yard.
> In that yard there is a house.
> In that house there is a room.

---

10 Offering choice for self-selection is often very successful for unobtrusive, 'natural' differentiation.

In that room there is a bed.
On that bed there is a basket.
In that basket there are some flowers.
Flowers in a basket,
Basket on the bed,
Bed in the room,
Room in the house,
House in the yard,
Yard in the lane,
Lane in the street,
Street in the town,
Town in the city,
City in the kingdom.
Of that kingdom this is the key.

You could try the following sequence of steps:

• Each pair is given a different keyword from the poem; KEY, KINGDOM, CITY, TOWN, etc. You make sure that the children who struggle have a CVC word like BED.

• The teacher asks who has KEY. Collectively, the class decides and once correct, the pair stick it somewhere visible in the classroom. This is repeated for each word.

• The next day the children are asked to describe the place where KEY is stuck on the wall, avoiding pointing with fingers. This is done with all the other words.

• The children copy the first two sentences from the blackboard, after which it is covered and they must write the rest from memory. The words are still stuck around the class.

> *Differentiated activity*: Pair struggling children together. Give keywords on small cards and the poem with those words missing at their desk. They stick the words with blue tack in the right places before copying it in their book

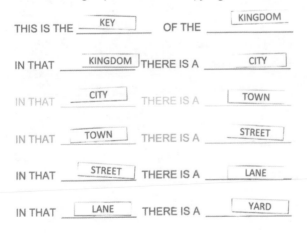

THIS IS THE _____KEY_____ OF THE _____KINGDOM_____

IN THAT _____KINGDOM_____ THERE IS A _____CITY_____

IN THAT _____CITY_____ THERE IS A _____TOWN_____

IN THAT _____TOWN_____ THERE IS A _____STREET_____

IN THAT _____STREET_____ THERE IS A _____LANE_____

IN THAT _____LANE_____ THERE IS A _____YARD_____

PART 5

Warming Up for Class 2

Chapter 19

Movement Work in Class 2

- Warming up routine for 7-year-olds
- Independence of left and right
- Clapping games

To help prepare children for learning each day, movement work should continue and develop in Class 2. The correlation between learning difficulties and movement co-ordination issues is well researched.[1] Aside from the general benefits of movement exercises for all children in your class, exercises specifically targeting independence of movement between left and right hands and between arms and legs, as well as crossing the midline, will be appropriate this year.

The use of poems or songs to accompany the movement exercises will help ensure that the movements are done in a breathing rhythm, bypassing the 'clever' brain and helping the exercises to reach a deeper level of automaticity. The eight spatial orientation exercises by Jean Hunt, as described in Part 2 and demonstrated on YouTube[2] (exercise 4), can be revisited, possibly with a different song.

The three preparation exercises for fine motor skills also in Part 2, Chapters 4 and 5 (The Baker poem) and demonstrated on YouTube[2] (exercises 1–3) also have a place in Class 2. These exercises help to increase the awareness a child has of the movement in the fingers, which, when followed by fine motor activities like handwriting or recorder playing, will enhance the effectiveness of this work.[3] In a class where children still struggle to achieve regularity and fluency in their letter formation, the 'Baker' exercise, or a different exercise involving strong physical activity like the press-ups described by Lois Addy, are still recommended.

Where exercises in Class 1 still mostly involved moving the left and right arms simultaneously in parallel or mirrored movement, the exercises in Class 2 develop independence between left and right.

---

1 Goddard Blythe, 2005.
2 See page 44 and Note 19.
3 Addy, 2004.

Practising Independence of Left and Right

Early childhood development with regard to independence between the left and right side of the body goes through certain phases. In the initial phase, tension on one side of the body automatically produces relaxation of the other side. Following this, the child begins to be able to perform symmetrical actions on left and right sides of the body. Subsequently, the child learns to differentiate the movement between the two sides, and is able to independently move one hand without the other having to perform the same task – e.g. when opening a jar, one hand holds it still while the other twists the top. At this point, proper dominance can develop and the child is free from involuntary reflex movements. The 'captain is now firmly on the ship'.[4]

In designing movement exercises, aim to recapitulate these earlier phases, especially for those children whose own development is delayed or incomplete.

For a group of Class 2 children, you need to build the exercise up by starting with movements where both arms/hands perform the same movement. Next, mirror movements can be practised: both hands performing the same movement, but in opposite directions. 'Passive' independence between left and right would be the next stage. This means that one side is active while the other is doing something different but is relatively still. Finally, once this has been achieved, the last stage is active independence. Do one thing on one side of the body whilst the other side performs a different task.

An example set out in more detail to achieve the goal of the exercise is Audrey McAllen's elementary juggling exercise,[5] an activity involving crossing the midline. The final activity is as follows:

- Stand with a beanbag in each hand. The right hand throws the beanbag in a gentle arc to the left whilst the left hand passes its beanbag straight to the empty right hand.
- The left then catches the beanbag thrown by the right hand.[6]

It can take a novice adult a little while to get the timing steady and correct for this, so if you were to ask all children to do this straight away you will lose several immediately, even if you repeat and repeat. Here is a pathway towards it.

Accompany this sequence of activities with a tongue-twister. By the time you have managed all the different stages of the exercise, you will be saying the tongue-twister twelve times in a row, one stage running smoothly after another without pause. The bold print indicates the rhythm of the movements (see Chapter 27 for how to use this poem for work with suffixes and prefixes).

A demonstration of this exercise (exercise 5) can be seen on YouTube.[7]

These exercises aim to develop independence of movement between the right and left hand and arm.

---

4 Goddard Blythe, 2005; also from the Dutch website http://www.motoriek.nl/motoriek/motorische-ontwikkeling/ (goo.gl/f3u3rm).
5 McAllen, 1985
6 This excellent exercise is recommended for children 7 years and older.
7 See page 44 and Note 19.

A TWISTER of TWISTS
Once TWISTED a TWIST
And the TWIST that he TWISTED
Was a THREE twisted TWIST [Pause]
NOW, [Pause] if a TWIST should UNTWIST
The TWIST that UNTWISTED
Would UNTWIST the TWIST

Start with the blue beanbag on the head and the red beanbag in the right hand, holding it out in front of you, palms open, elbows bent and relaxed. Repeat each action throughout the whole poem in time with the rhythm of the text – e.g. in the first exercise the right hand throws the red beanbag up on every word in capital letters (15 throws).

- Throw the red beanbag up with right and catch with the same hand.
- Swap the beanbags and put the blue beanbag in the left hand.
- Starting the poem again, throw the blue beanbag up with left and catch with the same hand.
- The next repetition of the poem; throw the beanbag from right to the left and back.

Now start with the red beanbag in the right and the blue beanbag in the left, holding them out in front of you, palms open, elbows bent and relaxed. Continue, repeating the whole poem for each action.

- Throw the red beanbag up with right and catch with the same hand whilst the blue beanbag lies still in the left hand.
- Throw the blue beanbag up with left and catch with the same hand whilst the red beanbag lies still in the right hand.
- Throw red and blue beanbags up alternately and rhythmically, each still catching with the same hand.
- Throw the red beanbag up with right hand and catch on the back of the same hand whilst the blue beanbag lies still in the left hand.
- Throw the blue beanbag up with left and catch on the back of the same hand whilst the red beanbag lies still in the right hand.
- Repeat with alternate hands.
- Throw the red beanbag in a gentle arc whilst passing the blue beanbag from left to right and catch the red beanbag with the left hand. Continue, all the time throwing with the right and catching and passing with the left.
- Repeat, now throwing with left and catching and passing with the right.

A second exercise to help develop independence between left and right is described here below and demonstrated on YouTube.[8]

To accompany it, the following poem can be used. Other poems with an anapaest rhythm would also be suitable.

I will work
All day long
With my head
Held up high
I will work
With great strength
With my hands
Side by side.
I will work
And will learn
How to read
And to write
All of that
I will ea-
si-ly take
In my stride.

The teacher speaks in a clear short–short–long rhythm while doing the movements.
 The children may be asked to speak as well, provided they can manage movements and speaking together.

- Clap, clap, jump – through the whole poem
- Stamp, stamp, clap – through the whole poem
- Touch head, shoulders and thighs with both hands simultaneously – through the whole poem
- Touch head, shoulders and thighs with right hand only – through the whole poem
- Touch head, shoulders and thighs with left hand only – through the whole poem
- Right hand starts, left hand follows one beat later, as in a round: Head, shoulders, thighs – through the whole poem
- 'Pingu feet'. Heels stay together throughout the poem:
Feet together, right foot out, left foot out: II I/ \/

8 See page 44 and Note 19.

- 'Pingu feet and Pingu's wings same side' – heels stay together throughout the poem:
  Feet together, right foot out and right arm stretches out simultaneously, left foot out and left arm stretches out.
- 'Pingu feet and Pingu's wings opposite side' – heels stay together throughout the poem:
  Feet together, right foot out and left arm stretches out simultaneously, left foot out and right arm stretches out.

Variations can be added, e.g. beanbag on the head, eyes closed, standing on a wobbly cushion.[9]

Many traditional clapping games are good for Class 2. They involve rhythmical co-ordination and often crossing the midline. Examples are:

This old man
Miss Mary Mack
A sailor went to sea
See, see my playmate[10]

---

9 See the Sitfit cushion supplied by Sissel, for example https://www.sisseluk.com/product/231_sitfit_by_sissel.php (goo.gl/ebsQOP).
10 http://funclapping.com/

Chapter 20

Assessment in Class 2

- Determining the starting point
- Free-writing assessment task
- Identifying and addressing individual needs

When you return to the classroom after the long summer break, it's a good idea to set the ground rules for the term ahead – not just for literacy! Usually delighted to see each other and be back at school, the class will also have developed and assimilated a great deal, cognitively speaking, in their absence. In addition to the data you have kept from the end-of-year spelling assessment described in Chapter 7, we recommend carrying out some baseline assessment tasks early on to give you up-to-date information. A 'free' writing task re-telling a fable the children will have heard on one of the first days might be a good way to see how much the children have retained. You will see from this what regular revision and practice of the skills they were taught in Class 1 is necessary.

Here are some examples with observations about the work. Note that prior to the task, some spellings will have been given.

Child 1

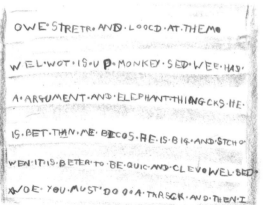

> WILL·TEL' YOU ·THE·ARNSER·VOT·IS·
> THE·TARSC·SAID·MONKEY·TO ·GET·
> THE·MANGO'S·ON·THE·UTHER·SID·OF·THE
> ·RIVER·SO·OF·THE·2·ANMOLS·WENT·
> AS·ONE·AS·THEY·RECHT·THE·RIVER
> MONKEY·LOCD·AT·THE·DEAP·WORT.

> AND·SAID·WE·MOST·GO·BAC·I·CANOT·
> CKROS·THE·WORTE·BOTH·ANOMOLS
> NAW NOUE THAT· THEY WARE THE SAME
> SO THEY WENT OF BEST OF
> FRENS·

- Initial and end consonants are in place.
- Blends are recognised and used mostly correctly.
- TH is in place, also in conjunction with a blend.
- Creative spellings show that this child is listening well and trying to use their phonological skills, e.g. 'bisnis' for 'business', 'throo' for 'through'.
- There are a few long vowel spellings in place, e.g. 'day' and 'tree', but silent 'e' spellings need to be taught – e.g. 'kam' for 'came' and 'mad' for 'made'.
- Common words 'the', 'was', 'on', 'his', 'them', 'at', 'you' 'and', all are in place. Common words used but misspelled are: 'there', 'they', 'were', 'their', 'said', 'we', 'what'.
- This child should continue with work on silent 'e' words and should learn these common words – 'there', 'they', 'were', 'their', 'said', 'we', 'what' – because she is using them. It would also be useful to tackle the choice between C and K, as this is quite an easy and consistent rule.

Child 2

> ONE ★ BRIGHT ★ DAY ★ OWL ★ WAS ★ DOZING ★ ON ★ A ★ BRANCH
> ★ SUDDENLY ★ A ★ LAOD ★ NOISE ★ BROKE ★ THE ★ SILENSE
> ★ IT ★ WAS ★ ELEPHANT ★ AND ★ MONEY ★ WOT ★ DO ★ YOU ★
> WONT ★ SAID ★ OWL ★ WE ★ ARE ★ HAVING ★ A ★ ARGUMENT ★

> SAID ★ MONKEY ★ COULD ★ YOU ★ TELL ★ US ★ WHAT
> ★ IS ★ BETTER ★ TO ★ BE ★ BIG ★ AND ★ STRONG
> ★ OR ★ TO ★ BE ★ QUICK ★ AND ★ CLEVER ★ YES ★ I ★
> CAN ★ SAID ★ OWL

- This child is conscientious and letter formation is much better.
- The care over the work does mean she is working more slowly, and she has only managed to write the beginning of the story.
- This child is using her phonetic skills confidently.
- She is using silent 'e' in broke.
- She is also using some doubling rules, as in 'better' and 'tell'.
- A lot of common words are in place. 'What' and 'want' should be on her list of words to start working with.
- This child should probably do some more work with long vowel spellings. Then more unusual vowels like OU and W influenced A, as in 'want', could be tackled.

Child 3

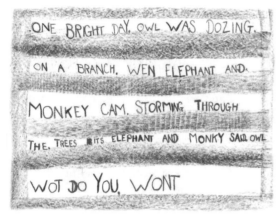

- Again, good use of phonological skills is evident.
- WH may need revising.
- Silent 'e' is not yet used and should be taught.
- W influenced A is also a problem for this child. 'Was', 'want' and 'what' are probably best taught as common words at this stage.
- QU may need to be revised.
- Common words – 'they', 'the', 'do', 'me', 'and', 'you', 'if', 'said' – are in place; 'when' and 'those' might be amongst the common words to tackle.

This, combined with the results of the diagnostic spelling assessment done at the end of Class 1,[8] will give a picture of the things you will have to revise thoroughly with the whole class and those that need revising only with some children. You could record individual needs as suggested on page 141.

Class Two Observation List

OBSERVATIONS *FROM WORDS THEIR WAY* SPELLING ASSESSMENT – DATE
Note:'/' means confuses.

Child A	New child – was not part of the assessment
Child B	Needs work on short u, short e, CH, SH and TH/F
Child C	
Child D	
Child E	Needs work on CH, TH. Also hearing ST/SD
Child F	
Child G	
Child H	
Child I	
Child J	Needs work on ST/SD
Child K	
Child L	
Child M	
Child N	Needs work on TH SH and TH/F
Child O	Needs work on short u, ST, DR, CH, SH, GR, F/TH, MP, LONG I/A
Child P	New child – was not part of the assessment
Child Q	
Child R	
Child S	Needs work on short e, short i, SH and blends BL, FR and CR
Child T	Needs work on CH and TH/FR
Child U	Needs work on SH and TH/F
Child V	

In your plans, include tasks for the whole class to revise all these skills, and during the practice, notice particularly how the individuals fare. If they still need it, arrange for some one-to-one time to rehearse these items. An assistant could help them carry out a sorting activity from *Words Their Way*,[11] or the parents can be asked to help at home. An explanatory note like the example on page 142 could accompany the materials:

---

11 Bear, Invernizzi, Templeton & Johnstone, 2012. Chapter 3 in this book gives extensive guidance for methods for working with words, including analysis of patterns in sorting activities. These are classroom-friendly and highly effective for building children's understanding of language and training spelling memory.

Dear parents

We have found that your child struggles hearing the difference between words starting with 'F' and words starting with 'TH'. I would like you to help by practising a little every day.

Attached is a document with cards for 'TH', 'F' and some odd ones out. These cards can be printed and cut out (it works best if they're printed on card or thicker paper).

This is how I would like you to practise:

- Put the 'TH' card and the 'F' card and the Odd One Out card on the table and practise saying those sounds. (Say the sound as you would hear it in a word without the schwa /uh/ sound – so /TH/ not /THuh/.) Let the child repeat the sounds and make them aware where their top teeth are: /F/ on the bottom lip, /TH/ on the tongue. I always say this is the only time they can stick their tongue out!
- Look at the cards with your child and sort them into words beginning with /TH/ and words beginning with /F/, and words beginning with neither. You will have to read the words as they are not all words that the children are able to read.
- Then you shuffle the cards, read the first card without the child seeing the word, and the child repeats the word and points to the correct spelling for the first sound.
- Then show the card and put it in the correct column.
- When this is too easy, you can do all the cards in the same way, but let your child place the cards in the correct column. Ask your child to check their columns at the end when all the cards are upside down.

When they say the words, keep watching that their top teeth are on the bottom lip for the /F/ and on their tongue for the /TH/.

I would like some feedback before the half term or earlier if there is a problem or an observation you'd like to share.

THANK	THINK	THIRST	THAW	THERMOS
THUNDER	THUMB	FIRST	FIN	FREE
THICK	THREE	THROW	THISTLE	THIN
THIRD	THIEF	THREAD	FAN	FISH
FIG	FOG	FUN	FLASH	FROG
FIST	FROST	FOND	FILL	FELL
CHAT	SHOW	SIT	CHAIR	SHOE
F	TH	ODD ONE OUT		

Chapter 21

Class 2 Revising of Work from Class 1

Games to play to revise work already learned:

- Whole-class games for CH, SH, TH
- Snakes and ladders for blends
- Ball games in a circle to split words into sounds and syllables

In your first weeks of Class 2, these would be useful revision activities to thread through your Main Lessons. There may also be new children in the class who have not yet played these games and need to know what you mean when you say 'do the troll game!'.

Revising CH, SH and TH

Create a CH, SH and TH area in a large room by sticking the letters to the wall near three corners. The children run, skip, jog, walk through the room. The teacher calls out words that begin with /CH/, /SH/ and /TH/, and the children run quickly to the marked areas. Other words are also included. If the word does not belong to the three groups the children must freeze. The following words could be used.

CH		SH		TH		OTHER
chin	chicken	shin	sharp	thin	third	big
chug	chocolate	shift	shell	thick	thirst	fin
chum	choose	ship	shock	three	thread	stick
chop	church	shop	shower	throw	thunder	stop
chair	chutney	shut	shout	thank	thumb	train
chain	check	shake	shovel	think		trampoline
change		shade	shrub	theatre		fish
cheer		shadow	shuffle	thaw		soap
child		share		thermos flask		try
children		sheep		thief		
chestnut				thistle		

At the end of this game, the children go back to their desks to make three columns in their Main Lesson book, at the top of which they write the three digraphs. Then the teacher can dictate the words in the top three columns. The children are reminded to 'use the troll game' to work out the spellings.

On the following day, repeat the game using the same words but standing next to the desk. When the teacher calls out a word starting with CH the children stand on their chairs. If the word starts with TH they stand next to their chair, and if the word starts with SH they sit down.

Then the class plays 'Snakes and ladders' in mixed-ability groups of four children. To differentiate effectively, the weakest group works with the teacher while others are managed by an able child. As happened in Class 1, each group has a reader who reads out a word. The player moves his or her counter while saying the *sounds* (not the letter names!) of the word. You may adjust the rules slightly to suit ability.

- The less able children may move the word a second time if they can tell whether the word starts with CH, SH or TH.
- You could challenge the middle group by printing the words on blue and red card. Easier words are on blue cards and harder on red; require the children to spell the blue words for a double move and just identify the initial letters of the red words. The first four rows (below) are easier to write, whilst the words that follw are a little harder.
- By contrast, give a piece of paper to the most able children, who may move the word twice only if they can write any word accurately.

CHIN	CHUG	CHUM	CHOP	SHIN
SHIFT	SHIP	SHOP	SHUT	THIN
THICK	THREE	THROW	CHILD	CHECK
SHELL	SHEEP	SHOCK	SHOUT	THREAD
THIRD	SHAKE	SHADE	CHAIN	CHANGE

THISTLE	SHADOW	CHILDREN	CHESTNUT	CHICKEN
THIEF	CHOOSE	CHURCH	CHUTNEY	SHRUB
THUNDER	THUMB	SHARP	SHOVEL	SHUFFLE
THANK	THINK	THIRST	THAW	THERMOS

Revision of Blends

The blends game described in Chapter 11 for Class 1 is worth repeating for those who still need to practise the blends a great deal. The others can play 'Snakes and ladders' with blends words. Use the method described on page 145 for differentiation and the words set out here. Again, the first rows are the simplest.

SPIN	SPOT	SLIP	SLIM	SLUG
TRIP	TROT	TRAP	TWIG	TWIN
DROP	DRUM	DRAG	GRAB	GRIN
GRAN	GRIP	GLAD	FROG	FLAG
FLAT	FLIP	PLAN	PLUM	PRAM

STOP	STUB	SNAP	CLIP	CLOG
CLAP	CRASH	FLASH	SPLASH	BRUSH
CRUSH	BLUSH	THRUSH	SWIM	SWIFT
CREST	FROST	TRUST	TWELFTH	CRISP
CRUST	CRUNCH	STRAND	SPRANG	STRENGTH
STRING	SPRING	STRONG	SHRINK	SPILL
GRILL	SHRILL	SMALL	SMELL	GLASS
CLASS	STRESS	STRUCK	TRACKING	SCRAPE
SCARE	STARE	STRIPE	SPINE	SLIDE
CLOTHE	PLANE	CRANE	STRODE	SPOKE
SPONGE	SPACE	TRACE	TWICE	SKELETON

Splitting Words into Sounds and Syllables

Playing the troll game once more to remind the children how to split words into sounds is a good idea, since it is such a useful skill (see Chapter 10). Whenever the children need to spell a word, encourage them to 'do the troll game' by tapping the sounds on their knees. We can also revise this in the following way:

Splitting Words into Sounds

You need a volleyball-sized ball (it is useful to have a red ball for syllables and a blue one for sounds).

- Stand in a circle. Tell the children what the theme is – for example, animals or sports – and remind them that we are splitting words into sounds. Model what you want them to do.
- Holding the blue ball, say 'CAT', then bounce the ball to the person to your left while saying the first sound.
- The next child bounces the ball left and says the next sound.
- The child who has the ball after the last sound has been said thinks of a new animal.

Splitting Words into Syllables

Repeat the game just described using a red ball for syllables. Show the children the red ball and remind them that now we are showing the 'beats' in a word. Grown-ups call them 'syllables'.

- Explain and model how you can work out the amount of syllables by holding your hand under your chin and saying the word in a normal way.
- Bounce the ball from child to child, with each child saying the next syllable. The child who receives the ball after the last syllable is said, thinks up a new word, and so on.

PART 6

Lesson Content for Class 2

Chapter 22

Cursive Script

- Introducing cursive script and handwriting
- Form Drawing
- What kind of cursive?

On the first day of Class 2, perhaps there will be a message for the children written in cursive script on the blackboard. Who can read it? Can we recognise some of the letters? What do we notice? The children might point out that all the letters in the words are connected, that the letters are all the same size, that there are some that are taller and some that go down but that these are also all the same size, that some have loops etc. What a mysterious start for children who feel well beyond the inexperience of a year ago!

Class 2 children will learn to identify several versions of the same letter: upper case, lower case, print and cursive. Obviously, it isn't functional to know only upper-case letters. Once the principles of sound and symbol correspondence have anchored, speed becomes the more essential characteristic. Indeed, historically as literacy became more democratic, cursive letters (both lower and upper case) were created out of a need for swift reproduction. As a child develops their handwriting capacity, they also develop a kinaesthetic memory of letter and word formation, so that spelling can become automatic, for example. We feel this to be especially important to maintain in our teaching and learning practice when so many of us now use keyboards. Fluency in handwriting might also become a major logistical factor in children's enthusiasm for authorship. What is the optimal relationship between thinking, wording the thoughts and the speed and ease with which one can set it down on paper? Potentially, a keyboard allows swifter release of thoughts, with easy revisions, but the steady pace of the hand might enable a deeper reflection.[1] If it's too slow, however, will it just be off-putting?

Of course, children must also know lower-case print letters for reading. How do we introduce all these sets of letters in the most economical way without confusing the children?

---

1 Chemin, 2014; Mueller & Oppenheimer, 2014.

As described at the beginning of Part 7, in one author's class the book letters were gently introduced at the end of Class 1. In the first weeks of Class 2, we suggest returning to this more fully to give the children practice in recognising the shapes.[2] This chapter shows you how to lead the children into good handwriting, and the next gives you examples for distinguishing between and becoming versatile with the different types of script they need to know.

We first prepare children for their own cursive writing with Form Drawing, following on from Class 1 (see Chapter 5).This Form Drawing is also a way to develop a sense for geometry.

Your aims are:

- Regularity
- Sticking to a straight line
- Fitting a pattern between two straight lines
- Straight backs slightly leaning forward

Here are some example running forms:[3]

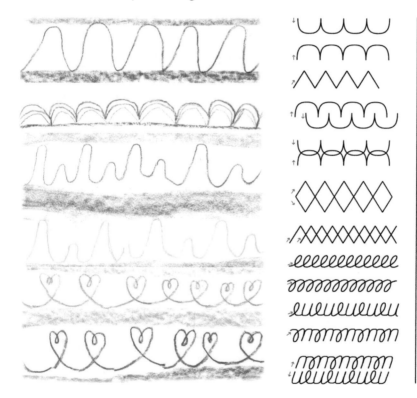

---

2 Do remember that the exact timing suitable for your class may vary. What we set out here as appropriate for the first term in Class 2 you may wish to introduce at another point.

3 These forms are from http://teachingfromatacklebox.blogspot.co.uk/2012/06/preparation-for-handwriting-form.html (goo.gl/b8A6ro). See also Lois Addy, 2004. Her book, *Speed Up!*, is an excellent handwriting resource.

Which Cursive Script?

For certain letters, a choice needs to be made; do we teach

b or *b*   *f* or *f*   *s* or *s*   *v* or *v*

w or *w*   *z* or *z* ?

You may have your own preferred aesthetic but here we also recommend that you consider the children with dyslexic difficulties. Many children with visual-processing difficulties reverse their letters both when they are writing and reading. You can help prevent this by your choice of script.

The shape of the 's' and the 'z' are more easily recognised in *s* and *z* .

The *b* has an advantage as it is more clearly distinguished from the *d* . It can be identified as the 'bucket letter' which further helps the reversal issue.

The *f* is also far more manageable than the *f* for children with dyslexia.

When you are ready to introduce the first cursive letters, we suggest doing so in groups, as follows:

i j t u y   *e*

l b h k   *s*

n m r   *f*

p   *v w*

c a o d g q   *x z*

Introduce the letter shapes in singular letters written quite large so that the children really feel the shape. Ask the children to draw them in various ways – for example, with their finger in the air, large on the desk, in sand trays and on individual blackboards.

- To get a real tactile experience of the letter, ask each of the children in the back row to choose a letter which they write on the back of the child sitting in front of them.
- This child writes it on the back of the child sitting in front of them. The front-row children write it on the blackboard.
- Check with the children behind; was it the letter they had written? Can we understand why the letter has changed?

Whilst practising the letters, use the opportunity to revise some of the spelling patterns the children have learnt. There is far more benefit in cursive writing with real words than writing lots of joined up *iiiii*, which is a pattern we never encounter.

Check Writing Position and Pencil Grip Regularly

As the children are developing their writing habits it is crucial that we continue to monitor writing position and pencil grip (see Chapter 5):
- Is the child sitting comfortably with good posture?
- Is the child leaning slightly forward?
- Are the feet flat on the floor?
- Are both arms resting on the table?
- Is the pencil guided by the thumb and index finger?
- Is the pencil grip relaxed (no white knuckles)?
- Is the paper positioned slanting to the left for the right-handed child or to the right for the left-handed child?

Chapter 23

Different Types of Script and Letter Recognition in Class 2

- Scripts – lower case, print and cursive
- Games for letter recognition

This chapter gives you more activities which link the letters shapes to each other in a clearly understandable way.

Making Bingo and Pairs Cards

- Display upper-case letters and book or print letters (that is, letters as found in printed material such as books) on the wall and photocopy the worksheets on pages 152–155 on card. Ask the children to write the upper-case letters next to the print/book letters on their cards. The cards can later be cut up and used for the bingo or pairs game below. Make sure the darker line is at the bottom of each card to give the correct orientation. A note of caution: some may not have written their upper-case letters neatly enough for others to recognise. You may need to print a version of the game for a few children.

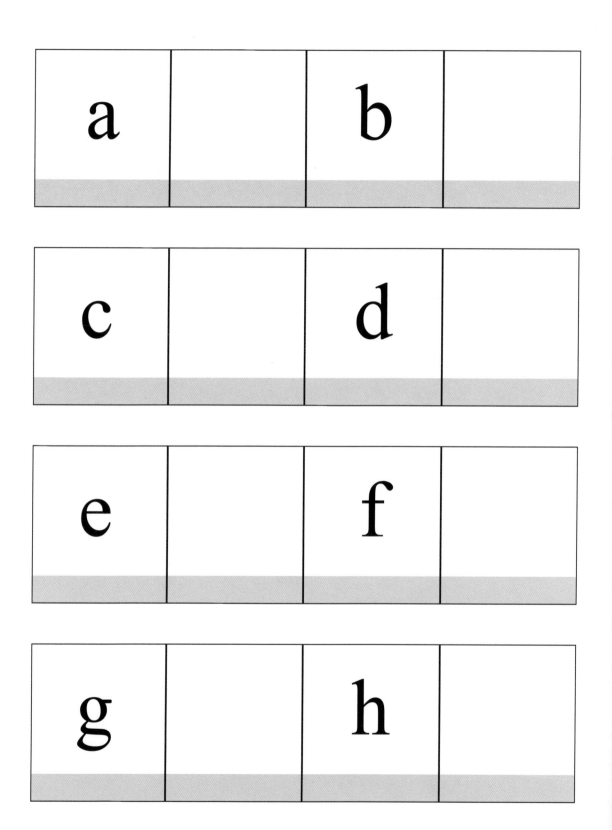

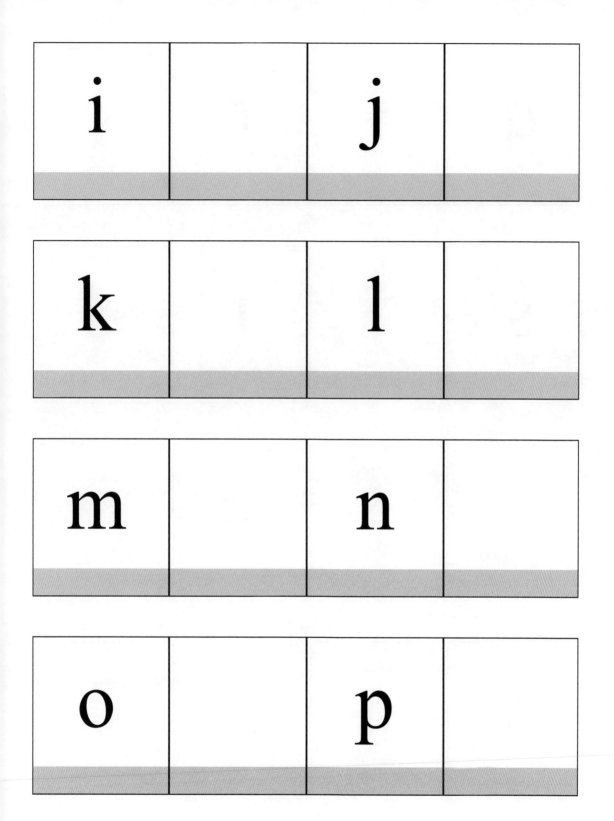

q		r	

s		t	

u		v	

w		x	

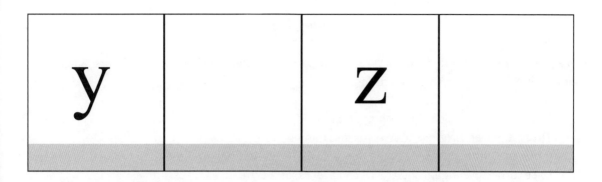

Scanning Text

Set a challenge with a poem that the children have been reciting. How many of each letter in the alphabet can you find? Scanning text for certain letters is a helpful activity for visual perception and helps develop speed of recognition. The children usually set to such a task with great enthusiasm. Here is an example.

The Fox and the Grapes

'What luscious grapes', mused a hungry fox;
'Fine good grapes', said he.
'If I jump as high as a clever fox can,
I'll have those grapes for me.'
He jumped and he leaped and he snapped with his teeth,
But only the air did he bite,
While the grapes sweet and juicy dangled above,
And swayed at a lofty height.
The fox grew mad, turned scarlet red,
But tossing his head said he:
'Those grapes are sour and full of worms —
Who wants those grapes? Not me!'

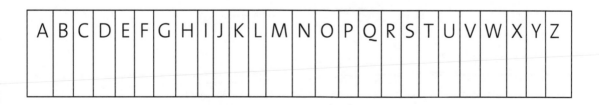

Playing Pairs

Using the previously prepared cards, this is a pairs memory game for work partners. Below is a printable grid. The game is played as follows:

- Place the cards upside down on the table.
- The first player turns over two cards and names the letters.
- If they match, the player can keep the cards and have another go. If they don't match, they need to be turned over again and the next player takes a turn.

Later, this game can be extended by including cards, also with cursive letters. We recommend finding a programme such as 'Handwriting for windows 3.0'[4] to allow you to print text out in cursive writing suitable for your class.

A	B	C	D

E	F	G	H

---

4 Font from a specialist dyslexia teacher such as this is available from Kath Balcombe. See Bibliography.

| I | J | K | L |

| M | N | O | P |

| Q | R | S | T |

| U | V | W | X |

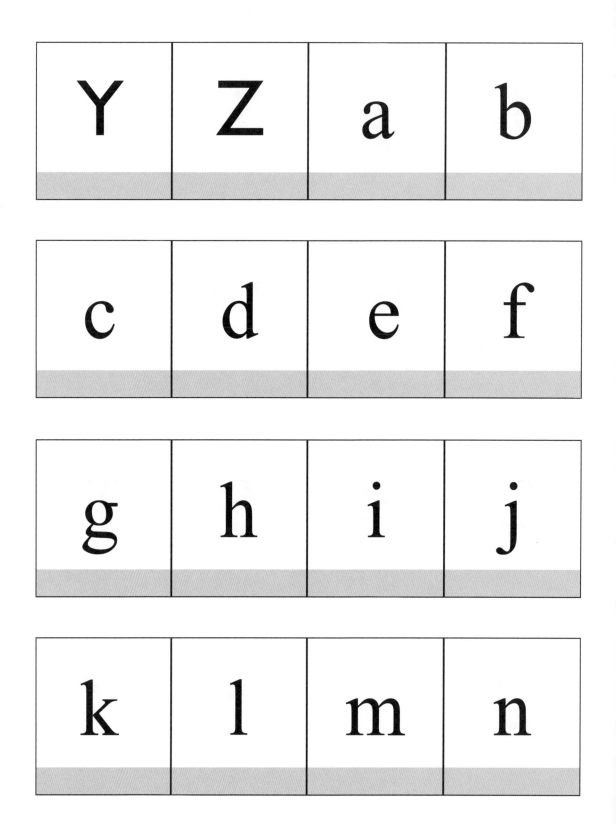

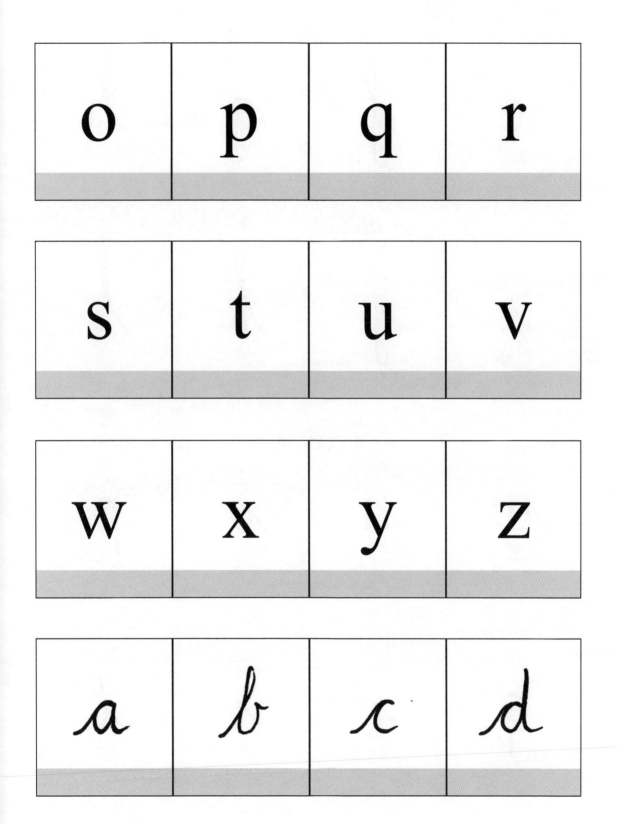

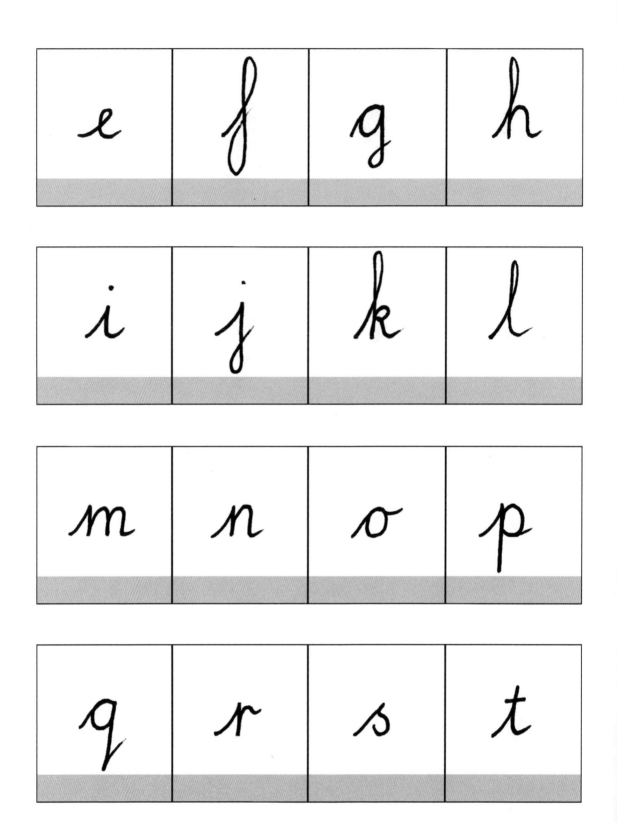

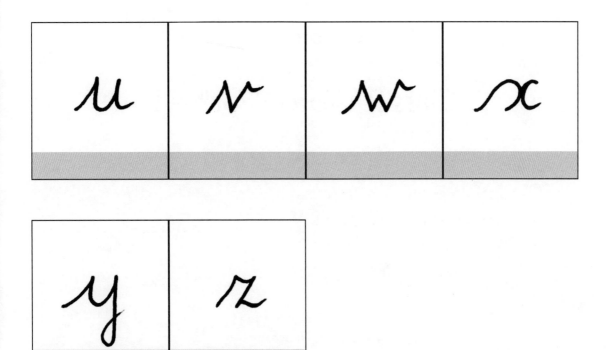

Bingo

The children draw a bingo grid with nine squares. They take their pack of letter cards as above, and choose nine book letters to put in the spaces on the bingo grid.

- The teacher calls out letter names, and when the children have a match they turn the card over.
- The first child to have all cards turned over calls out BINGO or KING or QUEEN.
- Check whether the turned-over cards are accurate.

This game can be played repeatedly with the same grid. Vary it by holding up the upper-case letters silently, or drawing them on the blackboard. Similarly, you could call out just the letter sounds.

Chapter 24

Class 2 Word Work – I

- Spelling teaching
- Working with common words
- Word walls

Spelling Teaching

In Class 1, you will have mostly been encouraging the children to write freely, using plausible spelling. You will notice that some children are very concerned to spell accurately, 'just like adults do', while others are not so aware or interested. Your aim has been to prioritise expression – that they put into writing whatever they want to say, unimpeded by worry about 'normal' spelling. Now that we are in Class 2, you will move towards dedicating more time to teaching specific phonic and spelling patterns, starting with the simplest.

A huge debate in the history of teaching of literacy has been that between whole-word teaching and phonics teaching.[5] The debate across the English-speaking world became highly polarised and politicised about best methods. Those who promoted whole-word techniques were insistent that children most needed meaning from reading; they needed to appreciate the art and beauty of the written word. They complained that splitting words into parts destroys enjoyment and squashes the life out of the learning. However, phonics advocates said that many children simply could not become effective readers without a good grounding in the phonic code, and that it was negligent to only give ad hoc phonics instruction rather than something systematic. Much research has been carried out to analyse how effective readers read, with the assumption that if weaker readers could be educated in the same strategies, they would progress. This research backs up the claims of the phonics advocates, showing that good readers automatically absorb phonic rules and can put them to use in a flexible way.

It ought to be simple, one would think, to combine the best of phonics teaching with whole-word approaches, so that all children get enough of what they need to effectively balance their

---

5 Adams, 1990.

absorption of the subject. What is a logical way to teach simple-to-complex elements of spelling progressively? How do you co-ordinate this with phases of writing or reading? How may you teach spelling so that it is effectively memorised for everyone, without boredom or disaffection?

In this book, we will be showing you appropriate spelling teaching for Class 2, using games and simple practice materials. This chapter focuses on common words teaching and the next on long vowels and their spelling patterns. Remember when designing your lessons:

*   Vary visual, auditory and kinaesthetic modes of learning
*   Use games to make learning fun
*   Practice should be brief (10 minutes or less) and frequent (daily)

Common-Word Practice

Make word wall cards in different scripts as shown here.

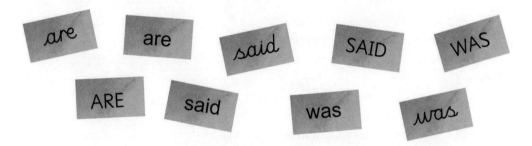

In Part 3, we described some games for working with a word wall in Class 1. Here, we develop these.

A Word Wall in Class 2

the	you	with	have	that
from	was	be	and	are
by	but	what	said	they
is	for	he	we	she
word	one	of	had	all

Word Wall Activity for Class 2

See this chart for words that you could work with, clues to give, and how to pace them day by day. Word walls are good for training the visual memory and linking it to auditory clues.

WEEK 1: that, they, friend, all, was

	Clue	Word Answers
Day 1	• A word that has two of the same letters that are next to each other	all
	• A word that has an 'A' in it that makes the sound /a/ (as in 'hat')	that
	• A word where 'e' and 'y' are friends and make the sound /a/ (as in 'cake')	they
Day 2	• A word that rhymes with 'bend'	friend
	• A word that rhymes with 'grey'	they
	• A word that rhymes with 'mat'	that
Day 3	• If you look at this word and also when you listen to it, you can find the word 'END' hidden in it	friend
	• If you look at this word and also when you listen to it, you can find the word 'HAT' hidden in it	that
	• If you look at this word you can find the word 'HE' hidden in it (you cannot hear it)	they
Day 4	• If you bounced this word with the blue ball (see page 148, Splitting Words into Sounds) you would bounce the ball five times	friend
	• If you bounced this word with the blue ball (sounds), you would bounce the ball three times and the word has four letters	that
	• If you bounced this word with the blue ball (sounds) you would bounce the ball twice and the word has four letters	they

WEEK 2: that, they, friend, all, was
have, when, said, why, are

	Clue	Word Answers
Day 1	• A word that has a 'Y' in it that makes the sound /i/ (as in 'hi')	why
	• A word that has an 'E' in it making the sound /e/ (as in 'bed')	when
	• A word that has an 'A' and an 'I' working as friends to make only one sound	said
Day 2	• A word that rhymes with 'try'	why
	• A word that rhymes with 'small'	all
	• A word that rhymes with 'then'	when
Day 3	• If you look at this word and also when you listen to it, you can find the word 'AT' hidden in it	that
	• If you look at this word you can find 'AS' hidden in it (you cannot hear it)	was
	• If you look at this word you can find the word 'HEN' hidden in it (you cannot hear it)	when
Day 4	• The word that could go in this sentence; 'I will invite _____ my friends'	all
	• The word that could go in this sentence; '_____ is your birthday?'	when
	• The word that could go in this sentence; '_____ you alright?'	are

At the end of two weeks, take the words off the wall and do a spelling dictation. Explain to the class that you need to know which words need to go back on the wall in the next block. Some of the words can be left or given to individual children in a 'practice pack'; others will have to return to the wall if a majority of children are still struggling with the spellings. Make sure that all the words reappear regularly in revision activities such as Five in a Row, set out on page 171.

Kinaesthetic Word Spelling Practice

You may notice that some children switch off during this whole-class common-word activity. They may be better off approaching common-word learning from a different angle if they have a weak visual memory and don't retain the 'whole word pictures'. You could try a more kinaesthetic approach for a handful of children in the class while the rest works with the word wall.

Gather appropriate practice words for these children specific to each one's needs. These common words can be collected from their writing or from word-wall assessments. For example, one child may end up with a list of words like this

> Was, are, for, word, once, how, do, were, which, will, like, about, what, many, some, other, make, into, use, them, said, so, would.

Depending on the child, 5–20 words may be tackled in this way each week.

At the start of each week, these children were given an A5 booklet with a rainbow writing task.

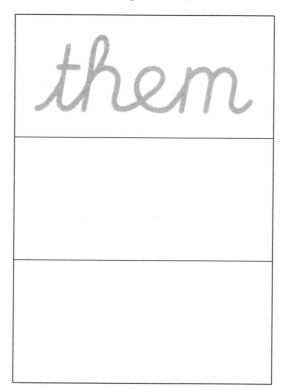

The children go over the faint printed word with five different coloured pencils. Then they copy the word again in five different colour pencils in the space below. They fold along the line and write the word from memory in the space below. Unfolding the paper, the work can be self-checked.

Once the booklet has been completed, the next stage of practice is as follows. Each of the week's practice words is on a card, and the children:

- Pick up the card
- Quietly read the word
- Look at the word intensely for three seconds – 'take a photo'
- Put the card upside down or cover it
- Write the word
- Check the spelling against the card
- If incorrect, re-write

At the end of the week, they pair up and, taking the other's pack of cards, dictate them one by one, showing the card once the word is written. A mini-tick is put on the corner of the card when the word is correct, a cross if it's incorrect.

The teacher checks the cards at the weekend. When a card has two ticks, it is kept aside with all 'known' words and a new card is added. A new rainbow writing booklet is made with the words for the next week. With a small group of children, this process is manageable for the teacher.

Flashcards

At times, you may wish to practise common words more quickly than with a word wall. Use flashcards with a mixture of upper-case, lower-case and print letters (see above). Hold the card up, count to three and the whole class chants the word, followed by the spelling. A very able child may be given the opportunity to stand so that they can't see the card and to chant the spelling after the class has called out the word. A fairly weak child could be the judge and check their accuracy.

'Five in a Row'

This really enjoyable game can be used to revise any spelling pattern or common words.[6]

Print 25 words to be revised on cards. Each child should have a blank bingo sheet of 5 x 5 squares. Share out the pack of 25 cards and ask the children to stick them all around the room with blue tack.

Give the children ten minutes to find all the words and copy each one correctly in any square on their bingo sheet. The rules are:

- You can walk to the words
- You may not take your book, paper or pen to the words
- You may not take the words to your desk
- The words have to be spelled correctly, otherwise it will not count when you have five in a row

---

6 The same game is described for Class 1 in Chapter 12.

The short time between studying the word where it is stuck on the wall and writing it down at their desk stimulates the short-term memory.

Ask a child to collect the words and read them out. The children tick the words to make sure they've not missed a word.

You could stop here and play the game another day or at a later time. For example, make the sheets at the beginning of the lesson and promise to play the game at the end if there's time or create it at the end of one lesson and play it the next.

Playing the game

The teacher has the pack of cards and the children have their bingo sheets and a pencil (a different colour to the one used to create the sheet).

The teacher reads out the words and the children circle them; the first one to have five in a row wins. Check their answers. The children very quickly catch on to the fact that they cannot win the bingo game with misspelled words. The accuracy with which they study the words on the cards before writing them down improves swiftly.

For any children who would still find this activity quite difficult, you could seat them near you and put the cards on their desk as you read them out. Those children can see the words as well as hear them, and don't just need to rely on auditory information, nor speed of response.

Chapter 25

Class 2 Word Work – II

- Long Vowel Spelling Patterns
- Poem, Game, Hunt-the-vowel, Write the Poem sequence for learning the differences

Long and Short Vowels

Before teaching the variety of ways to spell long vowels, you will need to revise what was learned in Class 1, reminding the children of the distinction between short vowels (bad, bed, bin, hut and sock) and long (plate, tree, pine, tune and hope.) See Part 3.

Long vowels can be quite confusing in English. In Appendix 1, you will see a chart showing the 44 sounds; there are 120+ ways of spelling those sounds. Most spelling errors are caused by vowels, because this is where there is most variation. We address this by first teaching the most common long vowel graphemes as seen here, followed by the less frequent ones:

- ay/ a-e /ai
- ee/ y/ ea/ e-e
- i-e/ igh/ ie/ y
- o-e/ow/oa/
- oo/ u-e/ ue/ ew

If children are able to become reasonably consistent with these patterns, then many frequent spelling errors will be avoided. In this chapter, you will see a sequence of learning that could be followed in the spring-term literacy lessons, to cover three of the long vowel sounds – /a/, /o/ and /i./ You could adapt them to address the other two, or refer to the next chapter for more ideas.

Consonant Vowel Consonant 'e' spellings (CVCe)

In the first term in Class 2, you could first introduce words of Consonant Vowel Consonant 'e' pattern. This pattern is often referred to as the 'magic-e' or 'silent-e' spelling. In one of our classes, the 'e' in this spelling pattern was introduced as the 'selfless' e, as it was very happy to help the main vowel say its name and did not insist on making a sound itself.[7] It is a very common way that English words are converted from short to long, especially for long 'a', 'i' and 'o'.

Make sure you precede this with revision of how to distinguish long and short vowels.

- Every morning children jump into position when the teacher calls out long and short vowel words (Chapter 9)
- Play 'Crows and Cranes' using long and short vowel words – see Chapter 10.
- Play run-to-the-vowel with long and short vowel words

Following the introduction, every morning dictate six words and ask the children to write them in the correct column. For example, they have two columns labelled 'A' and 'A-e'. You dictate MAT, MATE, FAT, FATE, CAP, CAPE. For children who need scaffolding, place a card on their desk with the six words in a random order. They will choose the word and copy it, instead of independently thinking up the spelling.

Introducing Other Regular Long Vowel Spellings

We suggest introducing the other common long vowel spellings in the spring term. Some established spelling programmes promote the teaching of each spelling pattern separately. In our class, however, we chose to teach up to three most-common patterns of spelling a long-vowel altogether, also instructing the children in making choices between the patterns.

This is a description of a whole sequence of work teaching the long vowel sound /a/. In morning warm-up, the children jumped long and short vowel words as the teacher called out words, as above. Then the children were introduced to the following poem (with a nod to Julia Donaldson), which they learned to recite:

The Tale of the Snail and the Whale

One day a snail met a great big whale.
Said the great big whale to the tiny snail
'If I may I would like us to play today.'
'Okay', said the snail and climbed on the tail
Of his friend the great big whale.

---

7 Note that most current synthetic phonics programmes do not separate out the CVCe spelling pattern from other long vowels, highlighting the special function of the 'e' in a particular way. Different programmes may well be underpinned by subtly different opinions as to the best steps on the literacy route. However, many other phonics programmes (sometimes analytic) use the one we followed in our class and we were satisfied with the results. In our opinion, this particular issue is not make or break. Choices need to be made to follow logical and intuitive learning sequences so that the chance of confusion is minimised. It is economical if children apply this knowledge straight away in their writing and reading, to secure their understanding.

'Stay still', said the whale. 'Hold on to my tail!
If you are very brave, I will show you the cave
Where I like to play with the waves every day.'
So he blew a spray and sailed away
And the snail and the whale had a splendid day.

While reciting, they soon learned to clap or jump every time they heard the long sound /a/. The children drew a picture of the meeting between the snail and the whale.

Make the Four-in-a-Row Sheet

A following day, the teacher hung cards with the long /a/ words from the poem all around the class, and the children drew a Four-in-a-Row page[8] in their Main Lesson book. They all walked through the class, reading the words and memorising the spelling, walking back to their desk to write the words in their Four-in-a-Row grid. Again, the rules are that they may not take the words to their desk, or their book to the words.

---

8 Like a blank bingo sheet.

day	may	play	today
okay	stay	spray	away
snail	tail	sail	whale
brave	cave	wave	great

When half the class has finished, the teacher collects all the words and reads them out. The children check whether they have all the words and underline those they know are correct. The children who need a longer time receive a sheet with the words to check them at their own pace, and to make sure their spellings are correct, also underlining them once they're sure.

Draw a Picture and Categorise the Spellings

Next, the teacher draws three pictures with the class; one of the whale, one of the snail and one of the spray. Then the children find the spellings that match in their bingo grid. They might notice which occur most frequently or where the /a/ sound is heard in each word.

sn ai l

snail Sale Tail

spr ay

stay sway today play
day okay May

Word-Hunt Categories

The next day, they're ready for a word hunt. The children draw three columns: one for whale words, one for snail words, and one for spray words. Some have drawn a fourth column. This can be used for odd-one-out words,[9] as some have already realised that the word 'great' is neither a whale, nor a snail, nor a spray word. Then the children took their reading books out and they hunted for words with the long sound /a/ and the spellings of the whale, the snail and spray.

Several children go home to hunt in their own books at home. One of them proudly announces in class the next day that he has found 37 words!

Play 'Four in a Row'

Now that they have done so much work with the words, they returned to their Four-in-a-Row grid that they'd made earlier in the week and played the game. Children who need support get a helper next to them, either an adult or another child who can handle searching through two grids. Now, when the words are dictated, the children circle the word. Whoever has four in a row may call out 'KING' or 'QUEEN'. Someone asks whether we can play on and have a KING and a QUEEN. Then they all want to play on until we have an EMPEROR.

The teacher explains that we all have the same words so we would all be EMPEROR at the same time. That sounds fun, and they all want to go on until they're all EMPERORS. The teacher

---

9 If you haven't got one already, it's a good idea to have a name for words that are irregularly spelled. Sometime they are referred to as red words (like a traffic light; regular words are green words). In a writing task, the teacher will often write up the red words and any unusual vocabulary on the board, for example.

agreed, but as one of the children has a headache we must call out 'EMPEROR' very quietly. They agree that there can only be one Queen and one King. Once a child calls out 'KING' or 'QUEEN', the teacher checks the spelling. You can't be a King or a Queen when you've misspelled a word. The next time they play a game like this, they'll check their spellings even more carefully.

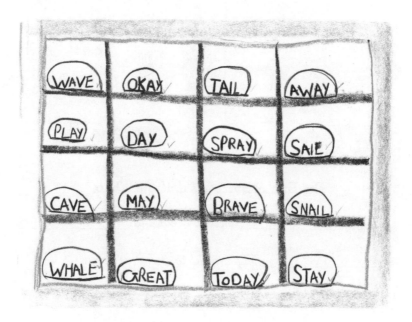

Write the Whole Poem Down

Finally, it is time to write the poem in the Main Lesson books. As further preparation, the teacher wrote lots of words on the blackboard. They are the words from the poem that don't have long /a/ spellings and don't have obvious spellings. The words are all mixed up. In pairs, the children choose two words and tell their partner in which sentences the words appear. The teacher asks some of the children to then tell the class which words they've read from the board, and in which sentences from the poem these words appeared.

The class agrees that they will try to write neatly, put capitals in the title and make sure all the long /a/ words are spelled correctly. Half-way through the writing time, the teacher beats the chime and partners check each other's work to make sure they've remembered those three things.

Some children who need support will get a cloze exercise to help them with their writing.[10] Most write the poem from memory. Everyone can do the task.

---

10 A cloze exercise is where text is written down with some words blanked out or left missing. The text forms a context, therefore, so that struggling readers can use their comprehension to work out what should be in the gap.

The tale of the Snail whale and the

one day a snail met

a great big whale said

the great big whale to

the tiny snail if I may

i would like us to

play today okay said

snail and climbed on

the tail of his friend

The Tale of the Snail and the Whale

One day a _____ met a great big _____.

Said the _____ big whale to the tiny snail

"If I may I would like us to _____ today."

"_____," said the snail and climbed on the _____

Of his friend the great big whale.

"_____ still," said the whale. "Hold on to my tail!

If you are very _____, I will show you the

_____

Where I like to play with the waves every day."

So he blew a _____ and sailed _____

And the snail and the whale had a splendid _____.

snail, spray, brave, whale, play, tail, away, cave, day, great, Okay, Stay

Other Possible Poems for Introducing Vowel Patterns

To introduce the long vowel choices one by one, the following poem by Martin Hardiman may be used to introduce /ai/:

A snail will not complain
When it starts to rain
He will not fail
To make a trail
With very little strain.

But when it starts to hail
A snail feels very frail.
He will refrain,
Because it's plain
Hail pains a snail's tail!

Introducing 'o-e', 'oa' and 'ow'

A possible poem to introduce the long 'o' sound, as in rose, toad and crow, could be the following:

The Rose

A toad met a goat and a frisky foal,
And a crow with feathers as black as coal.
Spoke the crow to the foal and the goat and the toad
'I will show you a rose that stands quite close'.
'Let's go!' spoke the goat and the frisky foal.
'Oh no!' croaked the toad, 'and how shall we go
To the rose you so want to show?'.
'I don't really know', spoke the coal black crow,
'I just spread my wings and am ready to go'.
'But we use the road', croaked Mr Toad
'And then there's the moat. We'll sure need a boat.'
And so the foal, the goat and the toad
Found a boat and round the moat did they float
So the coal black crow could the three of them show
The beautiful rose that stood in the snow.

The same process is followed. First the class learns the poem, then they jump on the long 'o' sounds while reciting. Once they've categorised the spellings, they could continue the recitation and instead clap on 'ow', jump on 'oa' and stamp on 'o-e'. In the mean time, a bingo sheet is prepared, a book hunt takes place and the bingo game is played. Again the poem is written from memory in the Main Lesson books with some children doing a cloze exercise before copying the poem into their book.

The Rose

A _____ met a _____ and a frisky _____,

And a _____ with feathers as black as _____.

_____ the crow to the foal and the goat and the toad

"I will _____ you a _____ that stands quite _____."

"Let's _____!" Spoke the goat and the frisky foal.

"Oh no!" _____ the toad, "and how shall we go

To the rose you so want to show."

"I don't really _____," spoke the coal black crow,

"I just spread my _____ and am ready to go."

"But we use the _____," croaked Mr Toad

"And then there's the _____. We'll sure need a _____."

And so the foal, the goat and the toad

Found a boat and round the moat did they _____

So the coal black crow could the three of them show

The beautiful rose that stood in the _____.

float

show

snow

know

rose

road

boat

moat

toad

foal

crow

close

coal

go

goat

Croaked

Spoke

wings

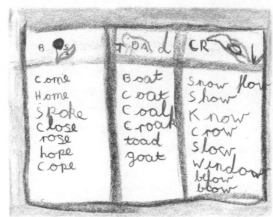

The Rose

A toad met a goat and a frisky foal and a crow with feathers as black as coal spoke the crow to the foal and the goat and the toad i will

show you a rose that stans cwite clos lets go spoke the goat and the frisky foal the crow spoke the toad and how shal we go to the rose you so wont to show

i dont really know spoke the coal black crow i just spred my wings and im redy to go, but we use the road croacd mrtoad and then there's the moat yell

sure need a boat, and so the foal the goat and the toad found a boat and round the moat did they float so

the coal black crow cold the 3 of them show the beautiful rose that stood in the snow

Introducing 'i-e,' 'igh,' and 'y'

The following nonsense poem could be used to introduce the long /i/ spellings, as in kite, fly and light:

The Kite and the Fly

'Come sit on my tail', said the kite to the fly
And I'll take you so high in the bright summer sky
'Alright', said the fly, 'I like to fly
So high in the bright summer sky'.
So they danced in the sky, the kite and the fly
But try as he might the fly got a fright
From flying so high in the bright summer sky.
He held on tight with all his might
That fly so high in the bright summer sky.
Then in the night they both went inside
And the fly heaved a sigh and told the kite
'I'll never again fly so high in the sky!'
While the kite lay aside, the fly buzzed all night
Around the bright light while the dark stayed outside.

The same process is followed.

fly sky thy

light, night, bright, might

Ongoing Practice

Stick cards with the different long vowel spellings on the classroom wall and refer to them regularly. When a child wants to know how to spell 'cake', for example, all the teacher need do is say, 'It is a whale spelling', or 'Do you think it could be a whale, a snail or a spray spelling?'.

Introducing Long /ē/

As an alternative to the scheme of work developed above, you could choose to work with a vowel spelling in a simplified way, using word sorts. Here is an example of what to do with the long vowel /ē/.

Prepare word sheets with a list that has the same number of short /ĕ/ words as the two most common long /ē/ forms, namely /ee/ and /ea/. Choose a few that use 'e' alone, such as 'me' and 'she', and then perhaps a couple of the less common long /ē/ forms /ie/ ('chief') and /e-e/ ('theme').

Include a couple of odd-one-out words such as 'head' or 'great' or 'friend', since these are frequent and confusing."[11] Here is a simple sheet example.

set	fed	red	mess
team	seat	feel	reed
creep	fell	read	he
sheet	meet	chief	great

Start by the whole class reading the words together and explaining any meanings or strange spellings. You may notice homophones and invite children to notice odd-one-out spellings. Ask the children to listen to you saying 'fed' and 'feed'. What sound difference can they hear? This is revising the difference between the short and the long vowel.

Ask the children to cut up the sheets into word cards and model how to initially sort the sounds into two vowel categories – 'fed' could be at the top of one column, 'feed' another. Show them how to put their odd-one-out words aside. Once all these have been read and working partners may have checked each other's work, you can talk about how the words in the column for the long vowel have different patterns. Can the children see patterns and choose a column header keyword for making more sub-categories?

Once the columns have been sorted once, keep only the headers and scramble all the words for a second lot of sorting. Don't do any corrections until the end and, if a mistake has been made, tell the children 'I can see two mistakes – can you find them?'.

You can keep the word lists for other activities later. Once children are familiar with this, you can leave the process more open. Give them a word list – perhaps with the same vowel sounds as above, but with new words – and introduce it once again by reading it out together. Then ask the children if they can work out how to sort the words themselves. Ask them what they notice, if

---

11 Word lists in books such as Bear, Invernizzi, Templeton, & Johnstone (2012) are invaluable here.

they can think of categories and find the odd-ones-out. Accept all reasonable categories, including sound and/or pattern.

Once categories are identified, agree keyword headers and ask open-ended questions. Also, see if there are any homophones. Again, it's a good idea to scramble and sort again.

Long Vowel /ū/

We suggest similar work with this long vowel. The most common ways of spelling this are /u-e/, /oo/ (boot,) and /ew/ (blew.) Less commonly, it is spelled /ue/ (blue) and /ui/ (suit).

There is also the ambiguous vowel /oo/, as in the word 'book'. We suggest teaching it at the same time as /oo/ in 'moon' and telling the children that this grapheme can make two sounds. Additionally, you will notice that the sound in 'tune' or 'unite' is different to that in 'flute', even though the spelling pattern is the same. Again, it's very good to create a situation where the children themselves can discover these subtleties. You want them to develop flexibility as well as an understanding of patterns and rules.

Word Hunt for /ū/

Instead of giving the class the words for a word sort, such as the one described for /ē/, you could organise a week-long word hunt whereby the children harvest words themselves. Once they know the word-sort technique, by working in any of the ways already described in this chapter you can start them off with a couple of rhyming sentences, such as:

> The man in the moon ate with a spoon
> He chewed his food and played a tune!

Or

> The animals came in two by two
> The elephant and the kangaroo
> Dear gnu, after you, said the cockatoo
> But the mule barged through
> Shoo! Or I'll show you my shoe!

There are several ways of spelling the sound here, with a couple of very irregular common words, namely 'two' and 'shoe'. If you say these rhymes out loud on the first day of the week, ask the children to repeat them back to you. Can they hear the /u/ words? How do they guess that the words are spelled? What sounds can they hear, and can they guess any effective spelling patterns, now that they have some experience with long vowels? Gather the answers up on the board. Prime the children that if they notice another word that has that sound, they can offer it to you at any time and you will write it up on the board with the spelling they think it might have. Hopefully, a few children will remember and spot words along the way during talking or other work.

On the next day, let the children come into the classroom and see their spelling with the correct spelling of that word next to it. There will be some surprises. Again, the children may give you /u/ words at any time during the day. At the end of the Main Lesson, or that morning, read all the words out that the class has so far gathered. Then ask a whole row to read them out before they go for their playtime/home time, followed by another row, and so on.

Continue this during the week so that there are plenty of words gathered. Try to find ways to include some key common words, such as 'do', 'to', 'two', 'you', 'use', 'new', 'good' and 'would'. At the beginning of the next week, prepare your pack of cards in the same way as above for the /e/, allowing opportunities for the children to hear the words and spell them without seeing, to notice subtleties of sound and strangeness of spelling, and to simply read the cards plenty of times.

Chapter 26

Class 2 Word Work – III

- Spelling teaching
- Working with common words
- Word Walls
- More vowels and sounds
- Word-building activities
- Hen to Fox
- Resources for work-sheets
- Images for memory

Working with Other Vowel Sounds and Spelling Patterns

The following sounds will still need to be introduced and worked with to enable children to write what they can say.

Vowels with 'r', 'w' and 'l':

- /ar/, /are/, /air/
- /or/, /ore/, /oar/, /our/
- /er/, /ear/ (dear,) /ear/ (earth)
- /ir/, /ire/
- /ur/, /ure/
- /wa/ (wash, warn), /wo/ (won, word)
- /all/, /alk/

Diphthongs /oy/, /oi/, /ow/, /ou/, /aw/, /au/

Consonant spelling patterns:

- Three-letter blends – /spr/, /shr/, /sch/, /spl/, /squ/, /str/, /thr/
- Silent consonants /kn/, /wr/, /gn/
- End blends – /ch/, /tch/, /ge/, /dge/
- Spelling teaching
- Working with common words
- Word alls

It would be impractical to introduce all of them with poems and pictures. In this chapter we give you a selection of games and activities, often using a central image that you can use to bring these patterns to the children's attention. You can use these games to facilitate spelling for a long time. For example, a child comes to ask you how to spell 'jaw' and you can refer to the AW spellings learnt.

> 'It is a SAW spelling. Do you remember the handle of the saw? What letter was hidden in the handle? What letter was hidden in the blade of the saw? Remember the zigzags of the saw blade making the W?'

Word-building exercises can also now be used effectively. Prior to this, the sequence of learning has tended to be from the whole to the parts. You started with a story or poem, moving to the whole words, then deriving a spelling pattern. The following games will be more 'synthetic' to help you make words from sounds, and can be adapted to suit which ever phoneme and grapheme you wish to target.

Word-building Activities

The Magician Game, or Hen to Fox

Which magician can change a CAT into a DOG by changing only one letter at a time and using only proper words? This game can be played early in Class 2 to help revise the first phonemes.
CAT
COT
DOT
DOG
This could also be called the 'Hen to Fox' game.

'Can you change a hen into a fox?', asks the teacher. She asks the children to write 'hen'. Then tell them to change 'hen' into 'pen'. How do you do that? Now, change a 'pen' into your 'pet'. Tell the children that the next one is harder: can they change 'pet' into 'pit'? This might require some partner discussion: see if the class can come to a consensus about which vowel change is required – can they convince each other until everyone hears it? Now change 'pit' to 'sit'. And the sequence then follows 'sit' to 'six,' to 'fix' to 'fox.' You can make up more using the short vowel CVC words in the Appendix 4, such as 'cat' to 'pig' – cat, hat, rat, rag, bag, big, dig, pig.[12]

Class Word Make

In one class, the teacher wrote a series of letters on the board each morning. On arrival, the children were challenged to find as many words as they could using only the letters on the board and write them down at their desk. After rhythmical time, the teacher picked up to ten names (randomly using lollypop sticks with the children's names on). Those children wrote one of the words they had found on the board. Everyone who did not have the words already added them to their list.
Here is an example:

i g n r s t was written on the board. The children discovered 'in', 'sit', 'ring', 'sting', but the word with all the letters was not yet found.

The teacher drew _ _ _ _ _ _ on the board and children were allowed to request a letter. The children tried hard to work out which word it was, and to make sure everyone had an opportunity to discover it, the rule was that as soon as someone had the word, they would put up their hand and could whisper the word to the teacher.

Worksheet phoneme practice

Once a phoneme and grapheme have been introduced, you can create games that children can complete independently or in pairs. Here are some examples for the sound /ir/.

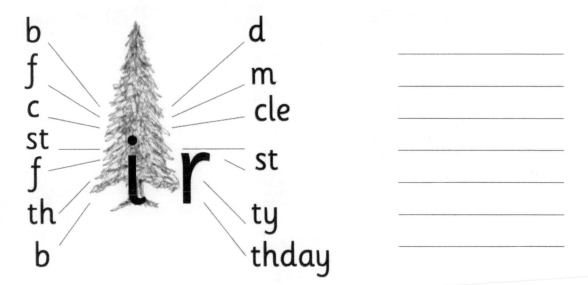

b
f
c
st
f
th
b

ir

d
m
cle
st
ty
thday

_____
_____
_____
_____
_____
_____
_____

---

12 Cunningham, 2013. This book gives many practical ideas that can easily be adapted for the Waldorf classroom.

This word search is taken from Key Spelling 1, part of a series published by Schofield & Sims, which we recommend.[13]

G	J	D	L	A	G	L	C	J	L	G	L	R	K	L	G	X	U	D	W	H	H	A	G	G
P	W	T	X	K	I	Y	X	U	F	A	I	L	R	T	W	H	T	H	I	R	T	E	E	N
P	Z	K	D	W	B	U	E	F	I	S	S	R	Z	G	K	P	U	Q	C	F	X	U	N	K
I	Y	H	B	V	Z	N	N	F	R	C	V	W	L	M	H	F	Z	X	J	K	F	Q	Y	Q
A	E	X	F	D	R	C	S	O	S	S	D	J	O	F	P	N	U	P	J	P	Y	K	H	B
Z	M	V	C	O	R	R	P	F	T	T	S	W	N	P	Z	C	C	I	N	J	S	M	T	I
L	W	C	B	I	R	D	X	D	X	E	X	P	V	C	N	W	J	C	G	U	C	B	H	R
N	F	K	I	W	H	T	R	S	A	W	G	E	J	Z	X	L	A	V	I	E	N	J	I	T
K	V	P	Z	R	B	R	F	I	R	Y	T	O	U	N	R	Z	V	L	A	R	Y	M	R	H
C	J	T	F	E	C	V	S	A	X	W	V	D	J	L	J	U	R	U	T	R	C	G	D	D
T	H	I	R	T	Y	L	R	T	L	Z	S	D	U	F	I	R	M	E	Z	L	H	U	F	A
L	O	I	P	K	T	C	E	X	I	D	H	P	I	O	U	Y	I	L	E	X	H	F	S	Y
X	R	J	R	Y	F	O	Q	V	T	R	I	P	N	R	G	S	N	X	Y	B	E	V	N	L
Z	D	C	U	P	X	K	F	T	I	L	R	E	V	T	T	R	I	C	V	W	Y	G	U	D
Z	N	X	K	O	D	M	Q	B	A	U	T	X	C	S	K	Y	T	H	I	R	S	T	Y	C

BIRD	FIRST
DIRTY	CIRCUS
GIRL	T-SHIRT
FIR	CIRCLE
THIRTY	THIRSTY
CHIRP	STIR
FIRM	THIRTEEN
THIRD	BIRTHDAY

---

13 Schoolhouse Technologies, Vocabulary Worksheet Factory 3 – http://www.schoolhousetech.com/.

ACROSS

1. Where you can see clowns
3. The day you were born
6. A is the ..... letter of the alphabet
10. Not soft
11. A type of tree
13. Animal with feathers and wings
14. 30
15. 10 add 3

DOWN

1. A sound some birds make
2. To mix with a spoon
4. Needing a drink
5. Comes after second
7. Something you wear
8. A round shape
9. Not clean
12. A young woman

Schoolhouse Technologies make educational software that can create word searches and crosswords suited exactly to your class and their different needs. The work-sheet here and on page 188 are both taken from the Vocabulary Worksheet Factory 3.[14]

14 Schoolhouse Technologies, Vocabulary Worksheet Factory 3 – http://www.schoolhousetech.com/.

Images for memory

Consolidate this work further by drawing the images in Main Lesson. These are examples for the sounds /ir/, /ar/ and /aw/.

The fir spelling; a fir tree with the little bird living in its branches.

The car /ar/ spelling; a Rolls Royce with the R on the bonnet.

The saw /aw/ spelling; an 'a' in the handle and the 'w' in the blade.

Homophone pear/pair tree

When you have studied long vowels and their friends for a while, it will become obvious to you and your class that sometimes, two words can sound the same but mean something different (a homophone.) While you might work on this more in Class 3, it could be enjoyable to make a homophone pear/pair tree for your classroom wall. Cut out pear-shaped pieces of paper and prepare a tree with branches for the wall or notice board. Every time that a homophone is discovered, you can write up the two spellings of the word on a pear and add it to decorate the tree. This encourages children to be alert to this possibility during their literacy work. Occasionally, there might even be three homophones (rode, road, rowed!). We recommend that you acquire a good homophones dictionary.[15]

---

15 There are many on the market. Another general book full of helpful pieces of language information is MacIver, 2013.

Chapter 27

Introduction to Suffixes and Prefixes

- Spelling two syllables
- Ground work for Class 3

Once children have acquired some confidence and ability with the core sounds and graphemes of English (there are commonly thought to be 44 phonemes), they can write anything they can say. As we've already explained, consonant sounds are relatively straightforward, with a few exceptions, and vowels are more difficult, with subtleties of auditory difference that make spelling highly variable. Somewhere in the middle of Class 2, let us say, we would want all the children in the class to have a plausible graphemic option to write every sound they want to convey in their writing.

As children start to gain confidence with writing, you may find it appropriate to help them understand more about how sections of words stick together. In English, words very often have a stem (which may have a common etymological root to others that mean something similar) and then either a prefix or a suffix. Prefixes and suffixes are very commonly the same as each other too, so there's a pleasing logic to the way they work, once children have grasped the concept. Teaching children about this process is a gentle extension work you'll have covered in Class 1 on syllables (see the Troll game in Chapter 10). It is also the precursor of grammatical information that you'll be working with in Class 3, where you will cover much more ground.

Simple Word Sums

The following is a good poem to work with for its demanding speech requirements, and because it demonstrates how a stem word can have a simple prefix or a suffix:

A twister of twists
Once twisted a twist
And the twist that he twisted
Was a three twisted twist
Now, in twisting this twist,
if a twist should untwist,
would the twist that untwisted
untwist the twists?

In rhythmical time at the start of the Main Lesson, teach the children to recite this poem with some beanbag juggling exercises. One day, take some wooden letters and ask five children to come to the front. They each close their eyes and get a wooden letter. They feel the letter, then go back to their desks and write the wooden letter they've felt on the back of another child. The five who have the letters written on their back now come forward and write them on the blackboard. The letters for the word 'TWIST' appear on the board. Can the children identify it?

Then ask, 'Who can make another word from the poem by adding some letters?'. One of the children might change 'TWIST' on the board to 'TWISTER'. In pairs the children soon have the whole list of words that can be made – TWIST+S, TWIST+ED, UN+TWIST, UN+TWIST+ED. Perhaps there are some slightly more advanced forms they can think of that aren't in the poem, such as 'TWIST+ING'? Model writing the first one 'TWISTER' as a word sum TWIST + ER = TWISTER. With some help on spelling the suffix 'ed', the children can work out the rest in their pairs and write down the word sums. Word Sums is a good game to play from now on in class!

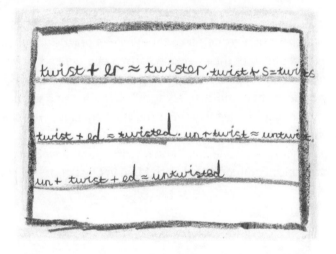

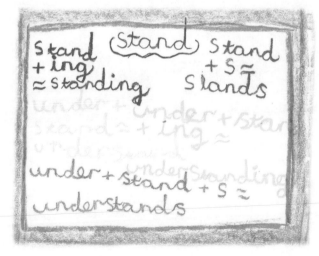

Chapter 28

Writing Stories

- Extending authorship with support
- No-copy story writing

In Class 2 the children continue to write stories in their own words. The stories might arise from one they've heard or from a poem they recite. Since they've been practising for some time, many will now be able to do this together with their working partner or independently.

For those who need more support we suggest providing a cloze exercise. Ask the children to read the whole story or poem first and then try to fill in the missing words. Once this has been achieved they can copy the text. This activity keeps the children active with the text and provides a good in-between stage.

The first examples here are of one child's own writing and a cloze (see Glossary page 328) exercise. The stories are fables, commonly told to children in Class 2.

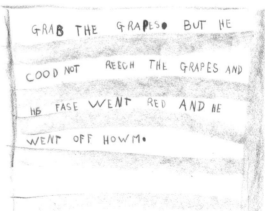

FOX WAS VERY HUNGRY.

HE RAN ON THE PATH AND SAW A BUNCH OF YUMMY GRAPES.

'I WILL EAT THOSE GRAPES', SAID THE FOX.

HE JUMPED AND HE JUMPED AND HE JUMPED.

HE SNAPPED AND HE SNAPPED AND HE SNAPPED.

'I CANNOT GET THOSE GRAPES', SAID FOX.

'THEY ARE SOUR AND FULL OF WORMS.

WHO WANTS THOSE GRAPES? NOT ME!'

FOX WAS VERY _____.

HE RAN ON THE PATH AND SAW A BUNCH OF YUMMY _____.

'I WILL _____ THOSE GRAPES', SAID THE FOX.

HE _____ AND HE _____ AND HE _____.

HE _____ AND HE _____ AND HE _____.

'I CANNOT GET THOSE GRAPES', _____ FOX.

'THEY ARE _____ AND FULL OF WORMS.

WHO WANTS THOSE GRAPES? NOT _____!'

EAT

GRAPES

HUNGRY

JUMPED

ME

SAID

SNAPPED

SOUR

Here follows examples of further cloze activities for use with other fables.

A BOY WAS WITH HIS SHEEP.

HE CALLED, 'THE WOLF, THE WOLF!'

THE BAKER CAME.

THE BUTCHER CAME AND THE LITTLE OLD LADY CAME.

THERE WAS NO WOLF TO BE SEEN.

A BOY WAS WITH HIS SHEEP.

HE CALLED, 'THE WOLF, THE WOLF!'

THE BAKER DID NOT COME.

THE BUTCHER DID NOT COME AND THE LITTLE OLD LADY DID NOT COME.

THE WOLF ATE THE BOY AND HIS SHEEP.

A BOY WAS WITH HIS _____.

HE CALLED, 'THE _____, THE _____!'

THE _____ CAME.

THE BUTCHER _____ AND THE LITTLE _____ LADY CAME.

THERE WAS NO WOLF TO BE _____.

A BOY WAS WITH HIS _____.

HE CALLED, 'THE _____, THE _____!'

THE _____ DID NOT COME.

THE BUTCHER DID NOT COME _____ THE LITTLE OLD LADY DID NOT COME.

THE WOLF _____ THE BOY AND HIS GOATS.

AND

ATE

BAKER

CAME

GOATS

OLD

SEEN

WOLF

THE FOX AND THE CROW

A CROW HAD FOUND A BLOCK OF CHEESE.

SHE SAT IN A TREE.

FOX CAME BY AND SAW THE CROW AND THE CHEESE.

FOX SAID, 'I WILL HAVE THAT BLOCK OF CHEESE'.

FOX SAID, 'MY DEAR CROW, YOU ARE SO PRETTY'.

THE CROW SAT UP AND LOOKED DOWN.

FOX SAID, 'MY DEAR CROW, YOUR BLACK FEATHERS SHINE'.

THE CROW SAT UP AND LOOKED DOWN.

FOX SAID, 'MY DEAR CROW, YOUR EYES ARE SO BRIGHT'.

THE CROW SAT UP AND LOOKED DOWN.

FOX SAID, 'YOUR SONG MUST BE PRETTY AS WELL'.

THE CROW SAT UP AND LOOKED DOWN.

THE FOX SAID, 'I WISH TO HEAR YOUR SONG'.

THE CROW SANG.

THE CHEESE FELL.

THE FOX HAD THE CHEESE AND RAN OFF.

A CROW HAD FOUND A BLOCK OF _____.

SHE SAT IN A _____.

_____ CAME BY AND SAW THE CROW AND THE CHEESE.

FOX SAID, 'I WILL HAVE THAT _____ OF CHEESE'.

FOX SAID, 'MY DEAR CROW, YOU ARE SO _____'.

THE CROW SAT UP AND LOOKED _____.

FOX SAID, 'MY DEAR CROW, YOUR _____ FEATHERS SHINE'.

THE CROW SAT _____ AND LOOKED DOWN.

FOX SAID, 'MY DEAR _____, YOUR EYES ARE SO BRIGHT'.

THE CROW SAT UP AND _____ DOWN.

FOX SAID, 'YOUR _____ MUST BE PRETTY AS WELL'.

THE CROW SAT UP AND LOOKED DOWN.

THE FOX SAID, 'I WISH TO HEAR YOUR SONG'.

THE CROW _____.

THE CHEESE _____.

THE FOX HAD THE CHEESE AND _____ OFF.

BLACK
BLOCK
CHEESE
CROW
DOWN
FELL
FOX
LOOKED
PRETTY
RAN
SANG
SONG
TREE
UP

THE LION AND THE MOUSE

A MOUSE RAN IN THE WOOD.
THE LION WAS ASLEEP.
THE MOUSE RAN OVER THE LION.
THE LION PUT HIS PAW ON THE MOUSE.
'I WILL EAT YOU', SAID THE LION.
'LET ME GO', SAID THE MOUSE.
'I MAY HELP YOU ONE DAY', SAID THE MOUSE.
'THAT IS FUNNY', SAID THE LION.
THE LION LET THE MOUSE GO.
THE LION RAN INTO A NET.
THE MOUSE CUT THE NET WITH HIS TEETH.
'THANK YOU. YOU HAVE SAVED MY LIFE', SAID THE LION.

A MOUSE RAN IN THE _____.

THE LION WAS _____.

THE _____ RAN OVER THE LION.

THE _____ PUT HIS PAW ON THE MOUSE.

'I WILL _____ YOU', SAID THE LION.

'LET ME _____', SAID THE MOUSE.

'I MAY HELP YOU ONE DAY', SAID THE MOUSE.

'THAT IS _____', SAID THE LION.

THE LION LET THE MOUSE GO.

THE LION RAN INTO A _____.

THE MOUSE CUT THE NET WITH HIS _____.

'THANK YOU. YOU HAVE SAVED MY _____', SAID THE LION.

ASLEEP	LION
EAT	MOUSE
FUNNY	NET
GO	TEETH
LIFE	WOOD

The story of St Giles

St Giles lived in a _____ in the forest. Around the place where St Giles lived grew a hedge of _____. A hind came every evening and gave him her _____ to drink. St Giles and the hind became _____. One day the king came to hunt in the _____. The hunting horns sounded and the hunters _____ the hind. The hind ran and ran. She escaped through the _____ of roses. The next day the hunters came again. The _____ saw the hind go through the hedge of roses and told the hunters to follow her. The hind lay trembling at St Giles' feet. St Giles stepped in front of the hind. One of the hunters shot an _____ and the arrow hit St Giles in his arm. The king saw what had happened and stayed with St Giles until he was _____.

spotted	king	milk	arrow	cave
friends	roses	forest	circle	better

The story of St Jerome

St Jerome lived in a monastery. One day he heard a noise. A _____ came out of the forest. He was limping. The monk went to the lion and saw that there was a _____ in its paw. He took the thorn _____ and turned to go back to the monastery. The lion _____ him and became the _____ of the monks.

The monk went every day with his _____ to fetch water for the monastery and the lion was always by their side. One day the monk was asked to help a _____ woman. He asked the lion to _____ the donkey. While he was away the lion fell _____ and the donkey was stolen. The monk thought that the lion had _____ the donkey.

From then on the lion was not treated well and had to carry the water as the donkey had done before. The lion was sad and his coat lost its shine.

Many weeks went by until the monk and the lion went to a town. There the lion _____ the donkey. He _____ to let the monk know what he had seen. The monk saw the donkey. Now he knew how _____ he had treated the lion.

The three of them went back to the monastery and from then on the lion was treated with the best care. When Jerome died the lion lay on his _____ and died too. They were _____ next to each other.

sick	thorn	donkey
spotted	unfair	grave
roared	followed	guard
pet	eaten	out
lion	asleep	buried

Chapter 29

Giving Feedback, Setting the Standards and Partner Work

- Plausible spelling and emergent planning
- Improving editing and accuracy
- Story writing

To encourage authorship, we celebrate children's exploration and expansion of phonetic strategies. For children to have a piece of work returned with lots of spelling mistakes picked out is demoralising and restricting. This child will be likely to limit their vocabulary next time to words she can spell. Of course the teacher needs to note children's mistakes to inform future teaching, but how do we strike a balance so that spelling instruction is a positive experience?

Success Criteria and Partner Feedback

We are taking ideas here from active-learning principles and recommend further reading on this methodology. We like to make it very clear to the class what skills they're practising at the beginning of a piece of work. If you can discuss 'success criteria' at the outset, it means that children know what to aim for and why they did well at the end. They also know what to aim for next time. Here's an example of what to do at the start of an English Main Lesson, Writing Saint Stories.

In the summer term of Class 2, the teacher handed out the following text so that each pair could read a copy, taken from a story the class had already heard.

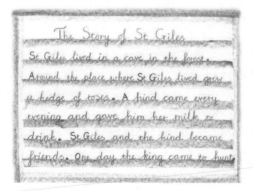
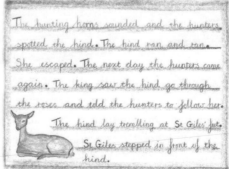

On the first day, the class read the story together. To make sure that all children followed the text, the teacher stopped regularly, asking individual children what the next word was. Then the class was given a partner task: talk for a few minutes with your partner and make a list of things you notice about how this writing looks. The class was given four minutes for discussion, after which the teacher gathered the ideas. The following list was written on the blackboard:

- Neat borders
- Neat cursive writing – all the letters are the same size and sit neatly on the line
- There is a picture.
- There are capitals for St Giles – capitals for names

The same day, the children were asked to write a story about another saint and to pay particular attention to the four points above. They were given about 25 minutes to write the piece in total but half way through, at about twelve minutes, they were asked to take a break and look at their partner's work. Could they comment on whether their working partner had managed to remember the four points? It is really important that this feedback happens before the piece of work is finished: improvements can then be made immediately and the things a child has noticed in their partner's work can be applied to his/her own work. 'Isn't it great that someone wants to copy your ideas? Your ideas are worth copying!' is the excellent unspoken message.

Improving Sentence Work

The following day, partners look at the St Giles story again, this time to have a closer look at sentences. At this stage of writing, many children have some difficulty with knowing exactly when it would be good for a sentence to finish. Quite often, they create 'run on' sentences that don't pause for breath. To help them learn the music of sentences, use this type of activity here.

Direct questions at the partners such as 'How many sentences can you find?', 'What is the shortest and what is the longest sentence?', 'What can you see at the start and at the end of each sentence?'. You could also ask a stylistic question such as 'What is a favourite / most unusual / most frequent word?'. The children may come up with:

- Full stops, capitals at the beginning of a sentence
- Number of words in a sentence
- Trembling, hind, roses etc.

You can then pull out a sentence with 'AND' in it (a sentence that has two clauses) and two, shorter sentences (that could be stuck together to make a compound sentence). Show partners how to split apart a compound sentence to make two simple sentences and vice versa. In future writing, you'll be able to say to children that they have a 'run-on' sentence somewhere and ask them to see if they can find it and split it.

You can also have a discussion about which words are most evocative and share different children's subjective experience.

These suggestions can raise curiosity and awareness among the children that it is possible to change their style to achieve a different impact when they're writing – the start of a long journey of experimentation.

Making Lists To Plan a Story

The following day the teacher has a piece of paper in her hand. She asks the class whether they remember that they made a list when they wrote the story about St Elizabeth. It looked something like this

- lived in Hungary
- princess
- noticed poor children
- took buns
- buns turned into roses

It helped to know what to write next when we wrote the story. Now the teacher shows the paper in her hand – 'On this piece of paper I have the list I wrote to help me write the story of St Giles. I wonder whether, with your partners, you can guess what was on my list.' The children scan the Story of St Giles and look for keywords. After about six minutes the class turns back to the front and teacher gathers the ideas. The children are really proud that they have managed to find most points on the teacher's list.

- cave
- roses
- hind – milk
- friends
- hunt
- escaped
- next day
- St Giles protects

The teacher observes that several pairs work very well together, but some are not too interested in their partner's thoughts.

Try a role play with the class assistant. The teacher and assistant model two kinds of partnership: first, where two children hide their lists from each other, and a second, a partnership that takes turns and where the stronger reader helps the other by putting a finger under the text. The class find this very funny. They are also very clear which of these two was a useful partnership.

In this way, several things have been modelled using the St Giles story. Children are writing by themselves and learning how to develop their work through being good partners and benefiting from others' feedback. They can begin to make lists so they include every important part of a story. They know to make neat work with essential basic sentences, capitals and full stops.

PART 7

Teaching Children to Read

Chapter 30

Supporting Early Reading Skills

- Books in Kindergarten and the home
- Three stages of reading: Emergent, Training, Fluent
- Average age of stages
- Reading practice

Here we discuss the teaching and practice of reading, concentrating on the early stages of literacy in Class 1 and 2, but we also sketch out how reading should develop in the first half of the lower school so that you know where you're aiming.

Before Class 1, children will usually have had many picture books read to them. Young children often associate reading a book with bedtime or otherwise peaceful times, so having a book corner can be a wise classroom ingredient from Kindergarten up. Enthusiasm for books and reading in the home environment is fundamental to children developing their own love of reading later. If parents model enjoyment of reading, children will want to do the same. Further, essential pre-reading skills that come from 'reading' at home include scanning the page from left to right and turning the pages in the right direction. Children will usually know the letters of their own names, or other familiar words, so they will understand that a symbol represents a sound. They will also be aurally literate: having heard and recalled many stories told with or without a book, perhaps also gaining practice in re-telling their own. We recommend that you have books in your classroom that are beautiful to look at, that children can 'read' independently, or that can be read and shown to the class, in addition to oral story-telling.

Parents of Kindergarten children sometimes wonder what to say when their children ask a technical reading-skills question such as, 'What does that say?' or 'How do you write ...?' Children with older siblings may be particularly aware and curious.[1] Parents may also ask how to respond when relatives want to introduce literacy-related materials to Kindergartners. As the teacher, you need to help your parents sing from the same hymn-sheet as the school.

---

1 See footnote page 212.

We suggest that as a rule of thumb, parents satisfy a child's curiosity to the best of their ability, without giving surplus information. This is a really important educational principle. As a teacher, and in your advice to parents, we suggest using an image of a facilitator. Think of yourself as removing obstacles to that child's own, natural learning impulse – let them determine the pace and the direction. This can require subtle observation and listening: it can be hard not to project your own excitement or preconceived ideas on to a young child in this situation. Parents don't tend to see their own children objectively and, especially when a child shows a particular aptitude or a weakness, this can trigger strong feelings. In our present-day culture, reading holds an emblematic place in our concept of success. Wouldn't life be different if we considered tree-climbing, weaving or emotional balance to be the epitome of strength and prowess? Later in this part, we give further guidance about helping parents with the challenge of their child being educated according to a different schedule from the mainstream.

Once children are in a whole-class learning environment and are being led by you, the teacher, we encourage you to give the parents information so that they may actively participate. For example, when asked a spelling question, tell them that it may be more effective to emphasise the sounds the letters make, rather than their names (e.g. /sss/ rather than /ess/.) Throughout the book, there are ideas for engaging parents with literacy practice, especially when children need extra help.

Reading Stages

Emergent reading

We find it useful to think of there being roughly three phases of learning to read for young children with average abilities.[2] With emergent reading, children use their auditory and visual memories for recognising regular and irregular keywords. They build up their 'bank' of knowledge about how the written language is put together. This phase requires structured, systematic teaching. It's also highly variable for children – some can absorb phonics seemingly without effort, while others need careful, highly repetitive instruction. Much research points to phonological and auditory processing being the key indicator of difficulty in this area, primarily because it prevents children from effectively memorising.[3]

---

1 Occasionally, you may hear of a child 'teaching themselves' to read. This is a bit misleading because, of course, they must have acquired the information somewhere. However, there indeed are some children who can retain information from a single explanation and apply it immediately. Parents in this situation will be likely to want to feed this child's strength. If you are called upon to give advice, suggest that parents observe the child closely: signs of fatigue mean stop and do something else, more questions mean perhaps more 'food'. Ask parents to consider the way the child is learning rather than the level of content. Ideally, you want a child to be having a whale of a time – it's play. At this age, it need have absolutely no suggestion of toil. We also advise keeping exclamations of the child's brilliance rather subtle: after all, if something is very easy for them, it's not such an amazing achievement. Use feedback about how much they are enjoying trying to learn rather than how 'successful' they are, and tell parents to think of the long term. Such restraint will pay off in preserving a child's own spontaneity, imagination and natural learning pace – you will be preventing cultural values boxing them into a corner. Childhood talent may presage adult brilliance but it may not – the spirit is a subtle animal.
2 A much-cited formal definition of reading acquisition was set out by LInnea C Ehri in 1995 in the *Journal of Research in Reading*. See Beech (2005) for a summary and critique of her model. Also see Wolf (2008) for a more detailed discussion.
3 Reid, 2009, p. 99. For an extended discussion of this issue, see Chapter 7 of Reid (2009) with detail on the variation for children with difficulties such as dyslexia, or in learning to read different languages.

In a Steiner Waldorf school, this phase usually lasts between the ages of approximately 6 and 8 years of age. The entire book so far has been dedicated to showing you how to teach children to become writers. Emergent spelling is particularly useful for reinforcing phonological acuity.[4] Via the active need to communicate their own interesting thoughts, emergent *reading* is an automatic by-product.

> Frith (2002) puts forward the view that writing and the desire to write helps to enhance the alphabetic stage of reading because spelling is linked more directly to the alphabetic principle and letter–sound relationships. This view is also supported by the work of Bradley and Bryant (1991), who found that beginner readers in the process of acquiring the skills of the alphabetic stage use visual strategies for reading, but phonological strategies for spelling.
>
> (Reid, 2009, p. 101)

In Class 1, children will be reading their own upper-case writing using poetry, as described in Part 6. You could also create your own readers for reading practice. The poems used for writing in Part 6 could be included in a poetry book that the children write themselves, and then read back. We have also seen an example of this where a teacher pasted upper-case words over the text of *Oxford Reading Tree* books. As their first experience of reading books, the children were 'safe' because they only met words that they'd been taught to decode in a font they knew.

It will depend upon when you decide to introduce lower-case, print and cursive letters, as to when you want to develop routine book-reading practice. In our case, this happened for quite a few children who were keen and beginning to read. Towards the very end of Class 1, the teacher decided to lightly introduce the 'book letters'. One day, they were stuck on the wall below the upper-case letters, and the class spent some time looking at them and finding similarities and differences. It was explained that we never have to write those letters, but they do appear in books so we must know them for reading printed books. An alphabet ruler was made which the children took home to use over the summer holidays.

A B C D E F G H I J K L M N O P Q R S T U V W X Y Z

a b c d e f g h i j k l m n o p q r s t u v w x y z

a b c d e f g h i j k l m n o p q r s t u v w x y z

---

4 Part 4; Adams, 1990; Reid, 2009.

The whole class then addressed this more formally early in Class 2.[5] Schedule reading practice in your timetable so that children are reading for at least ten minutes, five days a week. We achieved this with a combination of methods.

- Partners would read with each other, one using a pointer and the other reading out loud. This might involve pairing a more able pupil with a less able peer.
- Parents or a classroom assistant might read with a small group or a few children at a time for one-to-one, or a section of the Main Lesson or a subject lesson.
- The teacher could hear individuals or small groups read while the rest of the class has a free drawing activity.
- In addition, you may wish to create a system whereby children take home readers to read aloud to their parents and return.

Make sure that you have the opportunity to monitor progress regularly. We suggest you have your own record of how a child is reading every two weeks, not just the feedback from another reading helper.

Choose one or two full reading schemes for your shelves with appropriate numbers of copies for your class. Not everyone will be reading at the same level simultaneously. The virtues of a reading scheme are that phonics and keywords are systematically reinforced, and that progress is obvious and trackable.[6] However, if the children have been working solidly with phonics and keywords in earlier terms, you may find, as we did, that only a few children needed the reading schemes. Perhaps half the class used them in the first term, but after Christmas only a quarter of the class (with identified dyslexic-type difficulties) used them. Your shelf will also need plenty of simple chapter books, with some additional really good picture books for aesthetic enjoyment. Over the year, for most children you will see their reading capacity outstrip their writing. Hopefully, if the child's self-concept as a writer is well anchored, it ought to mean that writing confidence is not impaired but, rather, enhanced by their exposure to correct spellings and greater vocabulary. The lion's share of your timetabled work should still emphasise writing using advanced phonics and keywords.

Training Reading

In Class 2, most children will be crossing over from the emergent stage into the next phase of reading, which we have called 'training reading'. At this point the code is mostly mastered, but the child does not yet have speedy, automatic word-recognition (average Steiner Waldorf age 7 to 9 years). At this point there isn't much to teach, and yet reading may feel like a chore because it's not easy. Hundreds of words must gradually become completely effortless to read. Until reading is easy, the cognitive effort must be directed into the word-deciphering rather than only understanding the meaning of the text.

---

5 Again, the timing of this is flexible. We suggest that reading begins to be more strongly promoted in the classroom somewhere between Easter in C1 and Christmas in C2. We know that there is significant variability among Class Teachers in this matter.
6 There are many published schemes. We have used the Oxford Reading Tree books, Read Write Inc and others.

Similarly, texts that are unfamiliar in concept or difficult in wording or structure require active attention for comprehension. But to the extent that you are directing that attention to the mechanics of the system, it is not available to support your understanding. Only if your ability to recognise and capture the meanings of the words on a page is rapid, effortless, and automatic will you have available the cognitive energy and resources upon which skillful comprehension depends. (See Adams, 1990, p. 4)

Take care with book choice at this stage – you want books to be both attractive and pitched at the right level. Children are moving from sharing their reading with another person to working silently and independently. For this to happen, children ought to be able to accurately decode nine out of every ten words in a given text. If the book is more demanding than this, maintaining momentum will be too hard and motivation will drop.

Most reading schemes finish at a standard reading age of about 8 or 8.5. Children will move on to simple chapter books. Choose books with fairly big print, an appealing plot, some illustration and a small amount of text per page. For many children, a series that hooks them into the satisfaction of finishing book after book is very effective. Some of the most successful authors for this age range (publishers often sell them for the ages 5–8) use very repetitive language and plot. While it may seem uninspiring for adults, this style is perfect for trainee reader success. For those who take longer to master reading skills, look for specialist publishers such as Barrington Stoke, who publish books with an older interest but a lower reading level, on cream coloured paper using a dyslexia-friendly font. In addition, there are often 'large print' versions available of the normal books, sometimes stocked in local libraries, for children who have difficulty with visual tracking.

Parental help is now an essential part of ensuring that the children gain enough exposure to text.[7] Practically speaking, there isn't usually enough time in every school day to give over to reading practice once the children reach Class 3. Yet daily practice is still very strongly advised. Teachers will need to guide home-reading quite closely at this stage, setting book choice and reasonable targets for homework. Remember that reading time will be competing for attention with after-school activities, other homework and other social media.

Parents will probably appreciate some guidance on supporting their child. Good strategies include the following:

- Tell the parent to wait for five seconds before giving an unknown word
- Prompt a child to decode by sounding out the first 1–3 letters (usually the first syllable) to help them guess
- For an advanced word, just give it to them instantly to maintain momentum
- Only correct a mistake if it's necessary for a child to understand the meaning of the text; otherwise, let it go[8]

---

7 Clark & Picton, 2012.
8 This is in line with the tactics competent readers use: an unknown word is guessed or glossed over without concern as the reader continues with the narrative of the piece.

One way to keep tabs on progress is to issue children with a reading diary. There are some commercially available, such as one we have used published by edplanbooks.com, or you can make your own. The diary has space for information about each book, for setting reading targets and for parents to give feedback. For those children who are reluctant to practise at this stage, and who perhaps fall into a category of *can read won't read*, it can be important to close the loop of communication. Once children are in front of their own chapter books, they can appear to be reading but might not actually be making much progress. A reading diary prevents them from giving up too easily before they've cracked a book. It can be a fine line to encourage independence, while still providing enough support to enable persistence.

Fluent Reading

At this level, a child would achieve a standard reading age of 9+ years of age. This reader would be able to read the 200 most common words effortlessly. They would feel confident enough to tackle books with relatively sophisticated vocabulary, and could have a go at guessing unfamiliar words with less common phonological elements. Books at this level might have extended sentence structure, descriptive or atmospheric content, a smaller print size and no illustrations: they might now begin to be described as 'literature'. The reader is now likely to start asking what words mean, or making plausible guesses based on context. A child's thought-processes begin to expand and alter *because* they are now reading, and so their ability to learn is arguably affected symbiotically by their ability to access text.[9] Now, a reader will usually be developing personal taste about genre – fantasy, humour, suspense etc. They also absorb a great deal about how to write formally, imitating grammar and syntax without really having to think about it.

In a Steiner school, we expect this reading maturation to take place in Classes 3 and 4. This means that they begin to match standard reading levels and are no longer 'behind' because of the later start to formal learning. As far as the class teacher is concerned, the job of instruction of reading technique is mostly done. However, promoting reading for pleasure is not something to be taken for granted. Research shows that reading for pleasure is associated with many positive educational and social outcomes. Vocabulary and writing ability are, unsurprisingly, linked, but even when socio-economic and other variable background factors are taken into account, reading for pleasure correlates with all-round higher achievement. Further, there is a correlation between stronger social and emotional attributes, even such as adults being less likely to report feeling lonely.[10] As a life skill and a pillar to support all academic achievement, we believe that reading for pleasure is one of the single most valuable goals a school can have for its children. In recognition of this, many mainstream state schools now have a 'Drop Everything and Read' time held every day,

---

9 Keith Stanovich (1986) set out a highly influential argument termed the Matthew effect of reading level based on his research. This showed that at around the age of 9, children's IQ began to climb as a result of being able to read. If children failed to read fluently by this age, their IQ level measured by intelligence tests would not keep pace with their development.
10 Clark & Rumbold, Reading for Pleasure: A Research Overview, 2006; Department for Education, 2012.

where all children and staff must pick up their book and read silently. Perhaps in a digital age, this kind of intervention becomes vital.

A word about some readers with dyslexic-type difficulties: you may come across a student who can become fairly fluent in reading and possibly achieve a reading age of 9+, and yet they are still reluctant readers even at age 11+. There may be other reasons for this, but sometimes a high-functioning dyslexic child has a very strong photographic memory. They deploy this to acquire an impressive 'sight-bank' of the majority of the key words they need for reading. However, if they haven't fully mastered the basic code of phonics and syllables, they may continue to be poor spellers and slow writers. They may also, at an age of 11+ for example, dislike reading because as the vocabulary extends, they cannot decode and decipher meanings. Thorough teaching at the outset is therefore really necessary to prevent such difficulties. We would hope that this might arise when a new child joins your class, for example, rather than with someone who has had the benefit of your teaching after reading this book! However, use some of the strategies for earlier stages to fill in phonic gaps and hopefully, the situation can be remedied.

All children need encouragement to read and diversify their book diet as they mature. The fluent reader will usually respond well to peer enthusiasm for books and to a positive book culture in the school. Parents, teachers and students will need to work as a team to achieve it. Children can be encouraged to branch out into classical and contemporary genres and authors by verbal and written book reviews, book clubs and other activities where they can inspire each other. Here are a few ideas for promoting books:

- Hold half-termly book days where children bring in their current book and ask desk partners or small groups to share a few sentences each about them
- You can read a chapter of a recommended book as a 'teaser'
- Use a traffic-light recommendation system: use three different colour slips and ask the children to fill in a green slip if they liked a book, yellow if they did not like it much but thought someone else might, and red if they really didn't like it. We stuck them on the wall so others could see them and could choose a book that was popular. Vary this according to your age-group. In Class 3, children could just write the title and the author, but in Class 5 they would write a short summary, for example. This might lead to developing a recommendation list for each school year to leave behind for the next class.

Help parents by raising the subject of choosing 'good' books. At this fluent stage, matching difficulty level with appropriate content can be a fine art. Parents may feel clueless in the face of a sea of unknown authors in the bookshop, and publishers often exaggerate suitable age boundaries. Parents and teachers may also go through a reading Rubicon: a child's reading strengths will lead them into places one can't control. Adults haven't got time to read everything first, and sometimes children may read not-very-nice things. If some children are drawn to edgy or unfavourable subjects, we suggest that parents don't say 'no' but instead provide a greater variety and range of material to try. They might value accessing the websites – www.goodreads.com or the American site http://readingandwritingproject.org/. In addition, even though children at this level can read by themselves, we still value reading aloud in the classroom and at home, where possible. Accompanied in this way, children can access literature at a deeper level, and can be encouraged to branch out in style, as well as benefiting from mutual enjoyment.

In our school, we re-stocked classroom bookshelves using a variety of strategies. First, parents have been encouraged to bring in books that their children may have already been through and won't want to read again. To stimulate students in choosing new books, we held some one-off targeted reading lessons. In one Class 4, children came up with excellent suggestions for choosing a good book:

- Look at the front cover, title and the back cover summary and reviews
- Flick through and look at the print size or try a few pages
- Find authors you like and keep reading them
- Find types of books you like (genre) and try similar books
- Ask a friend for a recommendation!

We also began whole-school activities, centred around World Book Day[11] which is held in March every year. We ran a sponsored Readathon,[12] which enabled students to set a personal reading target for a two-week period, raise money against this target and then challenge themselves. They raised a small fortune for books and story-tellers for children in hospital, and a voucher for books for our school came back to us. Look on websites such as the National Literacy Trust or Book Trust for further information about resources. Other ideas include:

- Setting up a book club within school
- Reading-room lunch hours
- Running a book fair and inviting authors to speak or give workshops

In an age where children often have access to many types of media, books need to compete for their attention. In our experience, if a school can create a buzz about them, especially as children emerge into the excitement of independent reading, this can then provide a valid alternative.

---

11 See www.WorldBookDay.com.
12 See www.readathon.com.

Chapter 31

When Will My Child Read?
Communication with Parents

- What parents want to know – normal curriculum expectations
- How to support literacy learning
- Reassurance for SEN situations
- Assessment and results

Many parents who choose Steiner education for their child, however confident they are, may be under some sort of pressure to defend their choice. Family members may be unfamiliar with the education and feel doubtful, or even disapproving. Relatives' and friends' children may attain skills earlier than those in the Steiner school, which can lead to difficult comparisons. Indeed, it is counter-cultural to educate children 'slowly'. Teachers do well to take these worries seriously and find ways to support the parents in their choice. It will help if these worries are openly acknowledged at a parents' evening; 'We know that you might be dealing with these pressures and it isn't always easy.'

Your parents' evenings are about giving feedback to parents about what happens in classroom life, but you also have a role to play in educating the parents about the Waldorf learning journey. Explain that individual children's progress and needs will be dealt with separately. With respect to literacy – one of the most sensitive concerns that many parents have – Class 1 parents' evenings should include:

- Steiner's views on child development
- How the curriculum relates to this
- How and when literacy is taught
- When you expect the majority of the children to be at a level with mainstream education
- How you will support the potential dyslexic children and what to look out for
- How parents can support a child's writing and reading efforts at home

Give a clear picture of what lies behind the curriculum. Talk about the whole journey of story material in one of your first parents' evenings. Tell them how it moves from fairy tales to fables, legends, Old Testament, Norse mythology, Greek mythology and history, the ancient cultures, Rome etc., and explain how all these respond to the child's developmental stage. It is really useful for parents to see the grand scale of where you're heading. It gives them clear information to share (ammunition?!) in conversations with others outside the school. It also might be possible to ask them to reserve some stories for the appropriate age – e.g. please stay clear of the ancient Greek stories as we will enjoy these in Class 5. Referring to Class 1 in particular, explain how fairy tales feed the child's imagination. Apart from their entertainment value, they are imparting a sort of vocabulary of human archetypes, dark and light, and provide, in a dream-like way, a landscape of the unconscious. This is a hidden resource for adulthood imagination, a repertoire for their later conscious understanding of the psyche.

Give an account of what is different now that children have left Kindergarten and that their new capacities fit them for learning. For example, Rudolf Steiner said that at this age, the child's attention is freer for concentrating and manipulating concepts because of their physical maturation. He recommended sensory learning using concrete materials to enable deep absorption of new material, however abstract.[13] Share how you plan to introduce the different elements of literacy in quite some detail. You might choose to show how a letter comes out of the sound in the fairy tale, how blending sounds is practised through a game, or how writing will start. This will help parents understand that, although you're not practising reading in Class 1, you are doing all sorts of activities that will underpin the reading process when it eventually begins.

Early in the year it's a good idea to give your parents information about how to support their child's literacy learning along the way. In addition to the notes in Part 7 about how to support reading, explain to parents that they can expect their children to make spelling mistakes that you will not correct for a while. In line with the principle of encouraging authorship, let parents know that phonetic, plausible spelling is an excellent stepping stone for children towards writing whatever they can say. Pointing out spelling mistakes, even when it is done in the most friendly way, can be detrimental. You don't want children to confine themselves to very simple words they know they can spell.

So give parents some guidance on how to respond to their child's spelling requests. Sometimes it may be right to just give the correct spelling. At other times a parent may ask whether the child knows the first letter, or any of the sounds in the word. Usually, the trickiest part of the word is the vowel. For example, if a child asks how to write 'rain', their parent could respond with, 'The /ā/ is made by 'a' and 'i' working together. Do you know how to write the rest?'

If a child has already had a go and asks the parent if it is right, perhaps the best answer is, 'That is a good way to write that word. I can easily read it.' If the child persists, parents could say, 'The grown-ups usually write it like this. See, you have the beginning just right.' If the child shows their parent their writing proudly and does not ask about spelling, it's most encouraging if the parent

---

13 Steiner, 1996, p.23

just tries to read it or, if this is impossible, asks the child to read it to them.

Explaining to parents how to distinguish between letter sounds and names and showing them how to say the sounds clearly is a good idea. For example, we say /b/ as it sounds in the word 'bag' and not /buh/, /m/ as it sounds in 'man' and not /em/. You might also have told parents how we work on splitting words into sounds, possibly using the troll game described in Chapter 10, so you can explain how we say the letter sounds when we try to write a word.

Assessment and Results

It is very reassuring to give parents a rough benchmark of when to expect the majority of the children to achieve the different stages of writing and reading. In state schools, children are regularly tested for their progress, and while your parents may be happy that this isn't the way you do things, nonetheless a guideline gives parents confidence. Explain to parents what assessments you run in class and what they are used for.

You may also describe what sort of support there will be for those who struggle with literacy. Remember that there will be several parents in your parents group who will have experienced difficulty with learning, and who are possibly dyslexic. Emotions can run high for parents who have suffered from stigma or low self-esteem about this; they will be sensitive about whether their children will feel the same. Welcome parents' sharing of this sort of experience.

In our school, the class whose work is described in this book were assessed at the end of Main Lesson blocks with tests designed by the teacher. When they had their routine, bi-annual assessment from the learning support department, the median reading level at the end of Class 2 was above average for their age, according to a standardised test, despite not having had any formal reading instruction in Class 1.[14] All children enjoyed writing, though we did not carry out any formal test for this.[15] In Class 2, on the whole, those who had dyslexic-type difficulties were not strongly aware of their learning difference. In Class 3, in line with the growth of self-consciousness, they did become more aware that they found writing and reading harder than others in the class, but by then a solid scaffolding was in place and they experienced themselves as struggling but progressing. Part 7 on reading development gives more information about average progress for Steiner schools.

---

14 Salford Sentence Reading Test.
15 There were several children in the class struggling with difficulties of a dyslexic nature. Two of them were assessed by the learning support department in the Autumn term of Class 3. In response to the open question, 'What do you like most in class?' both independently replied, 'Writing!'.

APPENDIX 1

Need to Know Phonics

The English language is about 80 percent phonetically regular, though still complex. All class teachers should have a working overview of phonics for teaching literacy. The National Literacy Strategy (1998) and the subsequent Government reviews and revisions since, as well as all commercially available literacy schemes, agree on some essentials about phonics, despite many contentious debates. Phonological awareness is agreed to be the critical factor in a child's success with coding for writing and reading (Reid, 2009).

The 44 Phonemes of English and Some Common Ways of Representing Them

Consonant phonemes with consistent spellings

/b/	**b**at, ra**bb**it
/d/	**d**og, da**dd**y
/g/	**g**irl, gi**gg**le
/h/	**h**ot
/l/	**l**og, lo**ll**y
/m/	**m**at, su**mm**er
/n/	**n**ut, di**nn**er
/p/	**p**ig, su**pp**er
/r/	**r**at, ca**rr**y
/t/	**t**op, pa**tt**er
/y/	**y**ellow
/th/	**th**is (voiced) **th**ing (unvoiced)

Consonant phonemes with alternative spellings

/k/	**c**at, **k**ing, ba**ck**, **sch**ool, **qu**een (also the /k/ sound in bo**x**)
/s/	**s**un, pre**ss**, **c**ircle
/f/	**f**un, **ph**oto
/j/	**j**am, **g**inger, bri**dge**
/w/	**w**orm, q**u**een
/z/	**z**oo, pin**s**, **x**ylophone
/v/	**v**an (one exception: o**f**)
/sh/	**sh**eep, sta**ti**on, **ch**ef
/ch/	**ch**in, i**tch**
/ng/	si**ng** and also pi**n**k
/zh/	mea**s**ure, a**z**ure

Short and long vowel phonemes

/a/	b**a**g
/e/	b**e**t, br**ea**d, s**ai**d
/i/	b**i**g, c**y**linder
/o/	t**o**p, w**a**s
/u/	b**u**n, l**o**ve
/ae/	d**ay**, p**ai**n, g**a**te, gr**ea**t
/ee/	f**ee**t, s**ea**t, P**e**te, m**e**
/ie/	t**ie**, t**igh**t, fl**y**, t**i**me
/oa/	b**oa**t, gr**ow**, b**o**ne, t**oe**, g**o**
/ue/	bl**ue**, m**oo**n, gr**ew**, fl**u**te, y**ou**

Other vowel phonemes

/oo/	g**oo**d, p**u**t, c**ou**ld, w**o**lf
/ur/	ch**ur**ch, b**ir**d, h**er**b, **ear**th, w**or**d
/ar/	st**ar**t, f**a**ther
/or/	c**or**n, d**oor**, sh**ore**, r**oar**, y**our**
/aw/	p**aw**, t**au**t, t**a**ll, t**a**lk, t**augh**t
/ow/	cl**ow**n, sh**ou**t
/oy/	b**oy**, **oi**l
/ear/	n**ear**, d**eer**, h**ere**
/air/	ch**air**, sh**are**, th**ere**
'schwa'	see glossary: farm**er**, doct**or**, gramm**ar**, met**re**, col**our**, Americ**a**

APPENDIX 2

Further Letter Introductions

Other letter introductions could be made in the following ways. The *Rumplestiltskin* letter can be taken from the Grimm's fairy tale.

ROUND AND ROUND ROLLS THE REEL
RUMPLESTILTSKIN FILLS THE REEL
FILLS THE REEL WITH GOLDEN THREAD
BUT WHAT WILL RUMPLESTILTSKIN GET?
I'll HAVE YOUR CHILD, I'LL HAVE YOUR SON
UNLESS YOU NAME ME WHEN IT'S DONE
RUMPLESTILTSKIN RAN AROUND.
MY REAL NAME CANNOT BE FOUND.

The Tower letter could come from the Grimm's fairy tale *Rapunzel*.

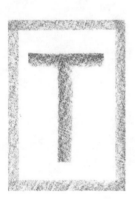

AT THE TOP OF HER TALL TOWER
TWISTING TWINE HOUR BY HOUR
RAPUNZEL SITS AND ALL SHE SEES
ARE THE TOPS OF THE TALLEST TREES.
TWISTING TWENTY TWINES A DAY
TILL THE PRINCE TAKES HER AWAY.

The H can be the Happy Hans letter with Grimm's fairy tale *Hans in Luck*.

HAPPY HANS HURRIES HOME,
HEAVES THE HEAVY GOLD ALONE.
HOW HAPPY MUST THAT RIDER BE,
THAT HANDSOME HORSE IS SURE FOR ME.
HOW USEFUL IS THE PLACID COW,
I'LL SWAP HIM FOR MY HORSE RIGHT NOW.
I'LL HAVE THE PIG THE HEAVY GOOSE,
THE HEAVY STONES I'LL NEVER LOOSE.
HERE'S TO LUCK SAID HAPPY HANS
AS THEY FELL IN THE WELL, JUST BY CHANCE.

The princesses letter with Grimm's fairy tale *The Twelve Dancing Princesses*.

PITTER PATTER PITTER PATTER GO PRETTY PRINCESSES FEET
PITTER PATTER PITTER PATTER DOWN THE STEPS THEIR PRINCE TO MEET
PIPES ARE PLAYING, DRUMS ARE POUNDING,
PRINCES DANCING, TRUMPETS SOUNDING.
PITTER PATTER PITTER PATTER GO PRETTY PRINCESSES FEET
PITTER PATTER PITTER PATTER DOWN THE STEPS THEIR PRINCE TO MEET

It is quite possible to teach a letter not from a story but from another image the children have strongly in their mind. In one class the teacher's youngest son Laurence was a keen unicyclist. The children in the class really looked up at him and so the L became the Larry letter.

LONG-LEGGED LARRY LEAPT LIGHTLY ON TO HIS UNICYCLE

The N could be the No Never letter with a poem the children said with gusto. The image was that of a farmer who needed to protect his fields.

NO NEVER SAID THE FARMER
NO NEVER YOU ENTER
NO NEVER YOU GO
INTO THE FIELD
IF THE FENCE TELLS YOU NO!

The Y has a number of common sounds and can either be a consonant or a vowel. Perhaps this one can be introduced without an image but with the following rhyme so that the children can remember the different sounds and the vowel or consonant character of this letter.

THE LETTER Y IS AN AWESOME FELLOW
IT LIKES TO SAY /Ŷ/ AS IN YES AND YELLOW
BUT WHEN AS A VOWEL IT WISHES TO BE
IT SAYS /Ῑ/ (rhythm), /Ī/ (why), OR EVEN /Ē/ (happy).

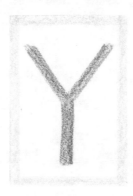

As you speed up towards the end of the collection of consonants, some can be introduced briefly with a tongue twister; you could also introduce several at one time.

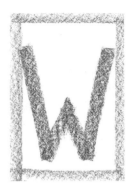

WILD WINTER WINDS
WHIP THE WATER IN THE SEA
WILD WINTER WATER
MAKES THE WAVES WASH OVER ME
I WILL WAIT UNTIL THE SUMMER
WHEN THE WATER'S NICE AND WARM
WHEN THE WEATHER IS MUCH BETTER
AND THERE IS NO WINTER STORM.

Perhaps the letters V, Z and Q can be introduced together in one story. Make sure to give the children a strong image of the Q needing the U to accompany her everywhere.

In one class a story was told about a queen living in a valley:

The valley could only be reached by a 'zig zag path' over the mountains. Often lightning and thunder accompanied such a journey. The queen was always scared and it became so bad that she could only stay in one room in the palace. One day a jester called Vincent came over the mountains to visit the palace. He was accompanied by a stray dog. The dog was also a very fearful creature and when they entered the queen's room to entertain her, the dog trembled and quaked and tried to hide behind the jester. The queen comforts the dog and forgets all about her own fears. She asks the jester for the dog's name but he says he never knew its name and always just called, 'hey you' when he wants it to come. The queen and the dog become inseparable and through looking after the dog the queen overcomes her fear.

The story is again followed by a picture and a poem.

VALIANT VINCENT TRAVELLED FAR
TO THE VAST VALLEY LED HIS STAR
THE QUEEN SAT QUIETLY QUAKING WITH FEAR
WHEN VINCENT, THE JESTER, AND HIS DOG CAME NEAR
THEY'D CROSSED THE MOUNTAIN PATH; ZIG, ZAG,
AS THE LIGHTNING FLASHED; ZIP, ZAP, ZIP ZAP.
WHILE THE DOG SAT QUIETLY QUAKING WITH FEAR
QUITE QUICKLY HE MADE THE QUEEN'S FEAR DISAPPEAR.
NOW THEY STAYED TOGETHER THE DOG AND THE QUEEN
WITHOUT 'U' THE Q IS NEVER SEEN.

There remains the X. This is a very difficult letter to find an image or to write a poem for. The image of xylophone could be used, perhaps with the musician lifting up her sticks in a cross every time she had finished playing. However the sound of X at the start of xylophone is /z/. This can be confusing rather than helpful. As the X mostly says its usual sounds /ks/ or/gs/ at the end of words a poem would not be so helpful. Perhaps this is one to introduce just by practising its shape and telling the children what sounds it can make. Make sure that later on you return to this sound and clarify the difference between six and sticks.

The Alphabet

APPENDIX 3

100 Most Common Words

100 Most Common Words

1 THE	2 BE	3 TO	4 OF	5 AND
6 A	7 IN	8 THAT	9 HAVE	10 I
11 IT	12 FOR	13 NOT	14 ON	15 WITH
16 HE	17 AS	18 YOU	19 DO	20 AT
21 THIS	22 BUT	23 HIS	24 BY	25 FROM
26 THEY	27 WE	28 SAY	29 HER	30 SHE
31 OR	32 AN	33 WILL	34 MY	35 ONE
36 ALL	37 WOULD	38 THERE	39 THEIR	40 WHAT
41 SO	42 UP	43 OUT	44 IF	45 ABOUT
46 WHO	47 GET	48 WHICH	49 GO	50 ME
51 WHEN	52 MAKE	53 CAN	54 LIKE	55 TIME

56 NO	57 JUST	58 HIM	59 KNOW	60 TAKE
61 PEOPLE	62 INTO	63 YEAR	64 YOUR	65 GOOD
66 SOME	67 COULD	68 THEM	69 SEE	70 OTHER
71 THAN	72 THEN	73 NOW	74 LOOK	75 ONLY
76 COME	77 IT'S	78 OVER	79 THINK	80 ALSO
81 BACK	82 AFTER	83 USE	84 TWO	85 HOW
86 OUR	87 WORK	88 FIRST	89 WELL	90 WAY
91 EVEN	92 NEW	93 WANT	94 BECAUSE	95 ANY
96 THESE	97 GIVE	98 DAY	99 MOST	100 US

Useful Mnemonics

PEOPLE People Eat Oranges, People Like Eggs.
WOULD Would Old Uncle Len Dance?
COULD Could Old Uncle Len Dance?
SHOULD Should Old Uncle Len Dance?
BECAUSE Big Elephants Can't Always Use Small Exits

APPENDIX 4

Words for Games

Words for Syllable Counting

In syllable counting we perform an action – clap, bounce ball, move counter – for each syllable of the word. In sound counting we perform an action – clap, bounce ball, move counter – for each sound (phoneme) of the word.

UPSET	TENNIS	INTO	MAGNET	TRUMPET
PROBLEM	BEYOND	DEFEND	EXPAND	CONTENT
TARGET	ARMY	HARDLY	GARDEN	MARKET
PARTLY	CARPET	SHARPLY	REPORT	REPORTER
ORDER	PERSON	PERHAPS	PERFECT	COLLECTOR
INSTRUCTOR	INSPECTOR	CONDUCTOR	RADIATOR	CALCULATOR
ADMISSION	PERMISSION	MUSICIAN	ESPECIALLY	EXPLOSION
TELEVISION	TELEPHONE	GEOGRAPHY	PHOTOGRAPH	FANTASTIC
PICNIC	GIGANTIC	PARACHUTE	MACHINERY	ARCHITECT
CHARACTER	ORCHESTRA	BEHAVIOUR	BEGINNING	FORGETTING

FORGOTTEN	ADMITTED	REGRETTED	MARVELLOUS	ACCIDENTAL
SPECIAL	SENTIMENTAL	HOSPITAL	EXCEPTIONAL	CATHEDRAL
ANIMAL	COURAGE	EXAMPLE	PRINCIPLE	IMPOSSIBLE
TERRIBLE	FURNITURE	CONSIDERATION	INSPECTION	EXAMINATION
ADVENTURE	COMPOSITION	PROCEDURE	INFORMATION	PREPARATION
CLOUD	DRAIN	SPROUT	SCRATCH	STREET
STRAIGHT	SPLASH	BRAIN	SWIM	TWIST
BREAD	CRAMP	POND	LAMP	JUMP
PLUMP	CLENCH	CRUNCH		

Words for Sound Counting

HAD	BED	HID	BUG	LEG
BIG	JAM	CAN	TEN	TIN
TOP	MAP	JET	FIT	SUN
CAT	YET	FOX	DESK	DUSK
SPELT	SPOT	TRIP	GRAB	FLAG
SPOT	NEST	SLUG	DROP	DRAG
FROG	BRUSH	SPLASH	SCRAP	CRISP
FROST	SCRUB	STRAND	TRENCH	STAMP
TRAMP	JUMP	STOMP	SCREAM	BLUE
SPRINT	SPRAY	BLACK	SPRAIN	SLOW
BROWN	SCRAPE	CROAK	CRUNCH	PLOT
PLANT	PLUG	CRAB	FRIEND	BREAK
SPOT	CRY	TRAIN	GREEN	TREE
SNOW	GRAB	TRAY	STRAP	STOP

TRAMP	PLAIT	PLOUGH	CREEPY	CLAP
CLOUD	DRAIN	SPROUT	SCRATCH	STREET
STRAIGHT	SPLASH	BRAIN	SWIM	TWIST
BREAD	CRAMP	POND	LAMP	PLUMP

Word Bingo

Here is a blank Bingo sheet for copying.

		WORD BINGO		

Possible words for Odd-One-Out

Rhyming

A child who has difficulties with discrimination of the sounds in words could do an 'Odd-One-Out' exercise. The adult says a short series of words to the child and the child must identify the word that does not rhyme or does not have the same initial sound etc.

DAD	BAD	HAD	SAD	PEG
CAN	FAN	MAN	LID	PAN
BED	HEAD	MUG	RED	FED
WIN	BIN	TWIN	PIN	HOP
CAT	SIT	FAT	HAT	SAT
FOX	PET	WET	YET	MET
HIT	FUN	PIT	SIT	FIT
GOT	COT	CUP	HOT	NOT
HUT	CUT	NUT	SHUT	BIG
DAD	BAD	HAD	SAD	MAP
CAN	FAN	MAN	CAT	PAN
BED	HEAD	LEG	RED	FED
CAT	MAP	FAT	HAT	SAT
LEG	PET	WET	YET	MET
HIT	WIN	PIT	SIT	FIT
GOT	COT	DOG	HOT	NOT
HUT	CUT	NUT	SHUT	BUG
BEST	TWIG	NEST	WEST	VEST
BRUSH	RUSH	BLUSH	CRUSH	BUG
JUST	MUST	FISH	TRUST	RUST
LAND	SAND	BRUSH	HAND	STAND
TENT	BENT	WENT	VENT	BIG
LAMP	TRIP	RAMP	STAMP	DAMP
SANG	RING	SPRANG	BANG	HANG
STING	STRING	SING	DOG	KING
WINK	DRINK	HUT	PINK	BLINK

Short Vowels

CAT	PAN	TAP	SAD	DOG
FED	MEN	BOX	PET	PEG
HIT	DIG	TOP	WIN	PIN
CUT	HUG	TEN	RUN	MUM
TOP	FOX	LOG	NOD	MAP
CAT	PAN	TAP	SAD	CUT
FED	MEN	WIN	PET	PEG
HIT	DIG	BAG	WIN	PIN
CUT	HUG	BAT	RUN	MUM
PET	LEG	YES	BUS	HEN
SLIM	RISK	SPLIT	GRAN	FLIP
SPOT	TROT	FLOP	TEST	CLOG
FROG	STOP	TWIG	SLOT	FLOP
DRAG	CLAP	DUSK	SNAP	GLAD
TEST	FELT	BAT	PET	PEG
DISH	SHIP	LEFT	LIFT	QUIT
MILK	SWIFT	BRUSH	CHIN	WISH
HUNT	LUNCH	TENT	BRUSH	SNUG
CRAMP	LIMP	HAND	SPLASH	TRAP
RENT	TRENCH	LENGTH	HINT	NEXT
SWIFT	SILK	SHIP	CRUST	CRISP
SHOP	LOST	FACT	POND	FROG
DRUM	SLUG	SNIP	TRUST	RUSH

Initial Letter

BAD	BEG	BIN	HUT	BRUSH
MAN	MIST	CAT	MUM	MUNCH
SAND	STILL	CUT	SIT	SELL
CAN	CUT	TIN	KIT	COD
DUST	DOLL	PIN	DESK	DOG
FILL	FELT	GET	FLUSH	FIST
GET	GO	DESK	GUST	GAP
HAT	HOT	POT	HILL	HUG
LAMB	LOCK	BACK	LET	LIFT
NOT	CAN	NIT	NAP	NUT
PACK	PUT	POND	PICK	SAT
RED	HAT	RUST	RICH	ROB
TICK	TOP	TAP	TEST	BEST
WISH	WHAT	LIFT	WEB	WILT
BAD	BEG	BIN	PICK	BUSH
MAN	MIST	NAN	MUM	MUNCH
SAND	STILL	ZIP	SIT	SELL
CAN	CUT	GET	KIT	COD
DUST	DOLL	TIN	DESK	DOG
FILL	FELT	THIN	FLUSH	FIST
GET	GO	KIT	GUST	GAP
NOT	MAP	NIT	NAP	NUT
PACK	PUT	POND	PICK	BACK
TICK	TOP	TAP	TEST	DEN
WISH	WHAT	VEST	WEB	WILT
SHIP	SHALL	FELL	SHOP	SHIFT
THIN	THRUSH	THICK	FIN	THINK
CHIN	CHUG	SHIP	CHUM	CHEST

Initial Blend words

More complete lists can be found on the internet.[1] Note that all words could be used for auditory games or dictations where the only thing that is written down is the blend, and the remainder of the word is either left out or represented by a line. In games or activities where the whole word is read or written one needs to stick to the spelling level that has been covered, e.g. use only the one-syllable short vowel and leave out any complex phonemes you have not yet covered, like end blends as in brand –dge in bridge or –sh in bush.

R-blends

BR	CR	DR	FR	GR	PR	TR

Short vowel

BR	CR	DR	FR	GR	PR	TR
brim	crab	drag	frog	grab	prod	trip
brick	crib	drip	from	grin	prop	trod
brand	crop	drum	fret	gram	press	tramp
brisk	crack	drop	front	grip	print	trick
bring	crust	dress	frost	grub	prince	track
brush	crisp	drift	fresh	grid	princess	truck
bridge	crash	drink	frill	grit	pram	tram

Long vowel

BR	CR	DR	FR	GR	PR	TR
brace	crane	drain	free	grain	praise	train
brain	creep	dream	fry	grape	price	trade
brake[2]	croak	drive	fright	green	pray	try
brave	crow	drove	freeze	greet	prune	trace
bride	crayon	dry	frozen	grow	prose	tree

More complex vowels

BR	CR	DR	FR	GR	PR	TR
brook	crawl	draw	frown	grass	proud	trout
brother	crowd	dread	fruit	grew	prowl	trowel
brought	crown	drew	friend	ground	prawn	troll
bruise	cried	draft	freight	growl	proof	trawl

---

1 http://www.enchantedlearning.com/consonantblends/.
2 Note the different spellings and meanings of break and brake. Make sure you avoid confusion.

APPENDIX 5

Class 1 Main Lesson

Yearly Overview

Appendices 5 – 20 include slightly adapted plans that the authors have used in real life. You will see that sometimes they are clearly working documents rather than polished products. They set out whole-year overviews for Classes 1 and 2. The termly plans are arranged according to the literacy skill benchmarks or learning outcomes that you will need to evidence for your classes, in categories of speaking and listening, reading, writing and spelling etc. The weekly plans give examples of how you organise daily routines of skills-teaching and practice combined with qualitative, experiential learning. There are also examples of notes about how things actually happened despite the best laid plan. In your plans, you can make a note of what never happened, what succeeded, what still needs practice and if you would do something differently next time.

WEEK	DATE	MAIN LESSON CONTENT	FESTIVAL/EVENT
1	Sept	Form Drawing	
2	Sept	Form Drawing / English Introduction to letters	
3	Sept	Form Drawing / English Introduction to letters	
4	Sept	Form Drawing / English Introduction to letters	September 29 Michaelmas
5	Oct	English Introduction to letters	
6	Oct	English Introduction to letters	
7	Oct	English Introduction to letters	

HALF TERM – 1 WEEK

WEEK	DATE	MAIN LESSON CONTENT	FESTIVAL/EVENT
1	Nov	Arithmetic Introduction to number	November 11 Martinmas
2	Nov	Arithmetic Introduction to number	
3	Nov	Arithmetic Introduction to number	
4	Nov	Arithmetic Introduction to number	
5	Dec	Home environment	Advent Spiral
6	Dec	Home environment	
7	Dec	Home environment	

CHRISTMAS – 3 WEEKS

WEEK	DATE	MAIN LESSON CONTENT	FESTIVAL/EVENT
1	Jan	English Introduction to letters, Writing/Reading	
2	Jan	English Introduction to letters, Writing/Reading	
3	Jan	English Introduction to letters, Writing/Reading	
4	Feb	English Introduction to letters, Writing/Reading	February 5 Open Day
5	Feb	Arithmetic Introduction to four processes	

HALF TERM – 1 WEEK

WEEK	DATE	MAIN LESSON CONTENT	FESTIVAL/EVENT
1	Feb	Arithmetic Introduction to four processes	
2	Mar	Arithmetic Introduction to four processes	Shrove Tuesday
3	Mar	Arithmetic Introduction to four processes	
4	Mar	Arithmetic Introduction to four processes	
5	Mar	Home environment	

EASTER – 3 WEEKS

WEEK	DATE	MAIN LESSON CONTENT	FESTIVAL/EVENT
1	Apr	English Writing/Reading	
2	Apr	English Writing/Reading	
3	Apr	English Writing/Reading	
4	Apr	Arithmetic	May Day Whitsun
5	May	Arithmetic	
6	May	Arithmetic	

HALF TERM – 1 WEEK

WEEK	DATE	MAIN LESSON CONTENT	FESTIVAL/EVENT
1	June	English Writing/Reading	
2	June	English Writing/Reading	
3	June	English Writing/Reading	St John's – Midsummer
4	June	English Writing/Reading	
5	July	Home environment	Class Play
6	July	Home environment	

SUMMER HOLIDAY – 7 WEEKS

This example is based on a cycle of teaching Literacy, Numeracy and Home Environment Main Lessons. Every year, the dates differ so you will need to adjust your balance accordingly. Four weeks at any one subject is usually enough but five weeks can be really successful if broken by a half-term. You will also need to take into account how much disruption there might be from festivals, or half-weeks at the beginning and ends of terms. (This number of weeks is based on a typical Steiner School in the UK, where privately funded schools are usually open for 36 weeks a year.)

In general, the first term is the best for introduction of unfamiliar topics, imparting information and new concepts. The mood shifts substantially once Advent has started, so changing Main Lesson topic at that juncture is a good idea. The Spring term can be a tricky term with less light and poor weather, although generally children concentrate reasonably well. Use this term for 'thinking' activities, reflection and discussion. The 'extrovert' summer term is better for revision and consolidation on the whole because the children are much more inclined to be physically active rather than sitting indoors!

APPENDIX 6

Class 2 Main Lesson

Yearly Overview

In this example, you can see how the teacher has made space on the original plan to record changes as they occurred through the year. Life obviously doesn't always go to plan!

WEEK	DATE	MAIN LESSON CONTENT	FESTIVAL/EVENT	TAUGHT / CHANGES
1	Sept	English, Form Drawing, cursive writing, fables, plays		✓
2	Sept	English, Form Drawing, cursive writing, fables, plays		✓
3	Sept	English, Form Drawing, cursive writing, fables, plays		✓
4	Sept	English, Form Drawing, cursive writing, fables, plays	Sept 27 Parents' Evening Sept 29 Michaelmas Rosh Hashana	✓
5	Oct	English, Form Drawing, cursive writing, fables, plays	Oct 8 Open Day	✓
6	Oct	Maths, the four processes and multiplication tables	Oct 16 Parents' Afternoon	English play
7	Oct	Maths, the four processes and multiplication tables		✓

HALF TERM – 1 WEEK

WEEK	DATE	MAIN LESSON CONTENT	FESTIVAL/EVENT	TAUGHT / CHANGES
1	Nov	Maths, the four processes and multiplication tables	November 6 Eid	✓
2	Nov	Preparing Martinmas lanterns	November 11 Martinmas	✓
3	Nov	Maths, the four processes and multiplication tables		✓
4	Nov	Maths, the four processes and multiplication tables	November 26 Advent Fair November 27 Advent Spiral	✓
5	Dec	English, saint stories, calendar, advent craft activities		✓
6	Dec	English, saint stories, calendar, advent craft activities		✓
7	Dec	English, saint stories, calendar, advent craft activities		✓

CHRISTMAS – 3 WEEKS

WEEK	DATE	MAIN LESSON CONTENT	FESTIVAL/EVENT	TAUGHT / CHANGES
1	Jan	Maths		✓
2	Jan	Maths		✓
3	Jan	Maths		✓
4	Feb	Maths	February 4 Open Day	✓
5	Feb	English		✓

HALF TERM – 1 WEEK

WEEK	DATE	MAIN LESSON CONTENT	FESTIVAL/EVENT	TAUGHT / CHANGES
1	Feb	English		✓
2	Mar	English	Shrove Tuesday	✓
3	Mar	Home environment/nature study		✓
4	Mar	Home environment/nature study		✓
5	Mar	Home environment/nature study		✓
6	Mar	Home environment/nature study		Maths

EASTER – 3 WEEKS

WEEK	DATE	MAIN LESSON CONTENT	FESTIVAL/EVENT	TAUGHT / CHANGES
1	Apr	English, play, stories, *St Fronto, St Bridget*		Maths
2	Apr	English, play, read *King of Ireland's Son*		Play
3	May	English, play		Play
4	May	English, play		Play
5	May	Maths	May 23 Whole school photo	Play
6	May	Maths. Start stories, *Saint Francis*	May 27 Whitsun	English

HALF TERM – 1 WEEK

WEEK	DATE	MAIN LESSON CONTENT	FESTIVAL/EVENT	TAUGHT / CHANGES
1	June	Maths		English
2	June	Maths	June 24 St John's – Midsummer	English
3	June	English		Maths
4	July	English		Maths
5	July	English	Class Play	Maths

SUMMER HOLIDAY – 8 WEEKS

APPENDIX 7

Class 1 English Year Plan

CURRICULUM CONTENT

SPEAKING AND LISTENING

AUTUMN TERM Main Lesson	SPRING TERM Main Lesson	SUMMER TERM Main Lesson
• Choral & individual speaking of verses • Listening to fairy tales, folk and nature stories and therapeutic stories • Recalling stories / recent events • Sharing news • Turn taking and partner work skills • Tongue twisters • Sequence of days of week, months, seasons; oral practice	As before Learn the alphabet	As before Practise the alphabet Play

WRITING

Introduce • B, C, K, D, F, G, M, HJ, L, N, P, R, S, T, W, Y – both sounds and names • A, E, I, O, U long and short sounds (no long vowel spellings yet) • In conjunction with Form Drawing • Introduce correct sitting position, tripod grip and page control • Practise patterns of straight and curved lines; use blocks first and then stick crayons • Develop letter shapes from pictures; practise correct formation using dominant hand • Copy learnt poems • Write labels for pictures, then sentences and then stories, partly using invented spelling • Write the word-wall words • Split words into sounds (aural, kinaesthetic activities) • Initial and end consonants: recognise, list, sort • Distinguish short vowel sounds (aural, kinaesthetic) • Introduce writing CVC words and first simple labels for pictures, own name, key words like birthday/ festivals etc., first essential irregulars	Introduce Q, V, X, Z – both sounds and names Practise Form Drawing patterns Revise correct letter formation Copy learnt poems Introduce writing CCVC words – creating, sorting, listing Practise 2-letter initial blends (aural, kinaesthetic, reading & writing) Distinguish B/P, T/D,	Introduce TH, CH, SH, WH, NG Practise 'running' Form Drawing patterns working towards cursive writing Introduce print lower-case letters List, recognise, sort initial and end consonants, blends (2 and 3) and short vowels of words Creating, sorting, listing, writing CCCVC words Distinguish F/TH, CH/ TR Introduce and practise the first long vowel spellings – VCe, AY; EE; IGH; OW; OO

READING

AUTUMN TERM Main Lesson	SPRING TERM Main Lesson	SUMMER TERM Main Lesson
• Memory reading • Draw attention to details of particular words in the 'memory reading' (whole to parts; synthesis to analysis) • Develop a word wall using the following words – THE, OF, AND, A, TO, IN, IS, YOU • Word-wall activities	As before Word wall with the following words – THAT, IT, HE, WAS, FOR, ON, ARE, AS Regular reading to the class Individual reading for those who are ready	As before Word wall with the following words – WITH, HIS, THEY, I, AT, BE, THIS, HAVE, SAID

Learning Objectives

Speaking skills so that children can
- enunciate individual speech sounds accurately for phonics work
- recount a simple story and recite verses clearly; recount recent events coherently
- take turns and successfully engage in partner work for learning
- improvise simple dialogue in dramas

Listening skills so that children can
- recall instructions, information or the narrative of stories accurately
- recall verses and sequences of information
- take turns and successfully engage in partner work for learning
- discern individual speech sounds accurately for phonics work, including vowels, consonants and digraphs using /H/, /NG/

Writing skills so that children can
- form letter shapes accurately and beautifully with the correct strokes
- using appropriate sitting position, pencil grip and page control
- write regular CVCs, words with blends and some common irregular words to form simple sentences and then short narratives

Reading skills so that children can
- read most of the 44 sounds of English accurately in and out of context, including knowing short and long vowel sounds, consonants and core digraphs
- read a known text from memory
- read their own writing and some common irregular words (from the word wall)
- enjoy being read to and looking at books in the classroom

APPENDIX 8

Class 1 Form Drawing Year Plan

FORM DRAWING CURRICULUM CONTENT

- Warm up at the start of the Form Drawing lessons with several gross and fine motor skills exercises to encourage awareness of the movement of the arm, hand and fingers
- Images are used to help children picture the form, e.g. 'rainbow', 'straight as a spear', 'Bird flying towards a crystal mountain wall'
- New forms should be moved thus: walking, drawing in the air or moving the hand over the paper, drawing with crayon
- Teacher alternates between drawing the shape in stages on paper or the blackboard and going round to help individual children

AUTUMN TERM	SPRING TERM	SUMMER TERM
• Vertical Straight Lines • Vertical and Horizontal Curved Lines • Vertical Symmetry Patterns • Circle and Spiral Patterns	As before Horizontal Straight Lines Vertical and Horizontal Symmetry Patterns	As before Linear Patterns in preparation for cursive writing Linear Patterns in preparation for cursive writing on double-sided blackboards

Learning Objectives

- To enhance hand–eye co-ordination
- To enhance fine motor skills
- To increase spatial awareness
- To encourage and work with the aesthetic sense of beauty
- To improve accuracy of the ability to express in colour and form

APPENDIX 9

Class 1 English Autumn Term Plan

SPEAKING AND LISTENING

When	Learning Objectives and Activities	Differentiation Strategies	Taught/Amendments
		This a new group of children and differentiation needs will still need to be established	
Every morning	Choral speaking Morning routine verses The morning verse with gross motor movement • *I lift my arms...* • *Round and round the windmills...* • *There once was a baker...* With fine motor movement... • *Once I made up...*	Encourage all children to participate in the choral speaking using descriptive praise	
Throughout Form Drawing and English Main Lesson	MI verses and tongue twisters • *Flounder, flounder* – F • *Oh my, a golden goose* – G • *Many masked men* – M • *Deep is the deed* – D • *Six swans* – S • *Can the boy* – K/C • *Hans in luck* – H		
Throughout Home Environment Main Lesson	• *Larry unicycle* – L • *No never poem* – N • Poem – Y Recitation with actions on the words beginning with the relevant letter		

SPEAKING AND LISTENING

When	Learning Objectives and Activities	Differentiation Strategies	Taught/Amendments

Every morning	Home Environment Main lesson
	
	Recitation with gross motor movements
	  • Days of the week
	  • Seasons
	  • Months
	
	Individual Speaking
	
	Morning news: Three children can give news each morning. Voluntary
	
	Gnomes: Every day two gnomes are hidden. Children are asked to find them. Two children each day can tell the class where the gnomes are hidden. Initially allow pointing; later, insist that the children describe in full sentences where the gnomes are hidden
		Keep a record of who has spoken individually and try to encourage those who don't speak much by asking them questions
		
		DD – reluctant speaker. Do not insist on speaking in front of the class but give him the opportunity if he puts his hand up
		Give him opportunities to speak to the adults in the class. Do not insist on eye contact. Make subject teachers aware of his problems with speaking
		
		Identify children who will need to have extra speech sessions. Refer to speech therapist	

Most Main Lessons	Listening to stories Once every two or three days, teacher completes a story (parts spread over days.) Children listen and are asked the next day to recall or re-create the story		

WRITING IN CONJUNCTION WITH FORM DRAWING

When	Learning Objectives and Activities	Differentiation Strategies	Taught/Amendments
Every time we embark on a writing task	Introduce correct sitting position, tripod grip and page control Use image of throne, demonstrate how to hold hand, then put the 'king on the throne' / the crayon in the hand. Regular reminders before writing tasks Lines on page, borders	SP, LS, MO said to be left handed Demonstrate left-handed grip for them Ask assistant/SENCo to assess handedness	
	Practising patterns of straight and curved lines See Form Drawing plan (see Appendix 8)		
English Main Lesson (ML)	Developing the letter shapes from pictures Tell story, next day recall story and draw picture; following day, draw letter and practise writing the letter • *Baker poem* – B • *The Fisherman and his Wife* – F • *The Golden Goose* – G • *Michaelmas Story* – D • *Semili Mountain* - M • *The Crystal Ball* – K and C • *Angel letters story* (vowels) – A E I O U Other letters as above also including • *Rapunzel* – R/T • *12 Dancing Princesses* – P/J		

WRITING IN CONJUNCTION WITH FORM DRAWING

When	Learning Objectives and Activities	Differentiation Strategies	Taught/Amendments
Towards end of English ML or during Home Environment	Copy learnt poems Write poems that the children already know on the blackboard to copy; also practise reading skills, see below		
Home Environment Main Lesson	Write word labels for pictures, sentences and stories, often using invented spelling. From stories they have heard. CVC words first		
Home Environment Main Lesson	Write the word-wall words THE, OF, AND, A, TO, IN, IS, YOU are stuck on the wall. Play mind-reading game giving clues like: • How many straight or curved lines in the word? • How many steps would we have to take in the gnome game (how many sounds)? • Which 'angel letter' (vowel) is in the word? • How many letters? • Rhyming clues • Initial and final letters		

WRITING IN CONJUNCTION WITH FORM DRAWING

When	Learning Objectives and Activities	Differentiation Strategies	Taught/Amendments
English and Home Environment Main Lessons as appropriate	**Keywords and CVCs** • Use opportunities to write CVC words for everyday functions of classroom life, e.g. for festivals, birthdays, seasonal activities • Practise keywords such as names and other essential irregulars		
English Main Lesson	<u>Letter sounds and names</u> • Regular rehearsal of identification and distinction between letter sound and letter name • Ditto, with vowel sounds distinguishing between letter name, long sound and short sound • Recitation of the letter poems with actions on the words beginning with the relevant letter. • Dictation of the letter poems – children write only initial letter of the words beginning with the letter the poem is about • Dictation of groups of words with two different initial letters. Children to write only initial letter of the words • In pairs, children think of words to give to another child to write. Choice of two or three initial letters	FP, ZK, RL, CC write whole poem or whole words FP, ZK, RL, CC write whole words	

When	Learning Objectives and Activities	Differentiation Strategies	Taught/Amendments
Towards end of the English Main Lesson	Activities to split words into sounds (aural, kinaesthetic) • Gnome game – children tap sounds of words on their knees. One child walks over the stepping-stone bridge – one step for every sound • Practice with the names of children – how many steps would you have to make if you were given xxx's name in the gnome game? • Ditto, with other words	Give FP, ZK, RL, CC, DK chance to read some of the words	
Towards end of the English Main Lesson	Activities to list, recognise, sort initial and end consonants of words using the consonants learned so far Dictation of groups of words with two different initial letters. Children to write only initial letter of the words In pairs, children think of words to give to another child to write. Choice of two or three initial letters	FP, ZK, RL, CC write whole words	
Towards end of English Main Lesson or during Home Environment	Activities to distinguish between the short vowel sounds (aural, kinaesthetic) • Create different vowel areas in the long room. Children run to the correct area when teacher calls out letter sounds (short and long) or words with long or short vowels • In pairs – model first, then one child has letter cards in front of her, second child says words. First child has to point to correct vowel		

READING

When	Learning Objectives and Activities	Differentiation Strategies	Taught/Amendments
Regular practice towards end of English Main Lesson or during Home Environment	Memory reading • Read a known poem from the blackboard • Read individual words from a known poem on the blackboard • Initially teacher follows poem with pointer, later the children do this		
Regular practice towards end of English Main Lesson or during Home Environment	Activities to draw attention to details of particular words in the memory reading Mind-reading games giving clues like: • How many straight or curved lines in the word? • How many steps would we have to take in the gnome game (how many sounds)? • Which 'angel letter' (vowel) is in the word? • How many letters? • Rhyming clues • Initial and final letters		

READING

When	Learning Objectives and Activities	Differentiation Strategies	Taught/Amendments
Regular practice throughout Home Environment Main Lesson	Develop a word wall using the following words: THE, OF, AND, A, TO, IN, IS, YOU Activities to draw attention to details of the word-wall words Words put up by the 'class gnomes' read the words Play mind-reading game giving clues like: • How many straight or curved lines in the word? • How many steps would we have to take in the gnome game (how many sounds)? • Which 'angel letter' (vowel) is in the word? • How many letters? • Rhyming clues • Initial and final letters		

EVALUATION

APPENDIX 10

Class 1 English Spring Term Plan

SPEAKING AND LISTENING

When	Learning Objectives and Activities	Differentiation Strategies	Taught/Amendments

Every morning	Choral speaking
	
	Morning routine verses
	• The morning verse with gross motor movement
	   I Lift My Arms...
	   Round And Round The Windmills...
	   There Once Was A Baker...
	With fine motor movement...
	• *Once I Made Up...*
		Encourage all children to participate in the choral speaking using descriptive praise as encouragement	✓

Form Drawing and English Main Lesson	MI verses and tongue twisters • Revise last term's tongue twisters • New poems for the remaining letters – Q, V, W, X, Z • *Wild Winter Water* – W • *Valiant Vincent* – V, Q, Z • *It's Spring* Recitation with actions on the words beginning with the relevant letter		✓
Home Environment Main Lesson	Home Environment Main Lesson Recitation with gross motor movements • Days of the week • Seasons • Months • Alphabet sequence		✓ (not done days of the week)

SPEAKING AND LISTENING

When	Learning Objectives and Activities	Differentiation Strategies	Taught/Amendments
Every morning English Main Lesson	**Individual Speaking**		
	Morning news: Three children can give news each morning. Only first week after the holidays, then news time to be stopped	Keep a record of who has spoken individually and try to encourage those who don't speak much by asking them questions	✓
	Letters: Every day three or more letters are hidden. Children are asked to find them. Three children each day can tell the class where the letters are hidden. Initially allow pointing; later, insist that the children describe in full sentences where the letters are hidden. Children to bring them to the front and say letter name and letter sound	DD – reluctant speaker. Has made huge improvement. Don't insist on him speaking in situations where he is shy, but encourage at other times	✓
		FP, ZK, RL, DD, DK, NR	
	Birthday verses: Individual children say their birthday verses for two weeks every day. Encourage clear rhythmical speech		✓ check whether children still have their verses at home
Most Main Lessons	**Listening to stories**		
	Once every two or three days teacher completes a story (parts can be spread over days). Children listen and are asked the next day to recall or re-create the story	Individual children to tell the whole story. TA makes notes as to the quality of their recall	✓ all children have had an opportunity to tell a story, except CC

WRITING IN CONJUNCTION WITH FORM DRAWING

When	Learning Objectives and Activities	Differentiation Strategies	Taught/Amendments
Every time we embark on a writing task	Correct sitting position, tripod grip and page control • Use image of throne, demonstrate how to hold hand, then put the 'king on the throne', the crayon in the hand • Lines and Borders on pages • Under page Line Sheet		Double check handedness SP and LS next term
	Practising patterns of straight and curved lines See Form Drawing plan		✓
English Main Lesson	Developing the letter shapes from pictures Tell a story, next day recall the story and draw a picture; following day, draw the letter and practise writing the letter • W: *Wild Winter Water* poem and image of water wind and waves • VQZ: *Valiant Vincent.* Own story for V, Z and QU – poem to be clear about Q always followed by U • X without story		✓

WRITING IN CONJUNCTION WITH FORM DRAWING

When	Learning Objectives and Activities	Differentiation Strategies	Taught/Amendments
English ML or Home Environment	Copy learnt poems Write poems that the children already know on the blackboard to copy – also practise reading skills *Upon A Hill There Stood A Tree* • 'Magic' blackboard words appearing: HILL, TREE, TRUNK, LIMB, BRANCH, TWIG, NEST, EGG, BIRD, WING, FEATHER, FLUFF • <u>Quiz</u> to work out what they say? Discuss strange spellings: double consonants LL, GG, FF needed help; LIMB silent letter • Find the right word for the gap, rubbing-out technique for memory		✓
Home Environment Main Lesson	Write stories, often using invented spelling From stories they have heard, CVCs, CCVCs, irregulars		✓
English and Home Environment ML	Write the word-wall words and stick them on the wall THE; THEM; IS; ALL; AND; YOU TO; IN; THAT; IT; WAS HE; ARE; AS; FOR; ON Play mind-reading game giving clues like: • How many straight or curved lines in the word? • How many steps would we have to take in the gnome game (how many sounds)? • Which 'angel letter' (vowel) is in the word? • How many letters? • Rhyming clues • Initial and final letters • Sentence clues		✓

WRITING IN CONJUNCTION WITH FORM DRAWING

When	Learning Objectives and Activities	Differentiation Strategies	Taught/Amendments
English Main Lesson	Revising Letters	FP, ZK, RL, CC write whole poem or whole words	
Regular questioning	• Ask the class for the name and sound of the letters learnt so far. Clear distinction between letter sound and letter name		✓
Rhythmical time quick activities	• Ditto, with vowel sounds distinguishing between letter name, long sound and short sound		✓
	• Recitation of the letter poems with actions on the words beginning with the relevant letter		✓
	• Regular writing practice with letters learnt		✓
	• Guessing games – feeling letters, walking letters, drawing letters on each other's backs		not done
	• 'I Spy' with letter sounds		✓
Towards end of the English Main Lesson	Activities to split words into sounds (aural, kinaesthetic)	Give FP, ZK, RL, CC, DK opportunity to read some of the words	
	• Gnome game: Children tap sounds of words on their knees. One child walks over the stepping-stone bridge – one step for every sound		✓ only couple of times but tapping used a lot.
	• Practice with the names of children: How many steps would you have to make if you were given xxx's name in the gnome game?		Not done
	• Ditto, with other words needed in their writing or in the common word-wall work		
	• Distinguish between B/P/T/D; 'Odd One Out' game		✓

WRITING IN CONJUNCTION WITH FORM DRAWING

When	Learning Objectives and Activities	Differentiation Strategies	Taught/Amendments
Towards end of the English Main Lesson	Word Building: list, recognise, sort initial and end consonants and blends • Dictation of groups of words with two different initial letters. Children to write only initial letter of the words • Ditto, in pairs children think of words they give the other child to write. Choice of two or three initial letters • Blends game • CVC, CCVC lists onset and rime games	FP, ZK, RL, CC write whole words	not done
Towards end of the English Main Lesson or during Home Environment	Activities to distinguish between the short vowel sounds (aural, kinaesthetic) • Create different vowel areas in the long room. Children run to the correct area when teacher calls out letter sounds (short and long) or words with long or short vowels • In pairs: One child has letter cards in front of him, other child says words. First child has to point to correct vowel. Model first centrally		✓ ✓ A/O and I/O should continue

READING

When	Learning Objectives and Activities	Differentiation Strategies	Taught/Amendments
English Main Lesson or during Home Environment	Memory Reading and Revision Read a known poem from the blackboard Read individual words from known poem on blackboard Mind-reading games giving clues like: • How many straight or curved lines in the word? • How many steps would we have to take in the gnome game (how many sounds)? • Which 'angel letter' (vowel) is in the word? • How many letters? • Rhyming clues • Initial and final letters		✓
English/ Home Environment ML Rhythmical time games	Word wall using the following words THE; THEM; IS; ALL; AND; YOU TO; IN; T HAT; IT; WAS HE; ARE; AS; FOR; ON Activities to draw attention to details of the word-wall words Words put up by the 'class gnomes'. Read the words Play mind-reading game giving clues like: • How many straight or curved lines in the word? • How many steps would we have to take in the gnome game (how many sounds)? • Which 'angel letter' (vowel) is in the word? • How many letters? • Rhyming clues • Initial and final letters		✓

READING

When	Learning Objectives and Activities	Differentiation Strategies	Taught/Amendments
Breaks/end of task times	Individual reading for those who are ready • Reading corner in the room for down-time/breaks • Reading books to class out loud in some spare story times / festivals		✓

APPENDIX 11

Class 1 English Summer Term Plan

SPEAKING AND LISTENING

When	Learning Objectives and Activities	Differentiation Strategies	Taught/Amendments
Every morning	Choral speaking Morning routine verses • The morning verse with gross motor movement • I lift my arms... • ALPHABET sounds and names		✓
Form Drawing and English Main Lesson	MI verses and tongue twisters • *Philippa* • *She Sells Sea Shells* • *Charlie* • *Betty One Bright Afternoon* • *Through the Thick* • *This is the Key of the Kingdom* • *Start with Your Tongue Between Your Teeth*		✓
Every morning	Individual Speaking Morning news: Three children can give news each morning. Only first week after the holidays, then news time to be stopped		✓
Every morning	Birthday verses: Individual children say their birthday verses for two weeks every day Encourage clear rhythmical speech		✓

SPEAKING AND LISTENING

When	Learning Objectives and Activities	Differentiation Strategies	Taught/Amendments
Most Main Lessons	Listening to stories Once every two or three days teacher completes a story (parts can be spread over days). Children listen and are asked the next day to re-call or recre-ate the story	Individual children this term to tell the whole story. TA makes notes as to the quality of their recall.	✓ all children have had an opportunity to tell story apart from CC

WRITING IN CONJUNCTION WITH FORM DRAWING

When	Learning Objectives and Activities	Differentiation Strategies	Taught/Amendments
Every time we embark on a writing task	Correct sitting position, tripod grip and page control • Remind King image • Lines and Borders on page for story writing • Under page Line Sheet	Check who needs under-page sheet	✓
Form Drawing lessons	Practising symmetrical and running patterns. See Form Drawing plan		✓
All day	Print letters Paste them up on the wall for Q&A spontaneously. Letters you find in books – not letters people write. Compare and contrast very similar and very differ-ent letters		✓

WRITING IN CONJUNCTION WITH FORM DRAWING

When	Learning Objectives and Activities	Differentiation Strategies	Taught/Amendments
English Main Lesson	Copy learnt poems Write poems that the children already know on the blackboard to copy – also practise reading skills, see below *This is the Key of the Kingdom*		✓
English Main Lesson	Write stories, often using invented spelling CVCs, CCVCs, irregulars Sentence modelling for stories. Sentence strips laid out, cut up and rearranged in correct order PAIRS drafting stories, e.g. *Cat and Mouse, This Is The Farmer*		✓
English Main Lesson	Write the word-wall words Mind-reading game giving clues like: • How many straight or curved lines in the word? • How many steps would we have to take in the gnome game (how many sounds)? • Which 'angel letter' (vowel) is in the word? • How many letters? • Rhyming clues • Initial and final letters • Sentence clues		✓

WRITING IN CONJUNCTION WITH FORM DRAWING

When	Learning Objectives and Activities	Differentiation Strategies	Taught/Amendments
English Main Lesson Regular questioning Rhythmical Time quick activities	• Revising letters • Ask the class for the name and (short / long) sound of the vowels and any still uncertain letters learnt so far (assess who needs this) • Regular writing practice with letters learnt • 'I Spy' with TH/ SH • Distinguishing between TH/F	TA to do 1:1 with few who still have some vulnerable letters/ sounds	✓
English Main Lesson	Activities to split words into sounds (aural, kinaesthetic) • Gnome game – children tap sounds of words on their knees. One child walks over the stepping-stone bridge – one step for every sound • Vowels dictation: Run to the vowel • Tap words needed in their writing or in the common word-wall work • Short vowel sorting and dictation activity – harder ones O/U • 'Odd-One-Out' rhyming game • Words Their Way assessment	Give FP, ZK, RL, CC, DK opportunity to read some of the words N/A/CH/C separate with TA I/A/O	✓

WRITING IN CONJUNCTION WITH FORM DRAWING

When	Learning Objectives and Activities	Differentiation Strategies	Taught/Amendments
English Main Lesson	Word Building: list, recognise, sort blends and digraphs • Blends dictation • Ditto – in pairs children think of words for the other child to write. Choice of two or three initial letters • Blends game • CVC, CCVC lists onset and rime games • CAT and DOG word-changing game • Gather words game CH/ TH/ SH/ WH/ NG/NT/NCH and other blend endings Find word families Entering classroom activity: using different short-vowel one-syllable word per day, e.g. *cross* • find two words hidden around the room • whisper to class helper what the words say • write them in light yellow book • think of several more in that word family	A,N,C,CH,Y,SH,M, E play 'Snakes and Ladders'	✓
English Main Lesson	Activities to distinguish between short vowel sounds (aural, kinaesthetic) Create different vowel areas in the long room. Children run to the correct area when teacher calls out letter sounds (short and long) or words with long or short vowels In pairs – one child has letter cards in front of him, other child says words. First child has to point to correct vowel. Model first centrally		✓

READING

When	Learning Objectives and Activities	Differentiation Strategies	Taught/Amendments
English Main Lesson or during Home Environment	Memory Reading and Revision • Read a known poem from the blackboard • Mind-reading games • Gather Word Family game		✓
Rhythmical time games English ML	Word-wall work Play mind-reading game		✓
Breaks / end of task times	Individual Reading for those who are ready • Reading corner in the room for down-time/ breaks • Reading books to class out loud in some spare story times / festivals • Pairs and individuals reading own written stories out loud to the class		✓

APPENDIX 12

Class 1 Week Main Lesson Plan

Summer Example A

Monday 6 June	Tuesday 7 June	Wednesday 8 June	Thursday 9 June	Friday 10 June
Entering activity • Find two words hidden around the room • Whisper to class helper what the words say • Write them in your light yellow book • Think of several more in that word family	As for Monday	As for Monday	As for Monday	As for Monday
Good morning song / Register/ news / Candle/ My feet I plant / verse	As for Monday but no 'news'	As for Monday but no 'news	As for Monday but no 'news	As for Monday but no 'news
Whitsun song	Whitsun song	Whitsun song	Whitsun song	Whitsun song
Birthday verses IS, RD, EY	As for Monday	As for Monday	As for Monday	As for Monday
Recitation *This is the House that Jack built* *She sells seashells* Alphabet	As for Monday	As for Monday	As for Monday	Make Whitsun doves
Gather Word family	As for Monday	As for Monday	As for Monday	Make Whitsun doves
Word-wall activity N/A/CH/C separate with TA	As for Monday	As for Monday	As for Monday	Make Whitsun doves
Long Room Play Run to the vowel Send children to individual vowels with a word Play Run to the vowel	Act the *Cat and the Mouse* story Write an initial sentence for the story – in pairs, gather	In pairs write the *Cat and the Mouse* story in pairs as draft N/A/CH/C separate with TA	Copy *Cat and the Mouse* story in Main Lesson book – first read to someone N/A/CH/C separate with TA	Make Whitsun doves

Monday 6 June	Tuesday 7 June	Wednesday 8 June	Thursday 9 June	Friday 10 June
Short-vowel sorting activity N/A/CH/C separate with TA Rest short-vowel dictation – which land etc. Short **i,a,o**	Short-vowel sorting activity N/A/CH/C separate with TA **i,a,o** Rest short-vowel sorting and dictation – in pairs **o,e**	Short-vowel sorting activity N/A/CH/C separate with TA **i,a,o** Rest short-vowel sorting and dictation – in pairs **o,u**	Short-vowel sorting activity N/A/CH/C separate with TA **o,e** Rest short-vowel sorting and dictation – in pairs **o,u,e**	10 am Class 3 play
Story *The Cat and the Mouse*	Story *The Three Hairs of the Devil*	Story *The Three Hairs of the Devil*	Recall story *The Three Hairs of the Devil*	

APPENDIX 13

Class 1 Week Main Lesson Plan

Summer Example B

Monday 20 June	Tuesday 21 June	Wednesday 22 June	Thursday 23 June	Friday 24 June
Entering activity with word *dish* • Find two words hidden around the room • Whisper to class helper what the words say • Write them in your light yellow book • Think of several more in that word family	As for Monday with word *chat*	As for Monday with word *brush*	As for Monday with word *splash*	As for Monday with word *thin*
Good morning song / Register / Candle / My feet I plant /verse/ A. alphabet sounds and names	As for Monday	As for Monday	As for Monday	As for Monday
Midsummer songs • *Rise up o flame* • *Behold* • *Summer Promises* • *Summer Is Acoming* • *Rose, Rose*	As for Monday	As for Monday	As for Monday	As for Monday
Recorder / *impompe* when handing out • *IncyWincy* • *Hot Cross Buns / Echoing* • *A Shepherd / Good Morning* • *Off to Market*	As for Monday	As for Monday	As for Monday	As for Monday
Birthday verses LH, CP, DK NR odd-one-out rhyming activity	As for Monday	As for Monday	As for Monday	As for Monday

Monday 20 June	Tuesday 21 June	Wednesday 22 June	Thursday 23 June	Friday 24 June
Recitation • *This Is the House that Jack Built* • *She Sells Seashells* • *Through the Thick* • *Start With Your Tongue Between Your Teeth* • *Alphabet*	As for Monday	As for Monday	As for Monday	As for Monday
Gather Word family	Gather Word family	Gather Word family	Gather Word family	Gather Word family
Word-wall activity N/A/CH/C separate with TA	As for Monday	As for Monday	As for Monday	As for Monday
• Write *This the Farmer* on the blackboard • Reading exercise • Read and follow / find certain words	*This the Farmer* Reading exercises from blackboard Put sentences in the correct order	Put cut-up words in the correct order for *This The Farmer* N/A/CH/C: one sentence at a time; reading whole sentence first, then cutting the sentences up into words, then copying into their Main Lesson book	Drawing for *This the Farmer*	Write *This the Farmer* N/A/CH/C: one sentence at a time; reading the whole sentence first, then cutting the sentences up into words, then copying into their Main Lesson book
Play blends game AR,NR,CP,CC,YS,SM,MO, ED play 'Snakes and Ladders'	As for Monday	Create pairs game with words from the poem	Play Pairs game	As above
Story *The Little Sea Hare*	Recall story *The Little Sea Hare*	Story *The Donkey*	Recall story *The Donkey*	Story *Star Money*

APPENDIX 14

Class 2 English Year Plan

CURRICULUM CONTENT
SPEAKING AND LISTENING

AUTUMN TERM	SPRING TERM	SUMMER TERM
	Regular revision of what is learned in previous terms	*Regular revision of what is learned in previous terms*
Main Lesson	Main Lesson	Main Lesson
• Choral & individual speaking of verses • Individual speaking of birthday verses • Listening to stories – fables, saint stories, nature stories • *The King of Ireland's Son* • Recalling stories / events • Sharing news – only in the first week after each holiday • Turn-taking • Tongue twisters • Reciting of fables • Fable plays	As before Seasons and months of the year	As before Legend play

WRITING

• Reminder of good pencil grip; regular checks • Introduce cursive script in conjunction with Form Drawing • Copy learnt poems • Write stories, partly using invented spelling • Write the word-wall words • Word-wall words: FROM, OR, ONE, HAD, BY, WORD, BUT, NOT, WHAT	As before • Practise cursive script • Copy learnt poems as handwriting practice • Write learnt poems from memory • Punctuation, capitals and full stops. Developing the sense for simple sentences • Make a calendar; months of the year, days of the week and seasons • Word-wall words: ALL, WERE, WE, WHEN, YOUR, CAN, SAID, THERE, USE	As before • Punctuation, including question marks • Word-wall words: AN, EACH, WHICH, SHE, DO, HOW, THEIR, IF

WRITING

• Spelling patterns: to be introduced by analogy, i.e. word families rather than rules. • Where possible spelling patterns will be linked to words we encounter in poems and stories, so if the mouse appears in a story and poem in term 1 we may already introduce the OU word family • Reminders of sound split-ting • Revision of consonant digraphs CH, SH, TH, WH, QU • Revision of consonant blends • Awareness of long and short vowels • Revise -CK, -LL, -SS, -ZZ, -FF straight after a short vowel as word families • Syllabification practice • Revise / introduce and practise end consonant blends; ND, NT, NCH, MP, NG, NK • 'Magic –E' for /A/ , /I/, /O/, /U/ AND /E/ • AY, AI for long A	As before • EE, EA for long E • IGH, Y for long I; include I on its own in long vowel, e.g. mind • OW, OA for long O; include O on its own in long vowel, e.g. hold • OU (sound); OW (how) • EA as in head • Introduce and practise suffixing just add rule only; -s, -ed, ing • Assess spelling levels using Words Their Way assessment • Assess retained common word spellings	As before • OO as in soon/ OO as in book • EW as in new / blew and UE as in blue • AR as in car / A as in father

READING

• Memory reading • Draw attention to details of particular words in the 'memory reading' • Reading word-wall words • Regular reading books to the class • Activities to link book letters, capitals and cursive letters Class reading of • Self-created class story books • Reading scheme • Class / paired / individual reading • Home reading instruction to the parents	As before • Weekly reading lesson and library visit	As before • Children team up with children from Class 7

Learning Objectives

Speaking skills so that children can
- Relate a story in detail to the class
- Recite a poem on their own in front of the class
- Perform a part in a simple play

Listening skills so that children can
- Recall main narrative and details of stories heard
- Recall verses, with accurate rhythm and confidence
- Distinguish all individual sounds in words
- Distinguish syllables
- Follow class reader
- Engage in effective partner / team work, taking into account moderate differences in learning styles

Writing skills so that children can
- Spell CVC, CCVC, CVCC words correctly
- Decide whether a vowel in a word they hear is short or long
- Spell long vowels correctly when they occur at the end of words, e.g. ay, ow, ee, y

- Know to choose a long vowel spelling for a one-syllable word with a medial long vowel, e.g. know that the spelling for pain should be either 'pane' or 'pain'
- Spell 80 percent of the common words introduced correctly
- Know the shape of all capital, cursive and print letters. Write cursive script using pencils
- Add a consonant or vowel suffix to cvcc words – Just Add rule – and spell the word correctly

Reading skills so that children can
- Read a simple book confidently out loud
- Recognise the base-word in a two-syllable word with an affix

APPENDIX 15

Class 2 Form Drawing Year Plan

FORM DRAWING CURRICULUM CONTENT

> • Method of warm-up and description of forms continues as per Class 1

AUTUMN TERM	SPRING TERM	SUMMER TERM
First Main Lesson at the start of the day • Daily dynamic linear patterns in preparation of cursive writing In the weekly Form Drawing lessons: • Rhythmical patterns of straight and curved lines • Creating patterns out of separate elements – dots, lines etc. • Geometrical shapes: square, rectangle, circle, oval, triangle, stars • Accumulative shapes	In the weekly Form Drawing lessons: • Revision of previous • Vertical symmetry patterns of increasing complexity • Horizontal symmetry patterns of increasing complexity	In the weekly Form Drawing lessons: • Revision of previous • Symmetry patterns where the symmetry line is crossed

Learning Objectives

• To enhance hand–eye co-ordination
• To enhance fine motor skills
• To increase spatial awareness
• To encourage and work with the aesthetic sense of beauty
• To improve accuracy of the ability to express in colour and form

APPENDIX 16

Class 2 English Autumn Term Plan

SPEAKING AND LISTENING

When	Learning Objectives and Activities	Differentiation Strategies *Identified SEN: AR, NR, CC* *Identified Gifted and talented: ED, DK*	Taught/Amendments
Every morning throughout term	Choral speaking Morning routine verses • The morning verse • The Earth Is Firm Beneath My Feet	Encourage all children to participate in the choral speaking using descriptive praise as encouragement • Give FP lines on his own to encourage his participation • TA to remind RB and FP to participate when they forget	✓
During English Main Lesson	English Main Lesson verses and tongue twisters Fables in rhyme • The Fox and the Grapes • The Shepherd Boy And The Wolf • The Crow and the Fox • The Wind and the Sun • The Fox and the Stork Recitation; recitation with actions – some performed as a little play		
Regular practice before cursive writing, Form Drawing or flute and lyre playing	Preparation for fine motor skill movements • The Windmill • The Baker		

SPEAKING AND LISTENING

When	Learning Objectives and Activities	Differentiation Strategies	Taught/Amendments
Every morning for about a week after each holiday	Individual Speaking • Morning news: Three children can give news each morning during the week after each holiday. Voluntary • Three children speak their birthday verse on their own in front of the class each morning for about three weeks • Give opportunities for individual speaking during fable recitations • Give opportunities to speak a whole fable either individually or in a small group.	CC – reluctant speaker. Do not insist on speaking in front of the class but give him the opportunity if he puts his hand up. Give him opportunities to speak to the adults in the class. Do not insist on eye contact. Make subject teachers aware of his problems with speaking Identify children who will need to have extra speech sessions. Refer to speech therapist. RB and AR have had speech therapy before. Communicate with the speech therapist and parents to see whether this should be picked up again	✓
Most Main Lessons	Listening to stories Once every two or three days teacher completes a story (parts can be spread over days). Children listen and are asked the next day to recall or re-create the story		✓

WRITING IN CONJUNCTION WITH FORM DRAWING

When	Learning Objectives and Activities	Differentiation Strategies	Taught/Amendments
Throughout the term when we are about to embark on a writing task	Remind of grip and page setting • Lines and borders • Under line pages	Check two new children: OW and AM CC: reminder of sitting position; try on writing slope Give RB writing slope	✓
Most Main Lessons	Introduce Cursive script in conjunction with Form Drawing • Prepare writing exercises with gross and fine motor exercises • Daily practice of running Form Drawing patterns aiming for regularity, keeping straight line ,fitting between two horizontal lines • Introduction of cursive-letter shapes following the sequence of letters i, j, t, u, y, e	TA to help RB and FP to stay focused on these tasks. RB and CC to use a writing slope for the smaller letter formation practice	✓
Most Main Lessons	Cursive writing practice • Large in crayon • Medium in coloured bands with coloured pencil • Smaller in pencil on handwriting sheets • Writing known words asap with newly introduced letters		✓
Throughout the English Main Lessons	Copy learnt poems For handwriting practice – also reading skills Emphasis on neatness and regularity in writing	Slopes for CC and RB	✓

WRITING IN CONJUNCTION WITH FORM DRAWING

When	Learning Objectives and Activities	Differentiation Strategies	Taught/Amendments
Throughout the English Main Lessons	Write stories, partly using invented spelling Children write stories they have heard using their own invented spelling	NR, AR, RB, CD: TA to read prepared text with them and then guide them through a cloze exercise which they will then copy in their Main Lesson book as handwriting practice	✓
Throughout the English Main Lessons	Write the following word-wall words: fROM, OR, ONE, HAD, BY, WORD, BUT NOT, WHAT Stick the words on the wall. Play mind-reading game giving clues like: • How many straight or curved lines in the word? • How many steps would we have to take in the gnome game (how many sounds)? • Which 'angel letter' (vowel) is in the word? • How many letters? • Rhyming clues • Initial and final letters	.	✓

WRITING IN CONJUNCTION WITH FORM DRAWING

When	Learning Objectives and Activities	Differentiation Strategies	Taught/ Amendments
Throughout the English Main Lessons	**Spelling** • Reminders of sound splitting • Revision of consonant digraphs CH, SH, TH, WH • Revision of consonant blends • Awareness of long and short vowels • Revise –CK, -LL, -SS, -ZZ, -FF straight after a short vowel as word families • Introduce and practise syllabification • Introduce and practise end-consonant blends; ND, NT, NCH, MP, NG, NK • Introduce and practise 'Magic –E' for /A/ , /I/, /O/, /U/ AND /E/ • Introduce and practise AY, AI for long A	.	✓
Throughout the English Main Lessons	**Sound Splitting** • In any writing task encourage children to 'do the gnome game' when they want to know how a word is spelt • Regular 'Snakes and Ladders' games where children need to split the sounds of the words	TA in group with NR, AR, CD and AM to encourage correct sound splitting. 'Snakes and Ladders' usually in ability groups so that harder tasks can be set for the more able children: DK, ED, IS and OA	✓
Week 2 1st English Main Lesson 2nd Main Lesson	Revision game for CH,SH and TH: Run to the correct spelling activity • Dictations sorting in correct column • 'Snakes and Ladder' game with sh, ch and th words • WH – introduce the question words as a group		✓

WRITING IN CONJUNCTION WITH FORM DRAWING

When	Learning Objectives and Activities	Differentiation Strategies	Taught/ Amendments
Week 3 1st English Main Lesson	**Revision of consonant blends** • Blends game made in Class 1 • Blends dictation	.	✓
Last 2 weeks of the first English Main Lesson	**Awareness of long and short vowels** • Practise distinguishing long and short vowels with movement – jump arms wide for long vowels and arms crossed for short vowels. With one-syllable words • Ditto whilst practising syllabification • Guessing games: Which word am I showing, jumping syllables and showing long and short vowels	TA to remind RB and FP to partici-pate when they forget	✓
Last 2 weeks of the first English Main Lesson	**Introduce and practise syllabification** • Circle game with ball bouncing to practise sound splitting and syllabification – different colour ball for sounds and syllables • Syllable jumping in conjunction with long and short vowel practice • Guessing games: Which word am I showing, jumping syllables and showing long and short vowels		✓

WRITING IN CONJUNCTION WITH FORM DRAWING

When	Learning Objectives and Activities	Differentiation Strategies	Taught/ Amendments
Last 2 weeks of the first English Main Lesson	Revise -CK, -LL, -SS, -ZZ, -FF straight after a short vowels as word families • Word families during cursive writing exercises • 'Snakes and Ladder' game with these spelling patterns	TA in group with NR, AR, CD and AM to encourage correct sound splitting 'Snakes and Ladders' usually in ability groups so that harder tasks can be set for the more able children – DK, EDIS and OA	✓
Last 2 weeks of the first English Main Lesson	Introduce and practise end-consonant blends; ND, NT, NCH, MP, NG, NK • Word families during cursive writing exercises • 'Snakes and Ladder' game with these spelling patterns	TA in group with NR, AR, CD and AM to encourage correct sound splitting 'Snakes and Ladders' usually in ability groups so that harder tasks can be set for the more able children – DK, EDIS and OA	✓
Last 2 weeks of the first English Main Lesson Second English Main Lesson	Introduce and practise 'Magic –E' for /A/, /I/, /O/, /U/ AND /E/ • Word families during cursive writing exercises • Poems with spelling pattern • Activities to change short-vowel spelling to long-vowel spelling		✓

READING

When	Learning Objectives and Activities	Differentiation Strategies	Taught/ Amendments
Throughout English Main Lessons	Memory reading Read a known poem from the blackboard Read individual words from a known poem on the blackboard Mind-reading games giving clues like: • How many straight or curved lines in the word? • How many steps would we have to take in the gnome game (how many sounds)? • Which 'angel letter' (vowel) is in the word? • How many letters? • Rhyming clues • Initial and final letters		✓
After painting and at other times when the work is finished. During the warming of the beeswax	Regular reading to the class • *The Faraway Tree* • *The Hedgerow*		✓
Throughout English Main Lessons	Activities to link 'book letters', capitals and cursive letters • 'Book letters' and upper-case letters on permanent display • Flashcards for high-frequency words practice in upper case, lower case and cursive • Worksheets writing upper case next to the 'book letters' • Pairs game • Scanning for 'book letters' – counting the number of letters in a known poem		✓

READING

When	Learning Objectives and Activities	Differentiation Strategies	Taught/ Amendments
Through-out English Main Lessons	Reading of • Self-created class story books, initially upper case • Whole-class reading, initially upper case • Paired reading • Home-reading instruction to the parents	Assess reading levels for differentiation Pair more able with weaker readers Possibly invite parents in to read with small groups of ability-paired children	✓

EVALUATION

Assessment Methods	• Observation of the children's work • Observation of the children's involvement in verbal work • Observation of the children's independence in doing the tasks • Words Their Way spelling assessment after the Christmas holidays • Specifically assess; short / long vowels, th, sh, ch, distinguishing short vowels, blends and sound splitting. Most through dictation and sorting • Assess reading levels through hearing individual children read
Success Criteria	By Christmas most children will: • Be able to recognise all 'book letters' • Be able to write all letters in cursive writing • Be able to write CVC, CCVC, CCCVC and CVCC with regular short-vowel spellings correctly • Write the common irregular words WAS, SAID, THEY, ONE, WHAT • Recognise the difference between short and long vowels • Begin to use most common long-vowel spellings in their writing • Be able to read the first three stories in the First Aid in English reading series, level A

EVALUATION

Notes: Extra individual work with TA at the start of the day in small groups using the *Words Their Way* method.

AR	• Needs work on short u, short e, CH, SH and TH/F ils read
CD	• Needs work on CH, TH. Also hearing ST/SD
HW	• Needs work on ST/SD
MO	• Needs work on TH SH and TH/F
NR	• Needs work on short u, ST, DR, CH, SH, GR, F/TH, MP, LONG I/A
RD	• Needs work on short e, short i, SH and blends BL, FR and CR
SM	• Needs work on CH and TH/FR
YS	• Needs work on SH and TH/F

APPENDIX 17

Class 2 English Spring Term Plan

SPEAKING AND LISTENING

When	Learning Objectives and Activities	Differentiation Strategies	Taught/Amendments
Every morning throughout term	Choral speaking Morning routine verses • The morning verse • *The Earth is Firm Beneath My Feet*	Encourage all children to participate in the choral speaking using descriptive praise as encouragement	✓

During English Main Lesson	English Main Lesson verses and tongue twisters
	• Poems to introduce long-vowel spellings
	  • A-e, AI, AY
	  • O –e, OA, OW
	• Recitation; recitation with actions
	• Recitation of the play text in preparation for the play in the summer term
		Give FP lines on his own to encourage his participation
		
		TA to remind RD and FP to participate when they forget	

Regular practice before cursive writing, Form Drawing or flute and lyre playing	Preparation for fine motor-skill movements • *The Windmill* • *The Baker* • *Impompe*		

SPEAKING AND LISTENING

When	Learning Objectives and Activities	Differentiation Strategies	Taught/Amendments
Every morning for about a week after each holiday	**Individual Speaking** • Morning news: Three children can give news each morning during the week after each holiday. Voluntary • Three children speak their birthday verse on their own in front of the class each morning for about three weeks • Give opportunities for individual speaking during fable recitations • Give opportunities to speak a whole fable either individually or in a small group	CC – reluctant speaker. Do not insist on speaking in front of the class but give him the opportunity if he puts his hand up. Give him opportunities to speak to the adults in the class. Do not insist on eye contact. Make subject teachers aware of his problems with speaking Identify children who will need to have extra speech sessions. Refer to speech therapist. RB and AR have had speech before. Communicate with the speech therapist and parents to see whether this should be picked up again	✓
Most Main Lessons	**Listening to stories** Once every two or three days teacher completes a story (parts can be spread over days). Children listen and are asked the next day to recall or re-create the story		✓

WRITING IN CONJUNCTION WITH FORM DRAWING

When	Learning Objectives and Activities	Differentiation Strategies	Taught/Amendments
Throughout the term when we are about to embark on a writing task	Remind of grip and page setting • Lines and borders • Under line pages	Check NR and RE regularly – communicate to TA CC and RD to use writing slope AR to have ruler with capitals, print and cursive on his desk	✓
English Main Lessons	Copy learnt poems For handwriting practice write poems that the children already know on the blackboard to copy – also for reading skills, see below. Emphasis on neatness and regularity in writing	Slopes for CC and RD AR to have ruler with capitals, print and cursive on his desk	✓
English Main Lessons	Write stories, partly using invented spelling Children write stories they have heard using their own invented spelling	NR, AR, RD, CF TA to read prepared text with them and then guide them through a cloze exercise which they will then copy in their Main Lesson book as handwriting practice AR to have ruler with capitals, print and cursive on his desk	✓

WRITING IN CONJUNCTION WITH FORM DRAWING

When	Learning Objectives and Activities	Differentiation Strategies	Taught/Amendments
English Main Lessons	Stick these words on Word-wall: ALL, WERE, WE, WHEN, YOUR, CAN, SAID, THERE, USE Play mind-reading game giving clues like: • How many straight or curved lines in the word? • How many steps would we have to take in the gnome game (how many sounds)? • Which 'angel letter' (vowel) is in the word? • How many letters? • Rhyming clues • Initial and final letters	Provide AR with a sheet with the words to have on his desk AR to have ruler with capitals, print and cursive on his desk	✓
English Main Lessons	Punctuation capitals and full stops Let children experience simple sentence structure in speech and encourage capitals and full stops in all writing tasks Encourage capitals for names and titles of poems		✓
Late Spring Term	Make a calendar; months of the year, days of the week and seasons		Done last term

WRITING IN CONJUNCTION WITH FORM DRAWING

When	Learning Objectives and Activities	Differentiation Strategies	Taught/ Amendments
English Main Lesson and writing tasks in Nature Study Main Lesson	**Sound Splitting** • In any writing task encourage children to 'do the gnome game' when they want to know how a word is spelled • Regular 'Snakes and Ladders' games where children need to split the sounds of the words • Ball-bouncing circle – children stand in circle, bounce ball around the circle saying the sounds or syllables. Different colour ball for syllables and sounds	TA in group with NR, AR and AM to encourage correct sound splitting. 'Snakes and Ladders' usually in ability groups so that harder tasks can be set for the more able children – DK, ED, IS and OA, LH	✓
Throughout English Main Lesson daily	**Practice 'Magic –E' for /A/, /I/, /O/, /U/ AND /E/** Jumping long and short vowels • Teacher calls out long-vowel word, children repeat and make star jump • Teacher calls out short-vowel word, children repeat and jump with arms crossed over chest and feet together • Teacher calls out short-vowel word, children repeat and jump with arms crossed and feet together, then straight away jump the long-vowel star jump while saying the same word with a long vowel • Ditto long-vowel word to short-vowel word • Ditto mixed Include CVCe words in the introduction of other long -vowel spellings		✓

WRITING IN CONJUNCTION WITH FORM DRAWING

When	Learning Objectives and Activities	Differentiation Strategies	Taught/Amendments

English Main Lesson and practice during English subject lesson
 	
Possible extension to summer term
	• Introduce and practise AY, AI for long A
	• Introduce and practise EE, EA for long E
	• Introduce and practise IGH, Y for long I; include I on its own in long vowel, e.g. mind
	• Introduce and practise OW, OA for long O; include O on its own in long vowel, e.g. hold
	• Introduce and practise OU
	• Introduce and practise OW (how)
	
	• Teach poem with all three common long-vowel spellings for A
	• Jump or clap on the long /a/ sounds while reciting. Draw characters from the poem and give visual image of the spelling, e.g. draw a snail with 'AI' written in shell and a whale with 'a' in body and the silent 'e' in the tail.
	• Refer to spellings as the whale, snail and spray spelling
	• Word bingo
	    • Hang 16 words around class. Children have to write these words into bingo grid without taking their book to the words or vv
	    • Pair-check of spellings and words
	    • Play Four in a Row or bingo
	• Word hunt – make columns with whale, snail and spray spelling at top. Hunt for words of these spelling patterns in books
	• Write the poem from memory in their Main Lesson books
	• Play 'Snakes and Ladders' with long /a/ choices
		Bingo – give AR a sheet with all words.
		Have extra sheet available in case needed for AM, RE, NR, CF
		
		Writing poem from memory – provide as cloze exercise for AR, NR and RE; optional for CC, SM, YS, AM and MO
		
		'Snakes and Ladders' – expect ED, OA, LH, DK, LS, AB to write whole words
		
		Ask AR, NR and RE only to identify whether the word is a spray spelling or another long-vowel spelling. Don't expect them to choose between ai and a-e yet
			✓

WRITING IN CONJUNCTION WITH FORM DRAWING

When	Learning Objectives and Activities	Differentiation Strategies	Taught/Amendments
English Main Lesson and practice during English subject lesson	Introduce and practise suffixing just add rule only; -s, -ed, -ing • Use Twister of Twist tongue twister • Recite – claps on every word that has TWIST in it • Pair task – identify all words that have a twist • Write all words as a word sum, e.g. 'twist + s = twists' • Write poem from memory in Main Lesson book • Let children create further word sums with STAND, JUMP, HUNT, REST, HELP, HAND, SAND	Encourage ED, OA, DK, LH, LS, AB to include prefixes and to write sentences with the words made	✓
Early March	Assess spelling levels using *Words Their Way* assessment		✓

READING

When	Learning Objectives and Activities	Differentiation Strategies	Taught/ Amendments
English Main Lesson	Memory reading Read a known poem from the blackboard Read individual words from a known poem on the blackboard Mind-reading games giving clues like: • How many straight or curved lines in the word? • How many steps would we have to take in the gnome game (how many sounds)? • Which 'angel letter' (vowel) is in the word? • How many letters? • Rhyming clues • Initial and final letters		✓
English Main Lesson	Word wall using the following words – ALL, WERE, WE, WHEN, YOUR, CAN, SAID, THERE, USE Read the words. Give three counts before each word to give slower readers the time to process Mind-reading games	Provide AR with a sheet with the words to have on his desk	✓
After painting and at other times when the work is finished During the warming of the beeswax	Regular reading to the class • *The King of Ireland's Son* • *The King of the Copper Mountain*		✓

READING

When	Learning Objectives and Activities	Differentiation Strategies	Taught/ Amendments
All term, Tuesdays	Class reading of: • Self-created class story books. • Weekly reading lesson and library visit Move reading lesson to coincide with whole-school orchestra lesson. Class 7 children who are not in the school orchestra to read with individual Class 2 children or with small groups Reading record to be filled in by Class 7 children Class 7 children to take the most able groups to the school library towards end of the term	CC, NR, RE, RD to do 'Snakes and Ladders' with CVC, CCVC, CCCVC and CVCC words for half the reading lesson	✓

EVALUATION

Assessment Methods	
	• Observation of the children's work • Observation of the children's involvement in verbal work • Observation of the children's independence in doing the tasks • Words Their Way spelling assessment after the Christmas Holidays • Specifically assess; short / long vowels, th, sh, ch, distinguishing short vowels, blends and sound splitting. Most through dictation and sorting • Assess reading levels through hearing individual children read

EVALUATION

Success Criteria	By Easter most children will:
	• Relate a story in detail to the class
	• Recite a poem on their own in front of the class
	• Perform a part in a simple play
	• Spell CVC, CCVC, CVCC words correctly
	• Decide whether a vowel in a word they hear is short or long
	• Distinguish all individual sounds in words
	• Distinguish syllables
	• Spell long vowels correctly when they occur at the end of words, e.g. ay, ow, ee, y
	• Know the shape of all capital, cursive and print letters
	• Read a simple book confidently out loud
	• Recognise the base-word in a two-syllable word with an affix
	• Add a consonant or vowel suffix to cvcc words – Just add rule – and spell the word correctly
	• Write the common irregular words ALL, WERE, WE, WHEN, YOUR, CAN, SAID, THERE, USE

Notes: Extra individual work with TA at the start of the day in small groups using the *Words Their Way* method.

AR	•	Needs to work on SH and CH, DR and FR. Give homework matching capital, cursive and book letter shapes (pairs game) and have 3-script-ruler on her desk
CF	•	Individual work on using long-vowel spellings – sorting tasks with TA
HW	•	Needs work on ST/SD
MO	•	Needs work on TH/F – home sorting tasks
NR	•	Needs work on short u, ST, DR, CH, SH, GR, F/TH, MP, LONG I/A
RD	•	Needs work on short e, short i, SH and blends BL, FR and CR
YS	•	Needs work on TH/F – home sorting tasks
OL	•	Needs work on TH/F – home sorting tasks
RE	•	Individual work on using long-vowel spellings – sorting tasks with TA
AM	•	Needs work on DR/GR – ask mum to work on this at home

APPENDIX 18

Class 2 English Summer Term Plan

SPEAKING AND LISTENING

When	Learning Objectives and Activities	Differentiation Strategies	Taught/Amendments
Every morning throughout term	Choral speaking Morning routine verses • The morning verse • *The Earth is Firm Beneath My Feet*	Encourage all children to participate in the choral speaking using descriptive praise as encouragement Give FP lines on his own to encourage his participation TA to remind RD and FP to participate when they forget	✓
During English Main Lesson	English Main Lesson verses and tongue twisters • Recitation; recitation with actions • *The Kite and the Fly* • Play rehearsals		
Every morning for about a week after each holiday	Individual Speaking • Morning news: Three children can give news each morning during the week after each holiday. Voluntary • Birthday verses • Play rehearsals • Whole-class discussion about good acting – speaking clearly, in part, face audience • Give opportunities to speak a whole poem either individually or in a small group	CC – reluctant speaker awareness	✓
Most Main Lessons	Listening to stories Once every two or three days teacher completes a story (parts can be spread over days). Children listen and are asked the next day to recall / re-create the story		✓

WRITING IN CONJUNCTION WITH FORM DRAWING

When	Learning Objectives and Activities	Differentiation Strategies	Taught/Amendments
Start of a writing task	Remind of grip and page setting • Lines and borders • Under line pages	Check NR and RE regularly – communicate to TA CC and RD to use writing slope AR to have ruler with capitals, print and cursive on his desk	✓
English Main Lessons	Copy learnt poems For handwriting practice write poems that the children already know on the blackboard to copy – also practise reading skills; see below. Emphasis on neatness and regularity in writing	Slopes for CC and RD AR to have ruler with capitals, print and cursive on his desk	✓
English Main Lessons	Write stories, partly using invented spelling Write from *King of Ireland's Son* Writing a Saints story book choosing which ones they like, page setting etc. Sentence analysis from St Giles story • How many sentences? • How many capitals – why are they there? • The sentence with the least words? • The sentence with the most words? Think up two sentences that could finish the story. Lists of words for Recall for St Francis story	NR, AR, RD, CF TA to read prepared text with them and then guide them through a cloze exercise which they will then copy in their Main Lesson book as handwriting practice AR to have ruler with capitals, print and cursive on his desk	✓

WRITING IN CONJUNCTION WITH FORM DRAWING

When	Learning Objectives and Activities	Differentiation Strategies	Taught/Amendments
English Main Lessons	Word-wall words • As before and from free-writing choices.	Provide AR with a sheet with the words to have on his desk AR to have ruler with capitals, print and cursive on his desk	✓
English Main Lessons	Punctuation capitals and full stops • As with sentence analysis above • Pairs correcting each other task	.	✓
English Main Lessons and extra English	Sounds • Anagram games • Odd-One-Out blends game • Star game	TA in group with NR, AR and AM to encourage accuracy	✓
English Main Lessons daily	Spelling • Keywords, mnemonics • Revise long vowels – gather words		✓

WRITING IN CONJUNCTION WITH FORM DRAWING

When	Learning Objectives and Activities	Differentiation Strategies	Taught/Amendments
English Main Lessons and extra English	Introduce and revise other common digraphs Revise long vowels • IR / ER / AR • OR / AW • OW / OU • Bingo • Word Hunts • Word-search games • Cloze • 'Snakes and Ladders'	Bingo – give AR a sheet with all words. Have extra sheet available in case needed for AM, RE, NR, CF	✓
English Main Lesson and practice during English subject lesson	Introduce and practice suffixing just add rule only; -s, -ed, -ing • Use Twister of Twist tongue twister • Recite – claps on every word that has TWIST in it • Pair task – identify all words that have twist in them • Write all words as a word sum, e.g. twist + s = twists • Write poem from memory in Main Lesson book • Let children create further word sums with STAND, JUMP, HUNT, REST, HELP, HAND, SAND	Encourage Erin, Orlando, Daniel, Luca, Louis, Amy to include prefixes and to write sentences with the words made	✓

READING

When	Learning Objectives and Activities	Differentiation Strategies	Taught/ Amendments
Regular practice throughout English Main Lessons	Memory reading Read a known poem from the blackboard Read individual words from a known poem on the blackboard		✓
After painting and at other times when the work is finished	Regular reading to the class *The King of Ireland's Son*		✓
All term, Tuesdays	Class reading of Self-created class story books Weekly reading lesson and library visit C7 helpers Library visit	CC, NR, RE, RD to do 'Snakes and Ladders' with CVC, CCVC, CC-CVC, and CVCC words for half the reading lesson	✓

EVALUATION

Assessment Methods	• Observation of the children's work
	• Observation of the children's involvement in verbal work
	• Observation of the children's independence in doing the tasks
	• Words Their Way spelling assessment after the Christmas Holidays
	• Specifically assess; short / long vowels, th, sh, ch, distinguishing short vowels, blends and sound splitting. Most through dictation and sorting
	• Assess reading levels through hearing individual children read
Success Criteria	By July most children will:
	• Relate a story in detail to the class
	• Recite a poem on their own in front of the class
	• Perform a part in a simple play
	• Spell CVC, CCVC, CVCC words correctly
	• Decide whether a vowel in a word they hear is short or long
	• Distinguish all individual sounds in words
	• Distinguish syllables
	• Spell long vowels correctly when they occur at the end of words, e.g. ay, ow, ee, y
	• Know the shape of all capital, cursive and print letters
	• Read a simple book confidently out loud
	• Recognise the base-word in a two-syllable word with an affix
	• Add a consonant or vowel suffix to cvcc words – Just add rule – and spell the word correctly
	• Write the common irregular words ALL, WERE, WE, WHEN, YOUR, CAN, SAID, THERE, USE

EVALUATION

Notes: Extra individual work with TA at the start of the day in small groups using the *Words Their Way* method.

AR	• Needs to work on SH and CH, DR and FR. Give homework matching capital, cursive and book letter shapes (pairs game) and have 3-script-ruler on her desk
CF	• Individual work on using long-vowel spellings – sorting tasks with TA
HW	• Needs work on ST/SD
MO	• Needs work on TH/F – home sorting tasks
NR	• Needs work on short u, ST, DR, CH, SH, GR, F/TH, MP, LONG I/A
RD	• Needs work on short e, short i, SH and blends BL, FR and CR
YS	• Needs work on TH/F – home sorting tasks
OL	• Needs work on TH/F – home sorting tasks
RE	• Individual work on using long-vowel spellings – sorting tasks with TA
AM	• Needs work on DR/GR – ask mum to work on this at home

APPENDIX 19

Class 2 Week Main Lesson Plan

Spring Example

Monday 5 March	Tuesday 6 March	Wednesday 7 March
Entering task • handwriting practice: a, b, c, d, e • poem line: '*To the Rose You So Want to Show*' • '*And a Crow with Feathers as Black as Coal*' • AR – Wooden-letter task – making words with SH and CH	Entering task • handwriting practice: f, g, h, i, j • poem line: '*I Don't Really Know Spoke the Coal Black Crow*' • AR – Wooden-letter task – making words with SH and CH	Entering task • handwriting practice: k, l, m, n, o • poem line: '*I Just Spread my Wings and Am Ready to Go*' • AR – Wooden-letter task – making words with SH and CH
Play recorder	Play recorder	Play recorder
Sing	Sing	Sing
Say 'Good morning'	Say 'Good morning'	Say 'Good morning'
Register	Register	Register
Verse	Verse	Verse
Hungarian rocking song / *I travel*	Hungarian rocking song / *I travel*	Hungarian rocking song / *I travel*
Play part	Play part	Play part
Birthday verses: IS	Birthday verses: IS	Birthday verses: IS
Word-wall activity – WILL, LIKE, ABOUT, WHAT, MANY AR, NR, CM, RE, HW rainbow drawing	Word-wall activity – WILL, LIKE, ABOUT, WHAT, MANY AR, NR, CM, RE, HW rainbow drawing / word-box practice	Word-wall activity – WILL, LIKE, ABOUT, WHAT, MANY AR, NR, CM, RE, HW rainbow drawing / word-box practice

Thursday 8 March	Friday 9 March
Entering task • handwriting practice: p, q, r, s,t • poem line: *'But We Use The Road', Croaked Mr Toad* • AR – Wooden-letter task – making words with SH and CH	Entering task • handwriting practice: u, v, w, x, u, z • poem line: *'And Then There's The Moat, We'll Sure Need a Boat'* • AR – Wooden letter task – making words with SH and CH
Play recorder	Play recorder
Sing	Sing
Say 'Good morning'	Say 'Good morning'
Register	Register
Verse	Verse
Hungarian rocking song / *I travel*	Hungarian rocking song / *I travel*
Play part	Play part
Birthday verses: IS	Birthday verses: IS
Word-wall activity – WILL, LIKE, ABOUT, WHAT, MANY AR, NR, CM, RE, HW rainbow drawing / word-box practice	Word-wall activity – WILL, LIKE, ABOUT, WHAT, MANY AR, NR, CM, RE, HW rainbow drawing / word-box practice

APPENDIX 20

Class 2 Week Main Lesson Plan

Summer Example

Monday 18 June	Tuesday 19 June	Wednesday 20 June
Entering task • Using A E K R S T, try to make as many words as you can • You don't need to use all the letters • Use each letter once in each word e.g. SKATER	Entering task • Using E I D P R S try to make as many words as you can • You don't need to use all the letters • Use each letter once in each word e.g. SPIDER	Entering task • Using E I B D R S try to make as many words as you can • You don't need to use all the letters • Use each letter once in each word e.g. BRIDES
Play recorder	Play recorder	Play recorder
Sing	Sing	Sing
Say 'Good morning'	Say 'Good morning'	Say 'Good morning'
Register	Register	Register
'Firmly on the Earth'	*'Firmly on the Earth'*	*'Firmly on the Earth'*
Verse	Verse	Verse
Song – Sing cuckoo Poem – *The Kite and the Fly*	Song – Rose / rose Poem – *The Kite and the Fly*	Song – Rose / rise up Poem – *The Kite and the Fly*
Recorders: *'A Shepherd'* while getting out recorder. Hands up to show they are in the right place *'Land of the Silver Birch'*	Recorders: *'A Shepherd'* while getting out recorder. Hands up to show they are in the right place *'Land of the Silver Birch'*	Recorders: *'A Shepherd'* while getting out recorder. Hands up to show they are in the right place *'Land of the Silver Birch*
Birthday verses: AM, MO, HW, AB. Old verse SM	Birthday verses: AM, MO, HW, AB, SM. Old verse OA	Birthday verses: AM, MO, HW, AB, SM, OA
Look back on entering task Spiral books out Lollypop sticks for children to write words on the blackboard Write in your spiral book if you have not got them all	Look back on entering task Spiral books out Lollypop sticks for children to write words on the blackboard Write in your spiral book if you have not got them all	Look back on entering task Spiral books out Lollypop sticks for children to write words on the blackboard Write in your spiral book if you have not got them all
Prepare Bingo sheet	Draw pictures in blue English Main Lesson books for IGH, I-e and Y: light, kite, fly	Gather words for IGH
Make a list for the next story you want to write OR do the cloze exercise for St Giles story.	Saint story	Saint story
Read *'King of Ireland's Son'*	Story – *'Saint Francis'*	Recall – in list form as in preparing to write a story Story – *'Saint Francis'*

Thursday 21 June	Friday 22 June
Entering task • Using E I D F N R S try to make as many words as you can • You don't need to use all the letters • Use each letter once in each word e.g. FRIENDS	Entering task • Using E I F G H N R T try to make as many words as you can • You don't need to use all the letters • Use each letter once in each word e.g. FRIGHTEN
Play recorder	Play recorder
Sing	Sing
Say 'Good morning'	Say 'Good morning'
Register	Register
'Firmly on the Earth'	'Firmly on the Earth'
Verse	Verse
Song – Rise up / behold Poem – *The Kite and the Fly*	Song – rose / behold Poem – *The Kite and the Fly*
Recorders: 'A Shepherd' while getting out recorder. Hands up to show they are in the right place 'Land of the Silver Birch'	Recorders: 'A Shepherd' while getting out recorder. Hands up to show they are in the right place 'Land of the Silver Birch'
Birthday verses: AM, MO, HW, AB, SM, OA, OL.	Birthday verses: AM, MO, HW, AB, SM, OA, OL
Look back on entering task. Spiral books out. Lollypop sticks for children to write words on the blackboard. Write in your spiral book if you have not got them all	Look back on entering task. Spiral books out. Lollypop sticks for children to write words on the blackboard. Write in your spiral book if you have not got them all
Gather words for I-e	Gather words for Y
Saint Story	Saint Story
Recall – in list form as in preparing to write a story Story – 'Saint Francis'	Recall – in list form as in preparing to write a story Story – 'Saint Francis'

Glossary

This jargon-busting section is heavily indebted to Palmer & Corbett, *Literacy: What Works?* 2003, p. 17. See also Townend & Walker, *Structure of Language: Spoken and Written English,* 2006 for detailed linguistic information.

Blends
Two or more consonant phonemes (see also Consonant cluster.) Initial blends – e.g. **tr**ip – tend to be the easiest for children to learn; end blends – e.g. ju**mp** – are harder to discern, and medial or middle sounds, whether consonant or vowel, tend to be the hardest of all for children to hear accurately.

Cloze
In language teaching, a cloze test is a test in which words are removed from a text and replaced with spaces. The student must fill each space with a suitable word.

Common words
The 100 or 200 most commonly used words in English. Also known as high-frequency or keywords.

Consonant cluster
Two or more consonant phonemes e.g. **twig** (CCVC), **lunch** (CVCC), **splash** (CCCVC). Sometimes these are also called 'blends'.

CVC word
Consonant-vowel-consonant word, e.g. **b**ed.

Digraph
Two letters representing one phoneme, e.g. /sh/, /ay/, /ar/.

Diphthong
A vowel sound which moves from one pure vowel to another such as /oy/ or /oi/.

Grapheme
Letter or group of letters that represent a phoneme.

Long Vowel
The five vowel sounds like the letter names: dāy, sēē, līght, blōw, flūte.

Morpheme
A unit of meaning, often related to grammatical function (e.g. -ed, -tion, -ly). Morphemes are important elements in reading and spelling, and often they are not phonetically consistent, e.g. -ed represents a different sound in jumped, listened, wanted.

Multisensory learning
SEN term for teaching the same material using varied methods, especially visual, auditory or kinaesthetic.

Onset and Rime
In a single syllable word, the onset is the part of the word that comes before the vowel (**c**at; **gr**and; **str**ong); the rime is the vowel and the rest of the word (c**at**; gr**and**; str**ong**). Once a child is able to blend and segment words easily, it is helpful to look at words in terms of larger units – first, onset and rime; later, syllables.

Overlearning
Differentiation term for practice exercises used to repeat the same learning in varied ways.

Phoneme
Individual speech sound.

Scaffolding
Differentiation term for providing prompts, aids and starters to remove blocks for a child learning a particular skill, e.g. writing frames, copy sheets, sentence starters.

Schwa
An indeterminate grunting sound like /uh/. The schwa is the most common vowel in the English language. Many child errors have been caused by a teacher pronouncing the phoneme for 'b' as /buh/ or 't' as /tuh/. Further, there is often uncertainty about how to represent it in many common words, e.g. seperate (separate,) definately (definitely). Demonstrate this for yourself by saying the sound /b/ for the first sound of the word 'bat'. Try to make a short, fricative sound using the lips as they come together; avoid saying 'buh'. Similarly, try not to say 'ler' for the first sound of 'lid'. The word is 'bat', not 'buh-at'; 'lid', not 'ler-id'.

Segmenting and blending
Taking a word apart into its individual phonemes (e.g. /c//a//t/) and putting it back together again ('cat'). The ability to do this is fundamental to the acquisition of literacy skills.

Short Vowel
The five vowel sounds in căt, běd, tĭn, hŏt, cŭp.

Sight Words
Common or high-frequency words that are phonically irregular and therefore need to be learned 'by sight.'

Split Digraph
A long vowel phoneme where a sounded and silent letter are plced apart from each other in a word but nonetheless together signify the vowel, e.g. gate, Pete, time, bone, flute. In the past this was often called 'magic e.'

Trigraph
Three letters representing one phoneme, e.g. /igh/, /ear/.

Bibliography

Adams, M. J. (1990). *Beginning to Read: Thinking and Learning About Print.* Cambridge, MA: MIT Press.

Addy, L. (2004). *Speed Up! A Kinaesthetic Programme to Develop Fluent Handwriting.* Hyde, Cheshire: LDA (Learning Development Aids).

Balcombe, K. (n.d.). *Handwriting for Windows,* 3. Shrewsbury: KBER. Retrieved from www.kber.co.uk.

Bear, D. R., Invernizzi, M., Templeton, S., & Johnstone, F. (2012). *Words Their Way: Word Study for Phonics, Vocabulary and Spelling Instruction* (5th edn). Harlow, Essex: Pearson.

Beech, J. R. (2005). Phases of development in learning to read words by sight. *Journal of Research in Reading,* 28: 50–58.

Bradley, L., & Bryant, P. (1991). Phonological skills before and after learning to read. In S. Brady & D. Shankweiler (eds), *Phonological Processes in Literacy* (pp. 37–46). London: Lawrence Erlbaum.

Brock, A., Jarvis, P., & Olusoga, Y. (eds) (2014). *Perspectives on Play: Learning for Life* (2nd edn). Abingdon: Routledge.

Brooking-Payne, K. (1996). *Games Children Play: How Games and Sport Help Children Develop.* Stroud, Gloucestershire: Hawthorn Press.

Brownjohn, S. (1994). *To Rhyme or Not to Rhyme: Teaching Children to Write Poetry.* London: Hodder Education.

Chemin, A. (2014). Handwriting vs typing: Is the pen still mightier than the keyboard? *Guardian Weekly.* London; *Guardian* Newspaper, Tuesday 16 December. Retrieved from goo.gl/LZB9Db.

Clark, C., & Picton, I. (2012). *Family Matters: The Importance of Family Support for Young People's Reading.* London: National Literacy Trust. Retrieved from www.literacytrust.org.uk.

Clark, C., & Rumbold, K. (2006). *Reading for Pleasure: A Research Overview. 2006.* London: National Literacy Trust. Retrieved from www.literacytrust.org.uk.

Clarke, S. (2008). *Active Learning through Formative Assessment.* London: Hodder Education.

Claxton, G. (1998). *Hare Brain, Tortoise Mind: Why Intelligence Increases when You Think Less.* London: Fourth Estate.

Cookson, P. (2004). *The Works 3: A Poet a Week* (3rd edn). Basingstoke: Macmillan.

Cookson, P. (2010). *The Works: Every Kind of Poem You Will Ever Need at School* (5th edn). Basingstoke: Macmillan.

Corbett, P. (2004). *Jumpstart! Literacy: Games and Activities for 7–14.* London: David Fulton.

Corbett, P. (2008). *Jumpstart! Poetry: Games and Activities for 7–12.* Abingdon, Oxon: Routledge.

Corbett, P., & Morgan, G. (2005). *The Works 4: Every Kind of Poem on Every Topic that You Will Ever Need for the Literacy Hour.* Basingstoke: Macmillan.

Corbett, P., & Strong, J. (2011). *Talk for Writing Across the Curriculum: How to Teach Non-fiction Writing 5–12 years*. Maidenhead: Open University Press/McGraw Hill.

Cowley, S. (2013). *The Seven Ts of Practical Differentiation*. Bristol: Sue Cowley Books.

Cunningham, P. M. (2013). *Phonics They Use: Words for Reading and Writing* (6th edn). Harlow, Essex: Pearson.

Daniel, A. K. (2011). *Storytelling across the Primary Curriculum*. London: David Fulton/Routledge.

Department for Education (DfE). (2012). *Research Evidence on Reading for Pleasure: Education Standards Research Team*. London: DfE. Retrieved from www.gov.uk.

Dodge, J. (2005). *Differentiation in Action: A Complete Resource with Research-Supported Strategies to Help You Plan and Organize Differentiated Instruction – and Achieve Success with All Learners*. New York: Scholastic.

Ehri, L. (1995). Phases of development in learning to read words by sight. *Journal of Research in Reading*, 18, 116–125.

Ehri, L. (2002). Reading processes, acquisition and instructional implications. In G. Reid & J. Wearmouth (eds), *Dyslexia and Literacy: Theory and Practice* (pp. 167–186). Chichester: John Wiley.

Elbow, P. (1998). *Writing with Power: Techniques for Mastering the Writing Process*. Oxford Oxford University Press.

Elbow, P. (2004). Write First: Putting Writing before Reading Is an Effective Approach to Teaching and Learning. *Educational Leadership*, 62 (October), pp. 8–14.

Elbow, P. (2012). *Vernacular Eloquence: What Speech Can Bring to Writing*. New York: Oxford University Press.

Fairman, E. K. (1996). *A Path of Discover: A Program of a Waldorf Grade School Teacher – Grade One* (Vol.1). Castle Cove, NSW, Australia: Self-published.

Finser, T. (1994). *School as a Journey: The Eight Year Odyssey of a Waldorf Teacher and His Class*. Great Barrington, MA: Anthroposophic Press.

Forster, A., & Martin, P. (1999). *Key Spelling 1*. Huddersfield: Schofield & Sims.

Frith, U. (2002). Resolving the paradoxes of dyslexia. In G. Reid & J. Wearmouth (eds), *Dyslexia and Literacy: Theory and Practice* (pp. 45–68). Chichester: John Wiley.

Gerver, R. (2010). *Creating Tomorrow's Schools Today*. London: Continuum.

Giesen, P. (2014). *Werkboek Vormtekenen: Leerplan vas clas tot clas*. Mercurius International: goo.gl/9O5Euj.

Goddard, S. A. (2001). *Reflexes, Learning and Behviour*. Eugene, Ore: Fern Ridge Press.

Goddard Blythe, S. (2005). *The Well Balanced Child: Movement and Early Learning*. Stroud, Gloucestershire: Hawthorn Press.

Goswami, U. (2013/2005). Orthography, phonology and reading development: A cross-linguistic development. In R. Malatesha Joshi & P. G. Aaron (eds), *Handbook of Orthography and Literacy* (pp. 463–480). New York and Abingdon, Oxon: Taylor & Francis (orig. 2005).

Graves, D. H. (1983). *Writing: Teachers and Children at Work*. Portsmouth, NH: Heinemann USA.

Hannaford, C. (1997). *The Dominance Factor: How Knowing Your Dominant Eye, Ear, Brain, Hand and Foot Can Improve Your Learning*. Arlington, VA: Great Ocean.

Heacox, D. (2012). *Differentiating Instruction in the Regular Classroom: How to Reach and Teach All Learners* (2nd edn). Golden Valley, MN: Free Spirit Publishing.

Healy, J. M. (1999a). *Endangered Minds: Why Children Don't Think and What We Can Do about It* (2nd edn). New York: Touchstone/Simon & Schuster.

Healy, J. M. (1999b). *Failure to Connect: How Computers Affect Our Children's Minds and What We Can Do about It*. New York: Touchstone/Simon & Schuster.

Healy, J. M. (2004). *Your Child's Growing Mind: Brain Development and Learning from Birth to Adolescence* (3rd edn). New York: Broadway Books.

Hollingsworth, S., & Ramsden, A. (2013). *The Storyteller's Way: A Sourcebook for Inspired Storytelling*. Stroud, Gloucestershire: Hawthorn Press.

Hornsby, B., Shear, F., & Pool, J. (2006). *Alpha to Omega: Teacher's Handbook* (6th edn). London: Heinemann.

House, R. (2013). What age should children start school? *The Mother Magazine*, 60 (Sept/Oct), pp. 32–34.

Janis-Norton, N. (2004). *In Step With Your Class: Managing Behaviour in an Inclusive Class*. Edinburgh: Barrington Stoke.

Koch, K. (1973). Rose, *Where Did You Get That Red?: Teaching Great Poetry to Children*. New York: Vintage/Random House.

Koch, K. (1999). *Wishes, Lies and Dreams: Teaching Children to Write Poetry*. New York: HarperPerrenial.

Kutzli, R. (2004). *Creative Form Drawing*. Stroud, Gloucestershire: Hawthorn Press.

MacIver, A. (2013). *The New First Aid in English*. London: Hodder Gibson.

Malatesha Joshi, R., & Aaron, P. G. (eds) (2005). *Handbook of Orthography and Literacy*. New York: Taylor & Francis.

Montessori, M. (1966). *The Secret of Childhood*. New York: Ballantine Books.

Moses, B., & Corbett, P. (2002). *The Works 2: Poems on Every Subject and for Every Occasion* (3rd edn). Basingstoke: Macmillan.

Mueller, P. A., & Oppenheimer, D. M. (2014). The pen is mightier than the keyboard: Advantages of longhand over laptop note taking. *Psychological Science*, 25 (6), pp. 1159–1168.

Myhill, D., Jones, S., & Hopper, R. (2005). *Talking, Listening, Learning: Effective Talk in the Primary Classroom*. Maidenhead: Open University Press.

Nash Wortham, M., & Hunt, J. (2008). *Take Time 2008: Movement Exercises for Parents, Teachers and Therapists of Children with Difficulties in Speaking, Reading, Writing and Spelling*. Stourbridge, UK: Robinswood Press.

O'Brien, T., & Guiney, D. (2001). *Differentiation in Action: Principles and Practice*. London: Continuum.

Palmer, S. (2006). *Toxic Childhood: How The Modern World Is Damaging Our Children And What We Can Do About It*. London: Orion (2nd updated edn 2015).

Palmer, S. (2016). *Upstart: The Case for Raising the School Starting Age and Providing What the Under-Sevens Really Need*. Edinburgh: Floris Books.

Palmer, S., & Corbett, P. (2003). *Literacy: What Works?* Cheltenham: Nelson Thornes.

Perrow, S. (2012). *Therapeutic Storytelling*. Stroud, Gloucestershire: Hawthorn Press.

Petrash, J. (2003). *Understanding Waldorf Education: Teaching From the Inside Out*. Edinburgh: Floris Books.

Rawson, M., & Avison, K. (eds.) (2013). *Towards Creative Teaching: Notes to an Evolving Curriculum for Steiner Education* (3rd edn). Edinburgh: Floris Books.

Reed, J., Maskell, K., Allinson, D., Bailey, R., Bates, F., Davies, S., & Gallimore, C. (2012). *The Adventurous School: Vision, Community and Curriculum for Primary Education in the Twenty First Century*. London: Institute of Education.

Reid, G. (2009). *Dyslexia: A Practitioner's Handbook* (4th edn). Chichester: John Wiley.

Robinson, K. (2009). *The Element: How Finding Your Passion Changes Everything*. Harmondsworth/London: Penguin.

Robinson, K. (2011). *Out of Our Minds: Learning to be Creative* (2nd edn). Chichester: Capstone.

Robinson, K. (2013, July 1). *How to Change Education – from the Ground Up*. London. Retrieved from goo.gl/QLDclS.

Robinson, K. (2015). *Creative Schools: Revolutionizing Education From the Ground Up*. Harmondsworth: Allen Lane.

Rose, M. (2007). *Living Literacy: The Human Foundations of Speaking, Writing and Reading*. Stroud, Gloucestershire: Hawthorn Press.

Ruth Miskin Literacy (2006). *Phonics Handbook: Read Write Inc Phonics*. Oxford: Oxford University Press.

Sahlberg, P. (2015). *Finnish Lessons 2.0: What Can the World Learn from Educational Change in Finland?* (2nd edn). New York: Teachers College Press.

Simmonds, D. (n.d.). *Form Drawing for Beginners*. Christopherus Homeschool Resources. Retrieved from http: waldorfbooks.com.

Smith, B. (1994). *Teaching Spelling*. Royston, UK: United Kingdom Reading Association (UKRA).

Stanovich, K. E. (1986). Matthew Effects in reading: Some consequences of individual differences in the acquisition of reading. *Reading Research Quarterly*, 21, 360–407.

Steiner, R. (1976). *Practical Advice to Teachers*, Stuttgart 21 August to 6 September 1919. London: Rudolf Steiner Press.

Steiner, R. (1995). *The Kingdom of Childhood, Torquay 12–20 August 1924*. Hudson, NY: Anthroposophic Press.

Steiner, R. (1996a). Education in the light of Spiritual Science, Koln. 1 December 1906. In R. Steiner, *The Education of the Child (and Early Lectures on Education)* (pp. 51–63). Hudson, NY: Anthroposophic Press.

Steiner, R. (1996b). The education of the child in the light of Spiritual Science, Berlin, 10 January 1907. In R. Steiner, *The Education of the Child (and early Lectures on Education)* (pp. 1–39). Hudson, NY: Anthroposophic Press.

Steiner, R. (1997). *Discussions with Teachers, Stuttgart 21 August – 6 September 1919*. Hudson, NY: Anthroposophic Press.

Steiner, R. (1998). *Faculty Meetings with Rudolf Steiner 1922–1924* (Vol. 2) (trans. R. Lathe & N. Parsons Whittaker). Hudson, NY: Anthroposophic Press.

Steiner, R. (2003). *Soul Economy: Body, Soul and Spirit in Waldorf Education, Dornach 23 December 1921 – 5 January 1922*. Hudson, NY: Anthroposophic Press.

Steiner, R. (n.d.). T*he Education of the Child in the Light of Anthroposophy*. Retrievable at goo.gl/rJ816s.

Suggate, S. P. (2009a). Research into early reading instruction and like effects in the development of reading. *Journal for Waldorf/ Rudolf Steiner Education*, 11 (2), pp. 17–20.

Suggate, S. P. (2009b). Response to Reading Instruction and Age-related Development: Do Later Starters Catch up? University of Otago, NZ: Unpublished Doctoral Dissertation.

Suggate, S. P. (2009c). School entry age and reading achievement in the 2006 Program for International Student Assessment (PISA). *International Journal of Educational Research, 48b* (3), pp. 151–161.

Suggate, S., & Reese, E. (eds) (2012). *Contemporary Debates in Childhood Education and Development.* Oxford: Routledge.

Topping, K. J. (1998). *Peer Assisted Learning: A Practical Guide for Teachers.* London: Routledge.

Townend, J., & Walker, J. (2006). *Structure of Language: Spoken and Written English.* Chichester: Whurr Publishers.

Vasagar, J. (2012). A different class: the expansion of Steiner schools. *Guardian* newspaper, 25 May. Retrievable from goo.gl/Tz4FFB.

Ward, H. (2008). Mouse deletes Literacy Hour. *Times Educational Supplement*, 11 May.

Wells, G. (2009). *The Meaning Makers: Learning to Talk and Talking to Learn* (2nd edn). Bristol: Multilingual Matters.

Whitebread, D. (2013). *School Starting Age: The Evidence.* University of Cambridge. Retrieved from goo.gl/oBGkxN.

Wiliam, D. (2011). *Embedded Formative Assessment.* Bloomington, IN: Solution Tree Press.

Wiseman, H., & Northcote, S. (1969). *The Clarendon Book of Singing Games.* Oxford: Oxford University Press.

Wolf, M. (2008). *Proust and the Squid: The Story and Science of the Reading Brain.* Cambridge: Icon Books.

Index

TalkforWriting™

Talk for Writing, developed by Pie Corbett and supported by Julia Strong, is powerful because it is based on the principles of how children learn. It is powerful because it enables children to imitate the language they need for a particular topic orally before reading and analysing it and then writing their own version.

Talk for Writing is a popular approach to teaching writing that is used in thousands of schools across Great Britain and, increasingly, around the world. It is based upon a few simple ideas such as the fact that it is impossible to write sentences unless you can say them!

There is a clear pattern to teaching which gives children confidence in their own ability to write. The use of story play and story maps from the Nursery onwards means that children quickly find their own voice. From the start, their oral stories, however humble, are celebrated and shared round the story telling circle. We believe that all children succeed in their own unique ways and the teacher's role is to work with their class to develop each child as a writer, reader and learner.

Talk for Writing uses formative assessment to focus teaching and learning so that progress in writing is visible. We use washing lines to hang up texts, story maps, banks of words and ideas as well as reminders of technique so that when children write they have plenty of scaffolding. Across a unit of work, the scaffolding is gradually taken away so that the children move towards becoming independent and confident writers.

A core aspect of the process involves learning orally a bank of stories, poems and nonfiction texts so that children internalise the language patterns that they need for writing, adding to their linguistic competency. Children from a very early age draw story maps and use actions to support memory and meaning. The oral learning and development of stories is central to the process of building the imagination as well as developing vocabulary, grammatical and text patterns.

Children spend time working with a story and process it through art, drama, play and discussion. In this way, by the time they come to read the text, everyone can read the words because they are familiar with the story. This multi-sensory, staged process means that teaching is inclusive. It has been used successfully with children who are deaf or have moderate learning difficulties. Children spend time reading the text for vocabulary as well as comprehension, deepening understanding before thinking about how the text is organised and how the writer has created different effects.

Time spent loitering with a story or nonfiction text has a pay off when children are led by the teacher through planning, drafting and editing their own versions. The teacher uses shared writing, revealing the thinking and creative processes used by writers to generate and craft writing. For many adult writers these processes come automatically but young children benefit from teachers making writing technique explicit. The teacher shows how to write by drawing on the core model as well as using other examples from the class's reading of quality books and allowing the imagination to take hold.

Talk for Writing is used across the curriculum as we recognise that every subject has its own particular vocabulary, sentence and text patterns. We use the process to aid memory, structure thinking in problem solving or organising writing as well as making explicit how to tackle the different demands of the curriculum both in primary and secondary schools. Because it is so carefully staged, progress is almost guaranteed and this builds writing stamina and confidence. Children develop a love of writing which spills into their reading. If nothing else, children leave primary schools with a bank of well-known stories from *The Gingerbread Man* to *Beowulf* plus hundreds of poems as an inner resource for the rest of their lives.

© Pie Corbett 2017
For more information visit **www.talk4writing.com**

Creating Storytellers and Writers: For 5-12 year-olds

Creating Storyteller and Writers: For 5-12 year-olds is the most recent *Talk for Writing* publication by Pie Corbett and Julia Strong, published January 2018. Priced £24.99 (+P&P), this long-awaited book comes with two DVDs and explains how to use the *Talk for Writing* method to teach fiction.

This book is only available through the *Talk for Writing* online shop: **www.talkforwritingshop.com**. It is not available from any other retailer. Payment can be made via card and PayPal. If you a UK school and buy three copies or more we can send an invoice for payment.

Creative Form Drawing with Children
Workbooks 1 and 2
Angela Lord

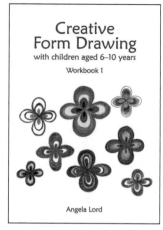

Creative form drawing helps children develop hand-eye co-ordination, spatial orientation, observations skills, confident movement, drawing skills and the foundations of handwriting. Originally developed by Rudolf Steiner, creative form drawing is widely used in Steiner/Waldorf schools to enable healthy child development and learning.

Workbook 1 is a form drawing resource for teachers working with ages 6-10, and is designed to be used with the Steiner/Waldorf curriculum from classes one through three. Workbook 2 is for ages 10-12, and is designed to be used for Classes four and five. These workbooks will also be valuable to home-educating parents using the Steiner/Waldorf ethos as their base.

"We believe that Angela Lord's workbooks are a very valuable investment and will carry a class teacher through Classes 1-6 without additional resources. That's £60 well-spent!"
Ann Gulbis and Paul White, Class teachers, Steiner Academy Frome.

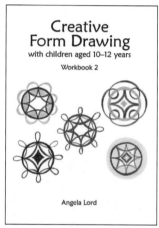

Workbook 1:136pp; 297 x 210mm; ISBN 978-1-907359-54-5; Paperback
Workbook 2: 96pp; 297 x 210mm; ISBN 978-1-907359-70-5; Hardback

Form Drawing and Colouring
For Fun, Healing and Wellbeing
Angela Lord

Originally developed by Rudolf Steiner, creative form drawing is widely used in Steiner/Waldorf education to support healthy child development and learning.

Rather than 'filling in the lines' as one would in a mainstream colouring book, the reader is provided with forms in varying stages of completion to copy, experiment with and develop. This approach offers more creative freedom and encourages the formation of new rhythmical and organic forms. The book features fourfold patterns of increasing challenge and complexity, and references Celtic, Moorish, Native American and Buddhist patterns.

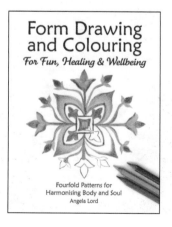

96pp; 246 x 189mm; ISBN 978-1-907359-78-1; Paperback

Free to Learn
Steiner Waldorf early childhood care and education
Lynne Oldfield

The approach of Steiner Waldorf kindergartens and childcare centres is that children's early learning is profound, that childhood matters and that the early years should be enjoyed, not rushed through. Lynne Oldfield, Director of the London Steiner Waldorf Early Childhood Teacher Training Course draws on kindergarten experience from around the world, with stories, helpful insights, lively observations and vivid pictures.

240pp; 216 x 138mm; ISBN 978-1-907359-13-2; Paperback

Games Children Sing & Play
Singing movement games to play with children ages 3-5
Joan Carr Shimer, Valerie Baadh Garrett

This treasury of both old and new games will help children feel at ease in their bodies and build relationships with others. The magic weaving of rhythms, movement, songs, stories and pictures invites children into worlds of vibrant wonder.

128pp; 200 x 250mm; ISBN 978-1-907359-20-0; Paperback

An A-Z Collection of Behaviour Tales
From Angry Ant to Zestless Zebra
Susan Perrow
Foreword by Georgiana Keable

Susan offers story medicine as a creative strategy to help children age 3-9 years face challenges and change behaviour. Following the alphabet, each undesirable behaviour is identified in the story title: anxious, bullying, demanding, fussy, jealous, loud, obnoxious, uncooperative, and more. The stories, some humorous and some serious, are ideal for parenting, teaching and counselling.

144pp; 234 x 156mm; ISBN 978-1-907359-86-6; Paperback

Making Waldorf Dolls
Creative doll-making with children
Maricristin Sealey

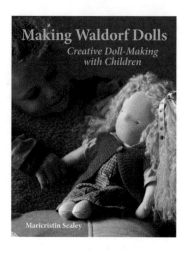

This comprehensive, well-illustrated book will give even the most nervous beginner the confidence to produce a unique, handcrafted toy from natural materials. Once you have mastered the basic baby dolls, you can progress to a more ambitious limbed or jointed doll. It includes ten doll designs, patterns for clothes and accessories, and information on tools, techniques and materials.

160pp; 246 x 189mm; ISBN 978-1-903458-58-7; Paperback

Making Woodland Crafts
Using green sticks, rods, beads and string
Patrick Harrison

This book is the perfect companion for any family outdoor day, a joyful introduction to the crafts available in any piece of woodland. It is guaranteed to get children (and their parents, siblings, grandparents...) out and about and enjoying nature. Through a series of visually stunning hand-drawn illustrations and simple instructions, you will learn to use simple tools, tie knots and develop your own designs. Projects include building masks and puppets, night torches, staffs, arrows, jewellery, ladders, shelters and chairs for stargazing.

120pp; 198 x 208mm; ISBN 978-1-907359-84-2 Paperback

Mask
Making, Using and Performing
Mike Chase

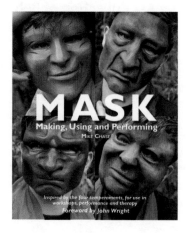

Drawing on the Four Temperaments, Mike Chase explores the transformative and regenerative power of masks in education, the arts and therapy. Highly illustrated throughout with colour photographs and line drawings, this exciting new book explores the history of the mask, different mask-making techniques and uses, and includes extensive workshop exercises for movement, voice work, games, improvisations and general acting skills.

176pp; 228 x 176mm; ISBN 978-1-907359-66-8; Paperback

Making the Children's Year
Seasonal Waldorf Crafts with Children
Marije Rowling

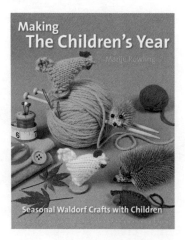

Fully revised and with colour illustrations throughout, this book draws on the creative ethos of Steiner Waldorf education, and is a gift for parents and adults seeking to make toys that will inspire children and provide an alternative to throwaway culture. Packed with all kinds of crafts, from papercrafting to building dens, there are projects to suit both beginners and experienced crafters.

240pp; 250 x 200mm; ISBN 9781907359699; Paperback

Festivals, Family and Food
Guide to seasonal celebration
Diana Carey, Judy Large

This family favourite is a unique, well loved source of stories, recipes, things to make, activities, poems, songs and festivals. Each festival such as Christmas, Candlemas and Martinmas has its own, well-illustrated chapter. There are also sections on Birthdays, Rainy Days, Convalescence and a birthday Calendar. The perfect present for a family, it explores the numerous festivals that children love celebrating.

224pp; 250 x 200mm; ISBN 978-0-950706-23-8; Paperback

All Year Round
A calendar of celebrations
Ann Druitt, Christine Fynes-Clinton, Marije Rowling

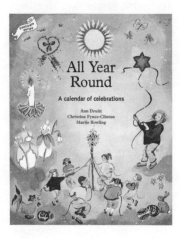

Observing the round of festivals is an enjoyable way to bring rhythm into children's lives and provide a series of meaningful landmarks to look forward to. This book is a festival store cupboard brimming with things to make, activities, stories, poems and songs to share with your family. It is full of well-illustrated ideas for fun and celebration: from Candlemas to Christmas and Midsummer's day to the Winter solstice.

320pp; 250 x 200mm; ISBN 978-1-869890-47-6; Paperback

ORDERING BOOKS

If you have difficulties ordering Hawthorn Press books from a bookshop, you can order direct from our website **www.hawthornpress.com** or from the following distributors:

UNITED KINGDOM
BookSource
50 Cambuslang Road, Glasgow, G32 8NB
Tel: (0845) 370 0063
Email: orders@booksource.net

USA/NORTH AMERICA
Steiner Books
PO Box 960, Herndon, VA 20172-0960, USA
Tel: (800) 856 8664
Email: service@steinerbooks.org
www.steinerbooks.org

Waldorf Books
Phil & Angela's Company, Inc.
1271 NE Hwy 99W #196, McMinnville, Oregon 97128, USA
Tel: (503) 472-4610
Email: info@waldorfbooks.com
www.waldorfbooks.com

AUSTRALIA & NEW ZEALAND
Footprint Books Pty Ltd 4 /8 Jubilee Avenue, Warriewood, NSW 2102, Australia
Tel: (02) 9997 3973
Email: info@footprint.com.au
www.footprint.com.au

Hawthorn Press

www.hawthornpress.com